Rethinking the Security–Development Nexus

This book critically examines the security–development nexus through an analysis of organised crime responses in post-conflict states.

As the trend has evolved, the security–development nexus has received significant attention from policymakers as a new means to address security threats. Integrating the traditionally separate areas of security and development, the nexus has been promoted as a new strategy to achieve a comprehensive, people-centred approach. Despite the enthusiasm behind the security–development nexus, it has received significant criticism. This book investigates four tensions that influence the integration of security and development to understand why it has failed to live up to expectations. The book compares two case studies of internationally driven initiatives to address organised crime as part of post-conflict reconstruction in Sierra Leone and Bosnia-Herzegovina. Examination of the tensions reveals that actors addressing organised crime have attempted to move away from a security approach, resulting in incipient integration between security and development, but barriers remain. Rather than discarding the nexus, this book explores its unfulfilled potential.

This book will be of much interest to students of war and conflict studies, development studies, criminology, security studies and international relations in general.

Sasha Jesperson is Research Fellow at the Royal United Services Institute, and has a PhD in Government from the London School of Economics, UK.

Routledge Studies in Conflict, Security and Development
Series editors: Paul Jackson
University of Birmingham
and
Mark Sedra
University of Waterloo

Designed to meet the needs of researchers, teachers and policymakers in this area, this series publishes books of new, innovative research in to the connections between conflict, security and development processes. The series encourages a multidisciplinary approach to the links between these thematic issues, including the nature of conflict itself and the underlying conflict drivers, the underlying characteristics and drivers of insecurity, and the effects and use of development strategies in post-conflict environments and how that relates to broader peacebuilding strategies.

Security Sector Reform in Conflict-Affected Countries
The evolution of a model
Mark Sedra

Rethinking the Security–Development Nexus
Organised crime in post-conflict states
Sasha Jesperson

Rethinking the Security–Development Nexus

Organised crime in post-conflict states

Sasha Jesperson

LONDON AND NEW YORK

First published 2017
by Routledge
2 Park Square, Milton Park, Abingdon, Oxon OX14 4RN

and by Routledge
711 Third Avenue, New York, NY 10017

Routledge is an imprint of the Taylor & Francis Group, an informa business

© 2017 Sasha Jesperson

The right of Sasha Jesperson to be identified as author of this work has been asserted by her in accordance with sections 77 and 78 of the Copyright, Designs and Patents Act 1988.

All rights reserved. No part of this book may be reprinted or reproduced or utilised in any form or by any electronic, mechanical, or other means, now known or hereafter invented, including photocopying and recording, or in any information storage or retrieval system, without permission in writing from the publishers.

Trademark notice: Product or corporate names may be trademarks or registered trademarks, and are used only for identification and explanation without intent to infringe.

British Library Cataloguing-in-Publication Data
A catalogue record for this book is available from the British Library

Library of Congress Cataloging-in-Publication Data
Names: Jesperson, Sasha, author.
Title: Rethinking the security-development nexus : organised crime in post-conflict states / Sasha Jesperson.
Description: Abingdon, Oxon ; New York, NY : Routledge, 2017. | Series: Routledge studies in conflict, security and development | Includes bibliographical references and index.
Identifiers: LCCN 2016028613| ISBN 9781138200081 (hardback) | ISBN 9781315515298 (ebook)
Subjects: LCSH: National security–Economic aspects. | Internal security–Economic aspects. | Postwar reconstruction–Economic aspects.
Classification: LCC HC79.D4 J47 2017 | DDC 355/.033–dc23
LC record available at https://lccn.loc.gov/2016028613

ISBN: 978-1-138-20008-1 (hbk)
ISBN: 978-1-315-51529-8 (ebk)

Typeset in Times New Roman
by Wearset Ltd, Boldon, Tyne and Wear

Printed and bound in Great Britain by
TJ International Ltd, Padstow, Cornwall

Contents

List of figures		vi
Acknowledgements		vii
List of abbreviations		viii
	Introduction: the security–development nexus – an uneasy relationship	1
1	A critical analysis of the security–development nexus	6
2	Tensions in the security–development nexus	30
3	Addressing organised crime through the security–development nexus in Sierra Leone and Bosnia	58
4	Tensions in the security–development nexus: Sierra Leone	86
5	Tensions in the security–development nexus: Bosnia	120
6	Inhibiting integration?	150
	Conclusion	185
	Index	191

Figures

2.1	Understandings of security and development by referent object and locus	34
2.2	Defining the relationship between security and development	40
2.3	Ideal types of security and development	47
2.4	Spectrum of motivations	51
4.1	Understandings of security and development in Sierra Leone	92
5.1	Understandings of security and development in Bosnia	126
6.1	How external actors perceive the linkage between security and development	155
6.2	The influence of development on the institutional underpinnings	159

Acknowledgements

This book is the end result of my PhD research in the Government Department at the London School of Economics (LSE), so its publication is down to the support and guidance of the LSE community, particularly my PhD supervisors Denisa Kostovicova and Mary Martin.

Since leaving the LSE I have also had the opportunity to further develop the ideas initiated by my PhD research and conduct further fieldwork in West Africa as a research fellow at the Royal United Services Institute, which has only strengthened the arguments advanced.

The research also benefitted from the generosity of the individuals interviewed in Sierra Leone and Bosnia, both for taking the time to speak with me but also in being open about their experiences in addressing organised crime.

Perhaps just as important during the research and writing process were the other parts of my life. Regents Canoe Club deserves a special mention for maintaining my sanity throughout this period: there is nothing like a wild river to stop thinking about organised crime and conflict.

Through kayaking I also met some of the most encouraging and supportive people I have had the fortune to spend time with. They have listened to me talk through the difficult areas, maintained my work–life balance, and even brought my beloved black and red Staedler pencils to Canada. My family, both in Australia and Canada, have also been of tremendous support, not least for packages of rescue chocolate.

The greatest contributor to bringing this research to publication has been Peter Bale. His unerring encouragement, the patient reading and rereading of every word, and keeping on top of everything else so I could focus, means this achievement is as much his as it is mine.

Abbreviations

BiH	Bosnia-Herzegovina
CARDS	Community Assistance for Reconstruction, Development and Stabilisation (EU)
CCYA	Centre for the Coordination of Youth Activities
CFSP	Common Foreign and Security Policy (EU)
CIDA	Canadian International Development Agency
CIVCOM	Committee for Civilian Aspects of Crisis Management (EU)
CPCC	Civilian Planning and Conduct Capability (EU)
DANIDA	Danish International Development Agency
DDR	Disarmament, Demobilisation and Reintegration
DEA	Drug Enforcement Agency (US)
DfID	Department for International Development (UK)
DG RELEX	Directorate of External Relations (EU)
ECOWAS	Economic Community of West African States
EEAS	European External Action Service
ESDP	European Security and Defence Policy
ESS	European Security Strategy
EU	European Union
EUFOR	European Force
EUPM	European Union Police Mission
FAO	Food and Agricultural Organisation (UN)
FCO	Foreign and Commonwealth Office (UK)
FDIDSL	Foundation for Democratisation and Development Initiatives
HDI	Human Development Index
ICITAP	International Criminal Investigative Training Assistance Program (US)
IcSP	Instrument contributing to Stability and Peace
IfS	Instrument for Stability (EU)
IMF	International Monetary Fund
INL	Bureau for International Narcotics and Law Enforcement Affairs (US)
IPA	Instrument for Pre-accession Assistance (EU)
IPTF	International Police Task Force (UN)

Abbreviations ix

JDITF	Joint Drug Interdiction Task Force (Sierra Leone)
MDGs	Millennium Development Goals
MoD	Ministry of Defence (UK)
NATO	North Atlantic Treaty Organisation
NDLEA	National Drug Law Enforcement Agency (Sierra Leone)
NGO	Non-governmental organisation
OECD	Organisation for Economic Co-operation and Development
ONS	Office of National Security (Sierra Leone)
PRSP	Poverty Reduction Strategy Process
PSC	Political and Security Council (EU)
RUF	Revolutionary United Front (Sierra Leone)
SAP	Structural Adjustment Programme
SIPA	State Investigation and Protection Agency (Bosnia)
SOCA	Serious and Organised Crime Agency (UK)
SSR	Security sector reform
TOCU	Transnational Organised Crime Unit (Sierra Leone)
UNDP	United Nations Development Programme
UNDPA	United Nations Department of Political Affairs
UNDPKO	United Nations Department of Peacekeeping Operations
UNIPSIL	United Nations Peacebuilding Mission in Sierra Leone
UNODC	United Nations Office on Drugs and Crime
UNOWA	United Nations Office in West Africa
USAID	United States Agency for International Development
VoIP	Voice over internet protocol
WACI	West Africa Coast Initiative
WACSI	West Africa Cooperative Security Initiative

Introduction

The security–development nexus – an uneasy relationship

The security–development nexus has received significant attention from policy-makers as a new trend in post-conflict reconstruction. Bringing together the traditionally separate areas of security and development, the nexus has been touted as a new strategy to achieve a comprehensive approach to post-conflict reconstruction. As a result, many actors engaged in post-conflict reconstruction have adopted the security–development nexus to frame their engagement to the extent that it has become a 'policy mantra' (IPA 2006). As Waddell (2006: 531) argues, 'it is becoming an article of faith that security and development are "inextricably linked"'. For example, the UN Secretary-General stated that 'we will not enjoy development without security, we will not enjoy security without development' (Annan 2005: 6).

The merging of security and development into a nexus goes beyond mere linkages. Actors are drawing on traditionally separate epistemological approaches and creating new policies and tools to address the complex challenges of post-conflict reconstruction. The security–development nexus moves beyond combining different areas of focus as actors conventionally associated with development are increasingly becoming involved in the security sphere, while security actors are also taking on development initiatives. Tschirgi *et al.* (2010: 2) outline how a wide range of actors, including the UN, the African Union, bilateral donors and NGOs, 'have enthusiastically embraced the refrain that security and development are interdependent and require integrated policies'.

Scholars have also acknowledged that security and development have become closely related, culminating in a historically specific attempt to institutionalise the two concepts into an integrated framework. Schnabel (2011: 44) contends that 'security and development agendas and requirements have been increasingly difficult to separate and a formerly antagonistic relationship has now evolved into mutually supportive coexistence to achieve cooperation'. The mutually beneficial relationship between security and development described by Schnabel is indicative of a comprehensive approach that shifts away from a preoccupation with the state to also acknowledge the needs of individuals in post-conflict states. This supports the enthusiasm of policymakers that the security–development nexus is able to meet both challenges through an integrated approach.

2 *Introduction: the security–development nexus*

Despite the enthusiasm behind the security–development nexus, it has also received significant criticism. Critics argue that rather than an integrated approach, the nexus results in the securitisation of development, where development is employed to further desired security outcomes. While the implementation of the security–development nexus appears to support these arguments, the critiques focus on the outcomes of the security–development nexus with little understanding of what contributes to these outcomes. This book seeks to address this gap to determine why the security–development nexus does not achieve the expectations attached to it. As critics focus on the dominance of security in the nexus, this book contends that the problem lies in the integration of security and development. As such, it investigates what in practice inhibits the integration of security and development into a nexus.

In contrast to the examination of outcomes in the literature on the securitisation of development, the focus here is on processes, investigating *how* security and development are integrated into a nexus, and what limitations exist. To do this, the book hypothesises and investigates four tensions that influence the integration of security and development. These tensions are analysed by examining how the security–development nexus is implemented in two case studies of internationally driven initiatives to address organised crime: Sierra Leone and Bosnia-Herzegovina (hereafter referred to as Bosnia).

Moving the debate forward

The primary critique of the security–development nexus is put forward by critical peacebuilding scholars, focusing on the securitisation of development. Rather than the integrated approach expected by policymakers, security continues to be the overriding concern. This is a valid critique, as international engagement framed by the security–development nexus often results in the securitisation of development in practice. The resulting analysis, however, while critical of international engagement, focuses solely on the outcomes of the nexus. Duffield (2007) expands on this to draw out several explanations of why the security–development nexus results in the securitisation of development, such as fears of security threats spreading internationally. Yet the focus continues to be on how policymakers have responded, such as curbing migration and encouraging self-reliance (Duffield 2010). Duffield (2010) also holds the security–development nexus responsible for a shift in how international actors control problems, aiming to control the actions of people in developing countries rather than the state in order to contain problems before they spread regionally and internationally. As such, the security–development nexus is taken as a fixed or given concept and analysis focuses on the result of the nexus and its policy implications. We are left with no understanding of how this outcome is arrived at.

From the perspective of the securitisation of development, the security–development nexus is understood to have a negative result. The securitisation literature calls for 'desecuritisation' in line with the Copenhagen School of Security Studies. These arguments run contra to the widespread adoption of the security–development nexus as a new, comprehensive approach. Stern and Ojendal (2010: 6) note that 'an ever-growing amount of economic resources and political will is being poured into the "security–development nexus" and the attendant revamping of national and multilateral institutions'. Regardless of criticisms, the nexus has become an important element of international engagement in post-conflict countries. Yet calls for 'desecuritisation' aim to discard the nexus without considering the potential benefits it can bring to post-conflict reconstruction.

In response, this research seeks to understand what causes these outcomes. The emphasis on a one-sided nexus by proponents of the securitisation of development argument suggests that the integration of security and development is not straightforward, but it is a negotiated and political process that has significant implications for resourcing post-conflict reconstruction. Yet the processes of the security–development nexus are not currently explored in the literature on the securitisation of development. This book seeks to fill this gap. The research is based on the premise that the outcomes described by critics are a function of the implementation of the nexus. In order to understand the outcomes of the security–development nexus as put forward by its critics, the book probes how security and development are integrated and the inner characteristics of the nexus, analysing the processes that underpin the nexus.

Beyond the critical literature on the securitisation of development and the developmentalisation of security, critiques have also emerged from orthodox peacebuilding scholars. Taking a problem-solving approach, these critics question how operational the security–development nexus is. Critiques have focused on the nature of security and development, as well as the difficulty of security and development actors working collaboratively (Chandler 2007; Stern and Ojendal 2010; Tschirgi *et al.* 2010a). These critiques begin to engage with the problematic relationship between security and development, but they focus on the effectiveness of the security–development nexus.

This research bridges the two areas of critique. It builds on the operational critiques of how the security–development nexus is put into practice, looking inside the nexus to analyse the role of security and development and their relationship. To understand why the nexus does not fulfil its potential, the research investigates how the security–development nexus is implemented, in particular analysing the dynamics of integration. No judgement is made on the effectiveness of the security–development nexus; rather this focus is solely on what limits the integration of security and development into a nexus.

The research is informed by the Welsh School of Critical Security Studies. From this perspective, the security–development nexus is imbued with the potential of a positive result. By integrating security and development concerns, the nexus holds the potential to shift away from the traditional security focus on post-conflict reconstruction, which sought to end violence, to bring in elements of development with a focus on the needs of individuals in conflict-affected states. This potential is operationalised through a human security approach, to expand the concept of emancipation pursued by the Welsh School. This book

4   *Introduction: the security–development nexus*

tracks the divergence of the security–development nexus from this potential and shows how the integration of security and development is inhibited.

Analysis of the security–development nexus is taken in a new and original direction by identifying and examining tensions that influence the integration of security and development. This approach disrupts the idea of the security–development nexus as 'something given, clear and shared' (Stern and Ojendal 2010: 10), and seeks to identify the difficult choices, underlying assumptions and conflicts that underpin the nexus. Although scholars have argued that security and development have moved beyond their 'formerly antagonistic relationship' (Schnabel 2011: 44), this research is premised on the assumption that rather than being straightforward, the integration of security and development is mediated by a series of tensions.

While security and development are both understood to be necessary for a new, comprehensive approach to post-conflict reconstruction, bringing them together is a contentious process, resulting in a series of conflicts and contradictions. Four tensions have been hypothesised that affect the integration of security and development into a nexus.

- Conceptual tension arises from the different understandings of security and development.
- Causal tension arises from the different applications of security and development and the linkages between them.
- Institutional tension arises from the way actors and institutions inform the implementation of programmes.
- Motivational tension arises from the drivers behind international involvement.

The analysis of these four tensions explains what in practice inhibits the integration of security and development, and why it results in the outcomes described by critics.

Chapter 1 sets out the conceptual framework for this research. It outlines the emergence of the security–development nexus and key debates, before discussing the use of critical security studies as a theoretical model to examine the nexus. Chapter 2 outlines the four hypothesised tensions, explaining what they are, how they are expected to affect the integration of security and development, and how they will be investigated. Chapter 3 discusses organised crime as a site of inquiry and provides background on the selected cases. The chapter sets out the comparability of the two case studies, the presence of organised crime in the two countries, and how the security–development nexus has been employed to address it. Chapters 4 and 5 investigate how the four tensions influence the integration of security and development in the two case studies, Sierra Leone and Bosnia. Chapter 6 brings the analysis of the tensions together, identifying the barriers that affect the integration of security and development. However, it also highlights the latent potential of the security–development nexus.

References

Annan, Kofi (2005). *In Larger Freedom: Towards Development, Security and Human Rights For All.* New York, United Nations General Assembly.

Chandler, David (2007). 'The Security–Development Nexus and the Rise of "Anti-Foreign Policy"', *Journal of International Relations and Development* 10(4): 362–86.

Duffield, Mark (2007). *Development, Security and Unending War: Governing the World of Peoples.* Cambridge, Polity Press.

Duffield, Mark (2010). 'The Liberal Way of Development and the Development Security Impasse: Exploring the Global Life-Chance Divide', *Security Dialogue* 41(1): 53–76.

IPA (International Peace Academy) (2006). *Building Partnerships for Crisis Prevention, Conflict Resolution and Peacebuilding between the United Nations and Regional Organisations.* New York, International Peace Academy.

Schnabel, Albrecht (2011). 'The Security–Development Discourse and the Role of SSR as a Development Instrument', in Albrecht Schnabel and Vanessa Farr (eds), *Back to the Roots: Security Sector Reform and Development.* Geneva, Centre for the Democratic Control of Armed Forces.

Stern, Maria and Joakim Ojendal (2010). 'Mapping the Security Development Nexus: Conflict, Complexity, Cacophony, Convergence?' *Security Dialogue* 41(1): 5–30.

Tschirgi, Necla, Michael Lund and Francesco Mancini (2010). 'The Security–Development Nexus', in Necla Tshirgi, Michael Lund and Francesco Mancini (eds), *Security and Development: Searching for Critical Connections.* Boulder, CO, Lynne Rienner.

Waddell, Nicholas (2006). 'Ties that Bind: DfID and the Emerging Security and Development Agenda', *Conflict, Security & Development* 6(4): 531–55.

1 A critical analysis of the security–development nexus

The security–development nexus has become a key feature of international engagement in post-conflict reconstruction, bolstered by statements that security and development are inextricably linked. In policy, the security–development nexus is proposed as a means to implement post-conflict reconstruction in ways that are more comprehensive. Despite the enthusiasm of policymakers, scholars have argued that the security–development nexus has not lived up to this promise. The gap between policy and practice has primarily been explained by the securitisation of development, where development is co-opted by security actors to deliver security objectives. However, this explanation engages with the outcome of the security–development nexus, rather than its inherent characteristics and dynamics.

This book takes a different approach, seeking to understand the causes of these outcomes by analysing the processes of the security–development nexus. The conceptual framework for this analysis is outlined in the next sections. The first section outlines the emergence of the security–development nexus, followed by an examination of the different approaches to study the nexus, and the approach taken in this research.

The security–development nexus as a framework for post-conflict reconstruction

Building on the increasing recognition that there will be no security without development and no development without security, external actors engaged in post-conflict reconstruction have been eager to merge security and development into a new, comprehensive approach. Since the early 2000s, the adoption of the security–development nexus has been accompanied by additional resources and the transformation of institutions engaged in post-conflict reconstruction (Stern and Ojendal 2010). As a result, the security–development nexus has become a guiding framework for external engagement in post-conflict reconstruction.

However, the connection between security and development is not new. Security and development have been linked historically in various permutations. Hettne (2010) tracks a genealogy of the linkages between security and development from the eighteenth century to the current day. In the eighteenth century, economic order was seen as a peace order; security was essential for economic prosperity (Hettne 2010). Development strategy shifted towards state capitalism in the nineteenth century, when it focused on strengthening the material base of the state through industrialisation reinforced by the security interests of the elite (Hettne 2010). At the end of the nineteenth century, with the failure of the League of Nations, development and security switched places; where previously order and predictability enabled development, in this period wealth served to reinstate order through the politics of war (Hettne 2010). Following World War II, the European Economic Community was developed as a security community, and development aid was used as a tactic of security in the struggle between the superpowers (Hettne 2010).

Other scholars have also highlighted earlier connections. Writing on South Africa, Mamdani (1996) argued that security and development were used to maintain the divide between the generally democratic, mostly white, urban areas and the indirectly ruled rural areas, through schemes to control the migration of rural populations into cities. After World War II, the development aid provided through the Marshall Plan was in response to concerns of further conflict in Europe (Stern and Ojendal 2010). Development was also a tactic in the Cold War to prevent the spread of communism (Duffield 2010). These examples highlight how security and development have been pursued in parallel throughout history.

The contemporary security–development nexus is qualitatively different. Rather than the parallel pursuit of security and development objectives, the nexus combines security and development in deeper, more institutionalised ways. For example, the UK, US, Netherlands and Canada have introduced inter-ministerial committees and funding mechanisms to address the security–development nexus. The UK government created Conflict Prevention Pools and, more recently, the Stabilisation Unit, plus the Conflict, Security and Stability Fund, which bring together the Ministry of Defence (MoD), the Foreign and Commonwealth Office (FCO) and the Department for International Development (DfID). The US government created the Office of the Coordinator for Reconstruction and Stability, which is jointly staffed by members of US government agencies traditionally associated with security and development, including the Agency for International Development (USAID), the Department of State and the Department of Homeland Security. The EU developed the Instrument for Stability (IfS), which was replaced by the Instrument contributing to Stability and Peace (IcSP) in 2014, both of which are rapid funding mechanisms designed to equip the EU with strategic tools to address global security and development challenges.

This institutionalised linkage between security and development has emerged at a particular historical point. The end of the Cold War resulted in a focus on other forms of conflict and insecurity. Until the 1990s, security threats were primarily directed at a state by another state. The preoccupation with the threat of 'mutually assured destruction' between the US and the Soviet Union obscured threats from non-state actors (Reisman 2003). However, during the Cold War

8 *A critical analysis of the nexus*

many internal wars were underway, often supported by the major powers. Unlike interstate wars, these internal wars featured paramilitary groups, gangs, foreign mercenaries and troops, disenfranchised civilians and forcibly recruited combatants as well as state armies (Akkerman 2009: 76). These conflicts also took a different form to interstate wars, blurring war, organised crime, human rights violations, guerrilla warfare and counter-insurgency (Kaldor 2006). Duffield (2010: 67) describes them as 'livelihood wars fought by non-state actors on and through the modalities of subsistence ... where the endemic abuse of human rights is part of the fabric of conflict itself'. While the state may still be under threat in internal wars, citizens also experience a significant threat. When the Cold War ended, these forms of insecurity gained more prominence.

The withdrawal of US and Soviet Union support from a number of countries, many of which had only recently become independent, also created a new challenge: weak or failed states. These countries had inadequate state structures, resulting in 'poorly guarded borders, weak law enforcement, incipient taxation, underdeveloped financial systems as well as a large presence of displaced people and refugees' (Kostovicova and Bojicic-Dzelilovic 2009: 9). Weak or failed states are prone to conflict and instability and contribute to global problems such as poverty, HIV/AIDs, drugs and terrorism (Fukuyama 2004; Kaldor 2009). These problems have had a considerable impact on how security is conceived. Security threats have shifted from strong states that may invade or attack another state, to weak states that cannot control factors that contribute to global problems. It became recognised that state weakness, once a problem of development, contributes to global insecurity through terrorism and criminal networks, as well as national insecurity, as weak states are rarely able to meet the welfare needs of their populations, which could result in conflict.

This period of instability and persistent conflict marked the post-Cold War interventionist stage. Without the veto power of the US and the Soviet Union, the UN Security Council mandated the international community to intervene in many internal wars to end conflict and build peace. Between 1989 and 2009, there were 20 major multilateral post-conflict operations (Paris and Sisk 2009). During this period, approaches to post-conflict reconstruction evolved rapidly. Early attempts at post-conflict reconstruction after the Cold War were security focused. However, the increasing recognition of the unique features of these internal wars – from the role of non-state actors, the impact of violence on civilians or the role of inadequate state structures – resulted in a broadening of approaches to post-conflict reconstruction. As Woodward (2003: 3) contends, by the early 2000s, security approaches were 'beginning to yield to the lessons of the 1990s – the neglect of human and social capital, gender relations and institutions'.

The problems created by early approaches to post-conflict reconstruction provided donors with a stronger understanding of the many factors that lead to conflict and state failure and the complexity in resolving them (Ottaway 2002). In response, external actors have expanded their mandates to address the interconnection of political, security and economic issues in comprehensive approaches to post-conflict reconstruction. As early as 1998 the UN was beginning to advocate for a comprehensive approach to post-conflict reconstruction. In his annual report on the work of the organisation, UN Secretary-General Kofi Annan defined post-conflict reconstruction as 'integrated and coordinated actions aimed at addressing the root causes of violence, whether political, legal, institutional, military, humanitarian, human rights-related, environmental, economic and social, cultural or demographic' (UN 1998).

During the post-Cold War interventionist phase, development actors also came to play a significant role in post-conflict reconstruction. The engagement of development actors in new areas has supported the institutionalisation of the security–development nexus. Early on, the humanitarian aid community discovered the impact their work could have on conflicts. The Biafran famine in the late 1960s highlighted how humanitarian relief could prolong conflict, and with it the death and suffering of numerous civilians and non-combatants. Smilie (1995: 104) refers to the airlift and the broader relief effort as 'an act of unfortunate and profound folly. It prolonged the war for 18 months.' The development community had a similar experience with the Rwandan genocide. In the early 1990s Rwanda was widely viewed as a development success following high economic growth (Krause and Jutersonke 2005). Once the genocide began in 1994, it was recognised that development assistance could reinforce social cleavages and actually cause conflict if wrongly distributed (Krause and Jutersonke 2005).

As violence and war became more visible with the end of the Cold War, the relationship of development and conflict has also become clearer. In 2003, Collier *et al.* described conflict as 'development in reverse'. Violent conflict destroys infrastructure, services and other development advances, creating billions of dollars' worth of damage (Ball 2001; Brinkerhoff 2005; Duffield and Waddell 2006). For Duffield and Waddell (2006), the destruction of infrastructure and livelihoods through violent conflict creates a disequilibrium that promotes further violence, severely undermining sustainable development. The potential to advance development during a conflict is also severely restricted. While progress may not completely stop, Ball (2001: 719) argues that 'what is possible to accomplish under conditions of war tends to be both very limited and under constant threat of reversal'. As a result, the post-conflict period is marked by widespread social and economic insecurity (Kostovicova *et al.* 2010).

Development has also been recognised as a contributor to the outbreak of violent conflicts. Underdevelopment has come to be acknowledged as a factor in insecurity, contributing to crime, terrorism and conflict (Duffield 2001). Since the 1990s, 80 per cent of the world's poorest countries have experienced violence (Tschirgi *et al.* 2010a). The *World Development Report 2000/2001* highlights how failed development in Bosnia and Sierra Leone contributed to conflict (World Bank 2001: 33). The role of poverty has also been recognised as a contributing factor to conflict, driving people towards violent leaders (Duffield 2001). Brinkerhoff argues that 'if youth are in school, job opportunities are available and families have hope that their wellbeing will improve, citizens are less likely to engage in crime or be recruited into insurgency' (Brinkerhoff 2005: 7). As a

10 *A critical analysis of the nexus*

result, economic inequality, underdevelopment and poor governance have become recognised by policymakers as a root cause of conflict (Buur *et al.* 2007).

In response, development actors have become involved in conflict prevention and post-conflict reconstruction alongside security actors. Development aid has been withdrawn from states in response to excessive military aggression or expenditure (Uvin 2002). Tools have also been developed to mobilise development resources for conflict prevention, such as early warning indicators in potential pre-conflict countries (Uvin 2002). Development actors have engaged in new areas following conflict, including justice, reconciliation, disarmament, demobilisation and reintegration programmes, policing, and governance reforms (OECD 1997). The increasing involvement of development actors in post-conflict reconstruction paved the way for a comprehensive approach that integrates security and development.

Although there is now broad recognition that a comprehensive approach to post-conflict reconstruction is needed, there have been different strategies to bring the different elements together. Some actors have sequenced the key elements of post-conflict reconstruction. Dobbins (2008: 68) sets out a hierarchy of tasks – security, humanitarian relief, governance, economic stabilisation, democratisation and development – arguing that 'unless higher priorities such as security are adequately resourced, sustainable progress on those falling lower on the scale are likely to be elusive'. A number of scholars agree that security should be addressed before other activities (Last 2000; Baker 2001; Jeong 2005). For example, Jeong states that 'adequately controlling physical violence and maintaining order, along with humanitarian activities, takes priority over qualitative, social development, such as economic and social processes' (Jeong 2005: 26).

Others actors have implemented elements of post-conflict reconstruction simultaneously. Berdal (2009: 96) argues that the priorities of post-conflict reconstruction, such as 'providing a secure environment, stabilising governing structures and ensuring basic life-sustaining services … are mutually reinforcing and need to be pursued in parallel'. This approach is evident in disarmament, demobilisation and reintegration (DDR) programmes. Disarmament and demobilisation of armed fighters must be accompanied with effective reintegration strategies to avoid a return to conflict. Kaldor (2007) argues that if not done simultaneously, ex-combatants with ready access to surplus weapons and no other form of income generation could potentially reignite conflict.

Despite the general acknowledgement of the need for components of post-conflict reconstruction to be implemented simultaneously, it remains a complicated process. Sisk (2009: 10) argues that some elements of post-conflict reconstruction 'are likely to interact in ways that have the potential to undercut, not advance, the goal of establishing legitimate, effective institutions in war torn countries'. As a result, approaches to post-conflict reconstruction have continued to evolve to improve comprehensive interventions in post-conflict states. The security–development nexus is one of these innovations, as it seeks to integrate security and development into a comprehensive approach.

A critical analysis of the nexus 11

New institutions, tools and approaches have been developed to merge the two traditionally separate areas. Actors conventionally associated with development, such as DfID, have become involved in the security sphere, and security actors are taking on development tasks. 'The security–development nexus has become a truism that inspires policymakers to make concerted efforts to overcome the established boundaries between sectorally defined institutions and policies by developing more coordinated, holistic strategies at the national and international level' (Tschirgi *et al.* 2010a: 406). In response, many governments and intergovernmental organisations have created mechanisms to bring together security and development components in their approach to post-conflict reconstruction.

By bringing together security and development elements, the security–development nexus is posited as a significantly different approach to post-conflict reconstruction. The nexus is understood as an avenue to more effective and sustainable approaches through coordinated, holistic strategies (Tschirgi *et al.* 2010b). Alongside security, development is viewed as an equally important objective to address insecurity in order to limit the effect on individuals. For example, DfID's 2005 aid strategy for security and development recognises the linkages between the two concepts, acknowledging that both need to be addressed to improve the lives of the poor (DfID 2005). This shifts the focus away from just securing the state to address individual needs, pointing to a balanced and people-centred approach.

The use of development strategies also fits within the growing acknowledgement that military means are inadequate to address security threats. In relation to organised crime it has become increasingly evident that it cannot be addressed without rule of law and good governance, areas that go beyond the remit of security actors. Rather than just another strategy to achieve security, rule of law and good governance programmes consider the impact of organised crime on individuals and communities, extending beyond a focus on the state. While development contributes to security outcomes, it brings in new tools and strategies that broaden the focus of post-conflict reconstruction. As a result, the security–development nexus can be understood as the pairing of hard and soft strategies to enhance post-conflict reconstruction and ensure positive outcomes for individuals and communities affected by conflict. As Stern and Ojendal (2010: 10) recognise, 'the notion of a "nexus" seems to provide a possible framework for acutely needed progressive policies designed to address the complex policy problems and challenges of today'. From this perspective, the security–development nexus is understood as a new and innovative strategy to achieve a comprehensive approach to post-conflict reconstruction.

The increased integration of security and development has aligned with significant changes in how security and development are understood and used by different actors. The Cold War period was dominated by realist interpretations of security. Realists define security as 'the absence of existential threats to the state emerging from another state' (Muller 2002: 369). The survival of the state and its sovereignty was the priority during this period based on the perception that states existed within an anarchic international system with self-help the only

12 *A critical analysis of the nexus*

avenue for recourse (Hettne 2010). The universally accepted belief that the two superpowers could destroy the world through their nuclear capacity powered this conception and provided a justification for the use of extreme measures. Buzan *et al.* (1998) interpreted the meaning of security as a threat to someone or something that has an inherent right to survive which justifies extraordinary measures appropriate for security threats only, such as secrecy, violence and conscription. Under this interpretation of security, labelling an incident a security issue depoliticises and adds urgency to the issue, giving states broad freedom to respond.

This 'traditional' understanding of security has had a strong influence on post-conflict reconstruction. During the Cold War, it limited international engagement in conflict and post-conflict states to ceasefire monitoring in countries deemed important to superpower interests. The first phase of interventions after the Cold War were also defined by this perspective of security. They focused on building peace in negative terms: ending violence and preventing a relapse to war in order to limit the impact on international security. However, the end of the Cold War revealed the inadequacy of the dominant perspective on security. Traditional understandings of security did not consider the impact of insecurity on individuals and communities, making it inadequate in addressing the civilian casualties and displacement caused by internal wars. This perspective also neglected the role of non-state actors in internal wars. These shortfalls and the identification of new security challenges triggered debates on the reconceptualisation of security (Brauch 2008).

The result was a new perspective on security that focused on the needs of individuals, which has been encapsulated by human security. Human security was put forward as a new paradigm of people-centred security that was in direct contrast to the state-centric focus taken during the Cold War. The UN Development Programme's initial conceptualisation highlighted seven areas of security, from economic to environmental, that needed to be considered by policymakers (UNDP 1994). However, the concept of human security has been heavily criticised. Critiques have primarily highlighted the lack of a clear definition and the vagueness of the concept (see for example Khong 2001; Rogers 2002; Douzinas 2007; Duffield 2007, 2010; Jabri 2007; Chandler 2008). Despite the critiques, Paris (2001: 88) acknowledges that the concept has brought together a 'coalition of "middle power" states, development agencies and NGOs – all of which seek to shift attention and resources away from conventional security issues and toward goals that have traditionally fallen under the rubric of international development'. As a result, human security has become the driving force of many actors engaged in post-conflict reconstruction. The focus on individual security and non-military strategies indicates a shift away from traditional understandings of security, creating space for the inclusion of development through the security–development nexus.

In parallel, approaches to development have also shifted to focus increasingly on individual needs, becoming closely related to new conceptualisations of security. Development became a focus of the international community in the 1950s and 1960s. Initially a tool for the reconstruction of post-war Europe after

A critical analysis of the nexus 13

World War II, the mandate of development quickly expanded. The 1950s and 1960s were marked by decolonisation, with many states in the developing world gaining their independence. The membership of the UN more than doubled between 1950 and 1970, growing from 60 to 127. However, many of these new states lacked the infrastructure, capacity and resources to grow into advanced economies. Against this backdrop, development became a major preoccupation of economists, drawing on contemporary growth models, such as those put forth by Keynes (Ranis 2004). The primary focus of development in this early stage was economic growth and modernisation.

By the 1970s, the economic approach to development was becoming recognised as inadequate as the results were not 'trickling down' to the poor as predicted. This triggered a focus on the needs of individuals. A study by the International Labour Organization in the 1970s found that economic growth and employment did not necessarily provide freedom from poverty, as many individuals were still unable to meet their basic needs (Deneulin 2009). A new approach was developed to ensure that the basic needs of all individuals in developing countries were met. Streeten (1979), a major proponent of the basic needs approach, argued that the direct provision of basic needs has a more immediate impact on poverty than economic approaches that focus on raising incomes and productivity. While the basic needs approach aimed to bring developing countries above the poverty line by directly providing goods and services in health, nutrition and basic education, it did not attempt to develop self-sufficiency in these areas. 'Some see the basic needs approach as the answer to the needs of world poverty, others as a plot by the rich countries to keep the poor in a constant position of inferiority' (Ghosh 1984: 4). Despite mixed perceptions of the underlying objectives and impact of the basic needs approach, it began a shift in development approaches away from economics towards a human-centred framework.

In the late 1980s, Amartya Sen's capability approach emerged as another alternative to economic approaches to development. Building on advances made with the basic needs approach, Sen adds dimensions of capability and agency, shifting development closer to a human-centred paradigm. 'The people have to be seen ... as being actively involved – given an opportunity – in shaping their own destiny, and not just as passive recipients of the fruits of cunning development programs' (Sen 1999). Within the capabilities approach, 'social arrangements should expand people's capabilities – their freedom to promote or achieve what they value doing and being' (Alkire and Deneulin 2009: 31). There are a number of criticisms of this approach; for instance, it lacks a coherent list of important capabilities, comparing wellbeing is not that useful, and there is a high informational requirement to make comparisons (Clarke 2002). However, the capabilities approach brings empowerment and agency into development. This addition shifts development from a focus on humans as subjects to humans as agents.

Human development consolidated the shift away from economic development. Human development promoted the idea that 'development is not about

14   *A critical analysis of the nexus*

economic performance alone, but most importantly about people and their well-being' (Jahan 2002: 1). Human development gained prominence in 1990 with the publication of the first UNDP Human Development Report. UNDP defined human development as 'both the process of widening people's choices and the level of their achieved wellbeing' (UNDP 1990: 9). The report criticised the continued focus on development economics in the World Bank's *World Development Report* as the 'excessive preoccupation with GNP [gross national product] growth and national income accounts has … supplanted a focus on ends by an obsession with the means' (UNDP 1990: 9).

Since the inception of human development approaches, development has evolved to include new areas, from gender, trade, democracy and climate change, with a strong focus on poverty alleviation (Alkire and Deneulin 2009). Development actors have also developed new programmes to achieve human development outcomes, such as through the Millennium Development Goals. While all of these shifts have been subject to intense debate and critique, which is beyond the scope of this book, it highlights a trajectory towards human-centred approaches.

This brief summary suggests a linear shift, from hard-edged approaches to something more emancipatory, which is not the case. Alongside these trajectories, other understandings and uses of security and development have emerged. In contrast to people-centred approaches to development, in the 1980s debt crisis, when several developing countries defaulted on their loans and many more were struggling with their repayments, the World Bank and International Monetary Fund (IMF) reverted to economic models of development. Structural Adjustment Programmes (SAPs), which were a condition of debt relief, required extensive economic liberalisation (Stromquist 1999). These programmes had a negative effect on the majority of countries that implemented them, reversing the social improvements of the 1970s (Cornia *et al.* 1992; Reimers and Tiburcio 1993; Samoff 1994). Programmes of the World Bank and IMF now aim to incorporate human development elements but principles of economic development remain important. The Poverty Reduction Strategy Process (PRSP) is 'country driven' and requires the broad participation of civil society (IMF 2003). In contrast to the 'harshly imposed borrowing conditions' of the SAPs, the PRSP is 'portrayed as "partnerships" based on mutuality and trust' (Gould 2005: 1). However, Craig and Porter (2003: 53) note that underlying the human development principles, neoliberal principles remain. This approach suggests that some actors still understand development in economic terms. Similarly, the increasing involvement of the private sector in development, particularly as contractors, heightens neoliberal drivers of development.

In relation to security, state security fears have remained present in the policymaking of donors, particular in relation to terrorism. After the terrorist attacks of September 11, 2001, the US government returned to a realist paradigm to frame their security policy, with many other states following suit. Unprepared to address a non-state-based enemy, the US National Security Council immediately began to develop plans to invade Iraq (Bergen 2011). Other countries were encouraged to join a 'coalition of the willing', with aid, arms sales, trade concessions and political patronage provided in return (BOND 2003). More recently, international involvement in Libya and Syria in particular has not focused on individual security in those countries, but rather on containing a threat.

A wide range of understandings and uses of security and development coexist, some of which are explored in more detail in relation to the conceptual tension. However, on both sides of the nexus, a trajectory has emerged towards people-focused approaches, which aligns with the enthusiasm attached to the security–development nexus – in that it can bring together the two traditionally separate tools into a comprehensive approach that shifts the focus away from the state to also engage with the needs of individuals.

Studying the security–development nexus

Although policymakers have enthusiastically adopted the security–development nexus, it has received significant criticism. Scholarly inquiry into the security–development nexus has emerged within the peacebuilding literature, and it fits within the two main approaches: critical and orthodox.

Critical approaches

Critical approaches see peacebuilding as inherently flawed and argue that it needs to be radically rethought. With the security–development nexus, rather than the innovative approach presented by policymakers, critical scholars argue that the relationship between security and development is not comprehensive and balanced as one side, whether security or development, continues to dominate the nexus. These arguments have resulted in two bodies of critique: the securitisation of development and the developmentalisation of security.

The primary critique of the nexus focuses on the securitisation of development. From this perspective, development is being integrated with security to achieve security outcomes rather than the comprehensive approach outlined on previous pages. Scholars argue that the 'trend seems to be that security at home is becoming the overriding priority of both [security and development] agendas' (Beall *et al.* 2006: 53). This is supported by the reframing of development objectives around terrorism, crime and conflict. For example, in 2004 the British Prime Minister Tony Blair claimed 'we know that poverty and instability lead to weak states which can become havens for terrorists and other criminals' (*Guardian* 2004). Underdevelopment has come to be understood as dangerous: '[T]he ripple effects of poverty, environmental collapse, civil conflict or health crises require international management, since they do not respect geographical boundaries. Otherwise, they will inundate and destabilise Western society' (Duffield 2007: 1). The result is a one-sided security–development nexus where development is simply another tool to achieve international security. Rather than an end goal, poverty reduction becomes a means to achieve security outcomes, shifting the focus away from individual wellbeing towards international security needs.

16   *A critical analysis of the nexus*

This critique focuses on the impact of the security–development nexus on development practices, arguing that the development agenda has been co-opted for security purposes, side-lining the key modalities of development, such as local engagement and a focus on individual needs. This argument is derived from earlier connections, such as the counterinsurgencies of the 1970s and 1980s which used development to 'win the hearts and minds' of populations by supporting communities once insurgents had been driven from an area (Buur *et al.* 2007). For example, in Malaya, only 25 per cent of time was spent on defeating insurgents, with the remainder dedicated to development activities (Duffield 2010). The extensive focus on development activities was designed to undermine and isolate insurgents rather than enhance the wellbeing of individuals and communities.

The concept of securitisation was developed by the Copenhagen School of Security Studies to describe the process where an issue is taken out of normal politics to justify extraordinary measures (Buzan *et al.* 1998). Aradau (2004) argues that normal politics is how things are done in liberal democracies. As such, securitising an issue allows decisions to be made outside of the democratic political process, beyond debate and deliberation (Aradau 2004). For development, this means that approaches focus on what decision makers – international donors – deem important, not that which is important for recipients. Beall *et al.* (2006) argue that the securitisation of development 'ignores certain crucial aspects of the development process, not least the development agendas of partner governments, and other regional, national and local organisations'.

In practice, there are many examples where the implementation of the security–development nexus adheres to the arguments on the securitisation of development. In 2010, the UK government demanded 'that projects in the developing world must make the "maximum possible contribution" to British national security' (Watt 2010: 1). This is now incorporated into the UK Aid Strategy: 'the government will invest more to tackle the causes of instability, insecurity and conflict, and to tackle crime and corruption. This is fundamental to poverty reduction overseas, and will also strengthen our own national security at home' (DfID 2015).

The US government has also used development to further their security interests. As part of the US War on Terror, many countries were offered aid, arms sales, trade concessions and political patronage in exchange for joining the 'coalition of the willing' (BOND 2003). For some countries, such as Yemen, participation in the War on Terror had the potential to undermine the fragile social and political situation in the country, which would negatively impact on development (Tschirgi *et al.* 2010a). Furthermore, an increasing amount of development assistance is being channelled through the military. Between 1998 and 2006 the share of the US aid budget provided to the Department of Defence increased from 3.5 to 21.7 per cent (Brown and Tirnauer 2009). These examples highlight the prioritisation of security over development.

These changes are also affecting practices on the ground. In Afghanistan security forces have used development tools to 'win the hearts and minds' of local communities, providing generators to households as part of their counter-insurgency strategy (Duffield 2011). While the provision of generators may be a useful tool for households in Afghanistan, in this case there was no local engagement to determine if they were needed. This suggests that development is being employed to achieve security objectives rather than improve wellbeing. Duffield (2001: 16) contends that for development actors 'the convergence of development and security has meant that it has become difficult to separate their own development and humanitarian activities from the pervasive logic of the North's new security regime'. As Donini (2010: 4) notes, NGOs in Afghanistan 'are allowing their universe to be defined by political and security considerations rather than by the humanitarian imperative to save and protect lives'. Duffield points out that approaches defined by 'enlightened self-interest' often gloss over contradictions between domestically oriented security interests and South-oriented development priorities (Duffield 2007: 128). While 'enlightened self-interest' brings in the tools and strategies of development, the focus is on security outcomes rather than development needs. This limits the contribution of development, in particular the focus on individual wellbeing, as development tools are employed to protect the state. As a result, the integration of security and development into a comprehensive approach is also limited.

The argument on the securitisation of development highlights the use of development by security actors to achieve their objectives. However, rather than just security involvement in areas that have been the responsibility of development actors, development actors have also become active in addressing security challenges. Through the security–development nexus, development actors engage in security initiatives to further their own agenda, improving the lives of individuals in developing countries. This raises the potential for the developmentalisation of security, as development influences how security initiatives are implemented. In contrast to the securitisation of development, from this perspective security is co-opted by development actors to achieve their desired outcomes – creating space for development. For example, DfID engaged in security sector reform (SSR) in Sierra Leone in order to create a secure environment to ensure the sustainability of development initiatives.

The literature on the security–development nexus is beginning to engage with this perspective. Chitiyo (2010: 26) argues that 'the developmentalisation of security is becoming the "new wave" in the security–development nexus'. Kuhn (2008) has set out how securitisation and developmentalisation influence each other. Pugh *et al.* (2013) have also assessed whether UK policy on the security–development nexus has shifted from securitisation of development to developmentalisation of security. This perspective resonates with the fears of security actors that they will lose their mandate and end up focusing purely on development tasks.

Both of these critiques suggest that the security–development nexus does not result in a comprehensive approach as one element, whether security or development, continues to dominate. Arguments on the securitisation of development have been accompanied by calls for 'desecuritisation'. This is aligned with

18   *A critical analysis of the nexus*

critical peacebuilding literature, which calls for a radical rethink of current approaches.

Orthodox critiques

In contrast to critical perspectives, a number of scholars take a problem-solving or conventional critique that revolves around effectiveness and aims to improve performance. For instance, in relation to peacebuilding, Paris (2009: 108) recognises that the record is 'mixed and full of disappointments, but missions have on the whole done considerably more good than harm'. This places the emphasis on identifying flaws and developing solutions.

Similar approaches have been applied to the security–development nexus, with some critics engaging with the flaws in order to identify solutions. Stern and Ojendal (2010) and Tschirgi *et al.* (2010b) question the value of the security–development nexus given that it draws on poorly defined and contested concepts. This raises concerns of ineffective action as it is difficult for security and development actors to work in collaboration when there is no shared understanding of the nexus. Chandler (2007: 362) has questioned the motives of external actors adopting the security–development nexus, arguing that it 'reflects a retreat from strategic policymaking and a more inward looking approach to foreign policy'. While these critiques engage with the problematic relationship between security and development, they focus on the effectiveness of the security–development nexus. These scholars are therefore broadly supportive of the security–development nexus as long as there is an attempt to identify and correct the flaws.

In line with the peacebuilding literature, critical approaches to the security–development nexus argue that it needs to be radically rethought. Many of the arguments from this perspective, particularly on the securitisation of development, do resonate with practice. Yet when it comes to the security–development nexus, critical approaches immediately overlook the potential of the nexus. Arguments on securitisation prompt very little probing of why the nexus results in that outcome and not the outcomes expected by policymakers.

In contrast, the orthodox critique engages with the effectiveness of peacebuilding and aims to improve performance. There is a risk that the ideas presented in this book fall into the conventional, problem-solving response that Duffield (2008) argues seeks to lift the security–development nexus out of its current malaise through 'more research, a better circulation of "good practice" and incremental reform'. While the orthodox scholars are broadly supportive of the security–development nexus pending coordination and sequencing, this book argues that what is required to bring security and development together into an emancipatory approach is more fundamental than just coordination and sequencing. Changes are required at conceptual, institutional and motivational levels because the underpinnings of the nexus, as outlined by the four tensions in the next section, limit its 'success'. The research analyses the security–development nexus from a critical perspective. In line with Newman, Paris and Richmond

A critical analysis of the nexus   19

(2009: 23), the book 'raises questions about existing institutions, policy assumptions and the interests they serve, and is ready to challenge these assumptions'.

As a result, the book challenges both critical and orthodox perspectives on the security–development nexus. With a starting point that engages with the positive potential of the security–development nexus, the research does not immediately call for a radical rethink of the nexus, and it challenges arguments on the securitisation of development. However, it acknowledges that there are no easy fixes for the security–development nexus, and the emphasis on emancipation is critical of the universal liberal blueprint put forward by orthodox scholars. This is achieved by adopting the Welsh School of Critical Security Studies as a theoretical model.

Examining the security–development nexus

In order to establish why the security–development nexus is more closely aligned to the critiques on the securitisation of development than the expectations of policymakers, this book investigates what inhibits the integration between security and development. Drawing on the enthusiasm of policymakers, the research engages with the positive potential of the security–development nexus to investigate why the relationship, or site of integration. between security and development is flawed. This investigation into the disjuncture between the theory and practice of the security–development nexus aligns with the assumptions of the Welsh School of Critical Security Studies.

Building on constructivist theories, critical approaches to security studies engage in a critique of traditional security approaches. Rather than a distinct theoretical perspective, critical approaches to security studies tend to be defined in contrast to the ontology, epistemology, starting point and assumptions of traditional approaches to security, particularly realism. This includes the

> emphasis upon parsimony and coherence; its privileging of a rational, state-centric worldview based upon the primacy of military power in an anarchic environment; its emphasis upon order and predictability as positive values; and its structural view of international politics as ahistorical, recurrent, and non-contextual.
>
> (Newman 2010: 83)

Critical theories also seek to move beyond a traditional approach to security. Critical security studies is based on the assumption that 'security can operate according to a different logic: that progressive ends can be achieved through security rather than outside it' (McDonald 2008: 71). The Welsh School of Critical Security Studies in particular takes a positive view of security. Rather than focusing on security in terms of threats, the Welsh School's interpretation is closer to Cicero's early interpretation as the 'absence of distress' (cited in Wæver 2008). As such, security is understood to be broader than just state security: 'Broadening securitisation will broaden "real" security (and bring

20   *A critical analysis of the nexus*

resources and attention) to a wider range of problems and actors beyond the state' (Newman 2010: 85–6). The Welsh School takes a normative approach, distinguished by its 'desire to radically reconceive security as the emancipation of individuals and communities from structural constraints' (Burke 2007: 6). As such, security is imbued with the potential to be emancipatory, rather than militaristic and state-centred.

As this research is situated within the disjuncture between the potential of the nexus and its critiques, it engages in immanent critique. A key element of critical security studies, immanent critique compares the outcomes – the securitisation of development – with the stated objectives – a comprehensive approach that integrates security and development (Stamnes 2004). The securitisation of development adheres to a traditional security perspective as it adopts development to the extent that it achieves security outcomes. A comprehensive approach that integrates the two shifts away from traditional security approaches to become more emancipatory.

For the Welsh School of Critical Security Studies, emancipation is the desired end goal of security but it is only vaguely defined, which weakens its value as an analytical tool. For Booth, emancipation is a process to be defined by those whose security is in question: 'what the world will look like must be settled by those future generations, when new and different possibilities and problems become clearer' (Booth 1990: 3). While Critical Security Studies provides some guidance as to what emancipation is, the actual conceptualisation should be derived from those experiencing emancipation. Such a conceptualisation is limited as an analytical tool without extensive research involving the intended beneficiaries of post-conflict reconstruction. As a result, a more concrete conceptualisation is required.

Within this research, emancipation is operationalised through human security. Human security provides the theoretical basis for the integration of security and development into a nexus that is emancipatory. Human security has been heavily criticised.[1] Tadjbakhsh (2014: 4) notes that 'what was supposed to be a simple, noble and obvious idea soon became engulfed in a cacophony of political and academic debates centred on its definitions, their advantages and weak points, and on its theoretical and practical applicability'. Despite these criticisms there remains value in the key tenets of human security.

Richmond (2007: 460) describes two versions of human security: 'the institutional approach and the emancipatory approach – and while one sees the creation of liberal institutions to protect human security as paramount, the other aims at empowerment of individuals and the removal of unnecessary constraints over their lives'. While policy communities have readily adopted the first version, resulting in what Christie (2010: 170) has labelled a 'new orthodoxy', the latter version still holds the potential to articulate what emancipation involves. Some scholars continue to challenge the emancipatory potential of human security (see for example Williams and Krause 1997; McCormack 2008). Taken out of its policy context there is still value in the concept. As Christie (2010: 170) argues, 'human security retains some limited critical potential for engaging with particular security problems and may be usefully employed for narrowly defined short-term goals'. For this research, human security is used as a lens to highlight the distinction between a traditional security approach and a new, emancipatory approach that reifies comprehensiveness.

Despite its critics, human security presents the opposite end of the spectrum from traditional security approaches. As such, it articulates in more detail what emancipation involves. This provides analytical grasp to the positive potential of the security–development nexus.

Operationalising the theory

The research takes a positive starting point based on the enthusiasm of policy-makers adopting the nexus. In contrast to a traditional security approach to organised crime, which engages with the threat posed by criminal activity to the state and seeks to disrupt it through law enforcement or military strategies, this research engages with the idea of an integrated and holistic approach that brings security and development together in an emancipatory approach. As well as focusing on the security threat posed by organised crime, such an approach would ensure that the impact of organised crime on development is also recognised, but also that development strategies are employed to address the factors that make a country conducive to organised crime. The inclusion of development is also expected to bring a new set of practices, particularly with the focus of many development actors on local engagement and people-centred approaches.

It is recognised that the security–development nexus is not perfect as it is still influenced by resources, the personality of personnel and other factors. Similarly, as outlined in the previous section, understandings and uses of security and development differ significantly. However, to analyse the security–development nexus and understand how the hypothesised tensions influence the integration of security and development, a spectrum is established between a traditional security approach and an integrated, emancipatory approach.[2] Analysis investigates what inhibits a shift away from a traditional security approach towards the other end of the spectrum, recognising that a complete shift is impossible.

Methodology

Methodologically, critical security studies is based on constructivist foundations where the security–development nexus is understood as a concept that is given meaning by the actors that employ it. As such, the nuances in how the security–development nexus is understood and applied by external actors engaged in post-conflict reconstruction are examined.

Critical security studies is distinguished from other epistemological approaches by its 'methodological flexibility' (Salter 2013: 17). The emphasis is on using the best tools for the specific research question. Increasingly, critical security scholars are drawing on different approaches to inform their research

22   *A critical analysis of the nexus*

design and choice of methods. Salter and Mutlu (2013) outline five different approaches to research within critical security studies: the ethnographic turn, the practice turn, the discursive turn, the corporeal turn and the material turn. As this research posits that the outcomes of the security–development nexus are a function of its implementation, it examines how the nexus is put into practice. As such, it fits within the practice turn.

Drawing on practice theory, the practice turn has its foundations in philosophy and sociology. It has only recently been applied to international relations, most notably through studies by Bigo (1996, 2002), Pouliot (2010) and Williams (2007). For Neumann (2002), practice theory provides a valuable tool for international studies as it entails a shift away from 'armchair analysis' to investigate how social action is enacted in and on the world. It draws on Wittgenstein's contention that the meaning of a concept is understood by analysing how it is used (cited in Collins 2001). Accordingly, this research engages with the security–development nexus as it is adopted and implemented by external actors addressing organised crime as part of post-conflict reconstruction. The research focuses on the integration of security and development into a nexus and why this might be problematic. Examining how the nexus is put into practice reveals tensions between the two components of the nexus and factors inhibiting their integration. The research posits that this produces a flawed integration that results in the outcomes that critics of the nexus have focused on, rather than a comprehensive approach.

As this research seeks to understand how the security–development nexus is implemented in practice, it draws on in-depth qualitative analysis. Two cases were selected of external actors addressing organised crime as part of broader post-conflict reconstruction efforts: the West Africa Coast Initiative (WACI) in Sierra Leone and the EU Police Mission (EUPM) in Bosnia. These cases were selected as they have sufficient similarities to facilitate comparison. However, they also have key differences that allow for an examination of the tensions in significantly different contexts.

In Sierra Leone, there were many and varied actors addressing organised crime connected through the WACI. The initiative was developed in response to the Political Declaration on the Prevention of Drug Abuse, Illicit Drug Trafficking and Organised Crime in West Africa and its accompanying regional action plan drafted by the Economic Community of West African States (ECOWAS). The WACI is an inter-agency project to address organised crime and illicit drug trafficking, bringing together the United Nations Office on Drugs and Crime (UNODC), the Department of Peacekeeping Operations (UNDPKO), the UN Department of Political Affairs (UNDPA) and Interpol. However, on the ground, implementation of the WACI was primarily driven by the UN Peacebuilding Mission in Sierra Leone (UNIPSIL) and UNODC officers based in the country. The focus of this research was the core WACI project in Sierra Leone, SLEU74 'Building Institutional Capacity to Respond to the Threat Posed by Illicit Drug Trafficking and Organised Crime in Sierra Leone', which was implemented from April 2010 to April 2013.

Until June 2012, organised crime was addressed in Bosnia by EUPM. The mission took over from the UN International Police Task Force (IPTF) in 2003 to continue the police reform process. Since then the mission has evolved through four phases. The focus of this research was EUPM IV, which commenced in January 2010 and lasted until the mission ended in June 2012. This fourth phase focused solely on organised crime and corruption. It also provides a better insight into the EU's initiatives within the security–development nexus as by 2010 the EU had articulated its policy in this area.

For both case studies, field research was conducted in the final phases of the programmes as key personnel were still in place but were beginning to reflect on implementation. Research was conducted in Bosnia in October 2011 and March 2012, and in Sierra Leone in January and February 2012. Research relied on two data sources: interviews with international, national and civil society actors, and official documentation from international actors addressing organised crime.

During field visits, semi-structured interviews were conducted with the key international actors engaged in initiatives to address organised crime. These interviews were designed to determine how individuals within international organisations engaging with organised crime witnessed and understood the implementation of the security–development nexus. They also sought to understand the factors that influence the security–development nexus, which will be set out in the empirical chapters that discuss the tensions. Interviews were also conducted with other actors connected to initiatives to address organised crime, including local law-enforcement agencies, international NGOs, diplomatic representatives and civil society actors. The aim of these interviews was to elicit a secondary perspective on how the security–development nexus is implemented. Particularly with actors that work in partnership with the key international organisations engaged with organised crime, these interviews provided another layer to triangulate the findings.

As previously stated, because this research is situated within the disjuncture between the potential of the nexus and its critiques, it engages in immanent critique. As Booth (2005: 11) points out, however, immanent critique cannot assess practices on the basis of blueprints that are not possible in reality. Rather, analysis needs to be based on unfulfilled potential that already exists. The focus on 'immanent, unrealised or unfulfilled possibilities' gives the analysis critical purchase, preventing recommendations that call for possibilities that are out of reach (Wyn-Jones 2005: 221). Postone and Brick (1993: 230) argue that this unfulfilled potential needs to be located within the existing society, not judged from outside as a 'transcendental ought'. While it can be argued that the integration of security and development 'ought' to result in a new, comprehensive approach, this needs to be possible, or immanent, in its existence to account for the unfulfilled potential. This 'unfulfilled potential' has been highlighted as the security–development nexus is adopted as a new form of comprehensive approach to post-conflict reconstruction. Chapter 3 engages with the selected case studies in more detail, outlining how the implementing agencies perceived the security–development nexus, thus establishing the benchmark for this 'unfulfilled potential'.

24 *A critical analysis of the nexus*

Through immanent critique, this book examines the security–development nexus from the standpoint of its positive potential operationalised through human security. From this perspective, four tensions are examined in Chapter 2 to track the divergence of the security–development nexus from this potential and show how the integration of security and development is inhibited.

Notes

1 The criticisms of human security have been addressed in detail by Tadjbakhsh and Chenoy (2007).
2 This spectrum is outlined in more depth in the discussion of each tension in Chapter 2.

References

Akkerman, Tjitske (2009). 'New Wars, New Morality?' *Acta Politica* 44(1): 74–86.
Alkire, Sabine and Severine Deneulin (2009). 'A Normative Framework for Development', in Severin Deneulin and Lila Shahani (eds), *An Introduction to the Human Development and Capability Approach: Freedom and Agency.* London, Earthscan.
Aradau, Claudia (2004). 'Security and the Democratic Scene', *Journal of International Relations and Development* 7(4): 388–413.
Baker, Pauline (2001). 'Conflict Resolution vs. Democratic Governance: Divergent Paths to Peace', in Chester Crocker, Fen Osler Hampson and Pamela Aall (eds), *Turbulent Peace: The Challenges of Managing International Conflict.* Washington DC, United States Institute of Peace.
Ball, Nicole (2001). 'The Challenge of Rebuilding War-torn Societies', in Chester Crocker, Fen Osler Hampson amd Pamela Aall (eds), *Turbulent Peace: The Challenges of Managing International Conflict.* Washington DC, United States Institute of Peace.
Beall, Jo, Thomas Goodfellow, and James Putzel (2006). 'Introductory Article: On the Discourse of Terrorism, Security and Development', *Journal of International Development* 18(1): 51–67.
Berdal, Mats (2009). *Building Peace After War.* London, Routledge.
Bergen, Peter L. (2011). *The Longest War: The Enduring Conflict Between America and Al-Qaeda.* New York, Free Press.
Bigo, Didier (1996). *Polices en Resaux: L'Experience Europeenne.* Paris, Presses de Sciences Po.
Bigo, Didier (2002). 'Security and Immigration: Toward a Critique of Governmentality of Unease', *Alternatives: Global, Local, Political* 27(1): 62–92.
BOND (2003). 'Global Security and Development', *BOND Discussion Paper.* London, British Overseas NGOs for Development.
Booth, Ken (1990). 'A New Security Concept for Europe', in Paul Eavis (ed.), *European Security: The New Agenda.* Bristol, Saferworld Foundation.
Booth, Ken (2005). 'Critical Explorations', in Ken Booth (ed.), *Critical Security Studies and World Politics.* Boulder, CO; London, Lynne Rienner.
Brauch, Hans Gunter (2008). 'Introduction: Globalization and Environmental Challenges: Reconceptualizing Security in the 21st Century', in Hans Gunter Brauch, Ursula Spring and Czeslaw Mesjasz (eds), *Globalization and Environmental Challenges: Reconceptualizing Security in the 21st Century.* Berlin, Springer.

Brinkerhoff, Derick W. (2005). 'Rebuilding Governance in Failed States and Post-Conflict Societies: Core Concepts and Cross-cutting Themes', *Public Administration and Development* 25(1): 3–14.

Brown, Keith and Jill Tirnauer (2009). *Trends in US Foreign Assistance Over the Past Decade*. Washington DC, USAID.

Burke, Anthony (2007). 'What Security Makes Possible: Some Thoughts on Critical Security Studies', *Working Paper 2007/1*, Australian National University.

Buur, Lars, Steffen Jensen and Fin Stepputat (eds) (2007). *The Security–Development Nexus: Expressions of Sovereignty and Securitization in Southern Africa*. Cape Town, HSRC Press.

Buzan, Barry, Ole Wæver and Jaap de Wilde (1998). *Security: A New Framework for Analysis*. Boulder, CO, Lynne Rienner.

Chandler, David (2007). 'The Security–Development Nexus and the Rise of "Anti-Foreign Policy"', *Journal of International Relations and Development* 10(4): 362–86.

Chandler, David (2008). 'The Human Security Paradox: How Nation States Grew to Love Cosmopolitan Ethics', presented at *Globalization, Difference and Human Securities Conference*, 12–14 March, Graduate School of Human Science, Osaka University, Japan.

Chitiyo, Knox (2010). 'African Security and the Securitisation of Development', in Nicholas Kitchen (ed.), *Resurgent Continent? Africa and the World*. London, LSE IDEAS.

Christie, Ryerson (2010). 'Critical Voices and Human Security: To Endure, To Engage or to Critique?' *Security Dialogue* 41(2): 169–90.

Clarke, David (2002). *The Capability Approach: Its Development, Critiques and Recent Advances*. Manchester, Global Poverty Research Group.

Collier, Paul, Lani Elliot, Havard Hegre, Anke Hoeffler, Marta Reynal-Querol and Nicholas Sambanis (2003). *Breaking the Conflict Trap: Civil War and Development Policy*. Washington DC, World Bank.

Collins, H.M. (2001). 'What is Tacit Knowledge?' in Theodore Schatzki, Karin Knorr Cetina and Elke von Savigny (eds), *The Practice Turn in Contemporary Theory*. Abingdon; NewYork, Routledge.

Cornia, Giovanni Andrea, Rolph Van der Hoeven and Thandika P. Mkandawire (eds) (1992). *Africa's Recovery on the 1990s: From Stagnation and Adjustment to Human Development*. New York, St Martin's Press.

Craig, David and Doug Porter (2003). 'Poverty Reduction Strategy Papers: A New Convergence', *World Development* 31(1): 53–69.

Deneulin, Severine (2009). 'Ideas Related to Human Development', in Severine Deneulin and Lila Shahani (eds), *An Introduction to the Human Development and Capability Approach: Freedom and Agency*. London, Earthscan.

DfID (2005). *Fighting Poverty to Build a Safer World: A Strategy for Security and Development*. London, Department for International Development.

DfID (2015). *UK Aid: Tackling Global Challenges in the National Interest*. London, Department for International Development.

Dobbins, James (2008). 'Towards a More Professional Approach to Nation-Building', *International Peacekeeping* 15(1): 67–83.

Donini, Antonio (2010). *Afghanistan: Humanitarianism Unravelled?* Boston, Feinstein International Center.

Douzinas, Costas (2007). *Human Rights and Empire: The Political Philosophy of Cosmopolitanism*. London, Routledge-Cavendish.

26 *A critical analysis of the nexus*

Duffield, Mark (2001). *Global Governance and the New Wars: The Merging of Security and Development.* London, Zed Books.

Duffield, Mark (2007). *Development, Security and Unending War: Governing the World of Peoples.* Cambridge, Polity Press.

Duffield, Mark (2008). 'Foreword', in Michael Pugh, Neil Cooper and Mandy Turner (eds), *Whose Peace? Critical Perspectives on the Political Economy of Peacebuilding.* London, Palgrave Macmillan.

Duffield, Mark (2010). 'The Liberal Way of Development and the Development Security Impasse: Exploring the Global Life-Chance Divide', *Security Dialogue* 41(1): 53–76.

Duffield, Mark (2011). 'Liberal Interventionism and the Crisis of Acceptance: From Protection to Resilience', *Centre for the Study of Global Security and Development Annual Lecture.* London, Queen Mary University of London.

Duffield, Mark and Nicholas Waddell (2006). 'Securing Humans in a Dangerous World', *International Politics* 43(1): 1–23.

Fukuyama, Francis (2004). *Statebuilding: Governance and World Order in the 21st Century.* Ithaca, NY, Cornell University Press.

Ghosh, Pradip K (1984). 'Introduction', in Pradip Ghosh (ed.), *Third World Development: A Basic Needs Approach.* Westport, CT, Greenwood Press.

Gould, Jeremy (2005). 'Poverty, Politics and States of Partnership', in Jeremy Gould (ed.), *The New Conditionality: The Politics of Poverty Reduction Strategies.* London, Zed Books.

Guardian (2004). 'Blair Demands International Action to Aid Africa', www.theguardian.com/world/2004/oct/07/politics.foreignpolicy accessed 12 February 2013.

Hettne, Bjorn (2010). 'Development and Security: Origins and Future', *Security Dialogue* 41(1): 31–52

IMF (International Monetary Fund) (2003). *Evaluation of Poverty Reduction Strategy Papers and the Poverty Reduction and Growth Facility.* Washington DC, International Monetary Fund Independent Evaluation Office.

Jabri, Vivienne (2007). *War and the Transformation of Global Politics.* Basingstoke, Palgrave.

Jahan, Selim (2002). *Measuring Human Development: Evolution of the Human Development Index.* New York, UNDP.

Jeong, Ho-Won (2005). *Peacebuilding in Postconflict Societies: Strategy and Process.* Boulder, CO, Lynne Rienner Publishing.

Kaldor, Mary (2006). *New Wars and Old Wars: Organised Violence in a Global Era.* Cambridge, Polity.

Kaldor, Mary (2007). *Human Security: Reflections on Globalization and Intervention.* Cambridge, Polity Press.

Kaldor, Mary (2009). 'The Reconstruction of Political Authority in a Global Era', in Denisa Kostovicova and Vesna Bojicic-Dzelilovic (eds), *Persistent State Weakness in the Global Age.* London, Ashgate.

Khong, Yuen Foong (2001). 'Human Security: A Shotgun Approach to Alleviating Human Misery', *Global Governance* 7(3): 231–6.

Kostovicova, Denisa and Vesna Bojicic-Dzelilovic (2009). 'Introduction: Persistent State Weakness in the Global Age', in Denisa Kostovicova and Vesna Bojicic-Dzelilovic (eds), *Persistent State Weakness in the Global Age.* London, Ashgate.

Kostovicova, Denisa, Vesna Bojicic-Dzelilovic and Francesco Strazzari (2010). *Multi-Stakeholder Partnerships for Socio-Economic Development in Post-Conflict Reconstruction.* Amsterdam, Multipart.

Krause, Keith and Oliver Jutersonke (2005). 'Peace, Security and Development in Post-Conflict Environments', *Security Dialogue* 36(4): 447–62.

Kuhn, Florian (2008). 'Equal Opportunities: Exploring the Turning Point between Securitization and Developmentalization', paper presented at the International Studies Association Annual Convention. San Francisco.

Last, David (2000). 'Organising for Effective Peacebuilding', in Tom Woodhouse and Oliver Ramsbotham (eds), *Peacekeeping and Conflict Resolution*. London, Frank Cass.

McCormack, Tara (2008). 'Power and Agency in the Human Security Framework', *Cambridge Review of International Affairs* 21(1): 113–28.

McDonald, Matt (2008). 'Constructivism', in Paul D. Williams (ed.), *Security Studies: An Introduction*. London; New York, Routledge.

Mamdani, Mahmood (1996). *Citizen and Subject: Contemporary Africa and the Legacy of Late Colonialism*. Princeton, NJ, Princeton University Press.

Muller, Harald (2002). 'Security Cooperation', in Walter Carlsnaes, Thomas Risse-Kappen and Beth A. Simmons (eds), *Handbook of International Relations*. London; Thousand Oaks, CA, Sage.

Neumann, Iver B. (2002). 'Returning Practice to the Linguistic Turn: The Case of Diplomacy', *Millennium* 31(3): 627–51.

Newman, Edward (2010). 'Critical Human Security Studies', *Review of International Studies* 36(1): 77–94.

Newman, Edward, Roland Paris and Oliver Richmond (2009). 'Introduction', in Edward Newman, Roland Paris and Oliver Richmond (eds), *New Perspectives on Liberal Peacebuilding*. Tokyo, United Nations University Press.

OECD (Organisation for Economic Co-operation and Development) (1997). *Guidelines on Peace, Conflict and Development Cooperation*. Paris, OECD-DAC.

Ottaway, Marina (2002). 'Rebuilding State Institutions in Failed States', *Development and Change* 33(5): 1001–23.

Paris, Roland (2001). 'Human Security: Paradigm Shift or Hot Air?' *International Security* 26(2): 87–102.

Paris, Roland (2009). 'Does Liberal Peacebuilding have a Future?' in Edward Newman, Roland Paris and Oliver Richmond (eds), *New Perspectives on Liberal Peacebuilding*. Tokyo, United Nations University Press.

Paris, Roland and Timothy D. Sisk (2009). 'Introduction: Understanding the Contradictions of Postwar Statebuilding', in Roland Paris and Timothy Sisk (eds), *The Dilemmas of Statebuilding: Confronting the Contradictions of Postwar Peace Operations*. London, Routledge.

Postone, Moishe and Barbara Brick (1993). 'Critical Theory and Political Economy', in Seyla Benhabib, Wolfgang Bonß and John McCole (eds), *On Max Horkheimer: New Perspectives*. Cambridge, MIT Press.

Pouliot, Vincent (2010). *International Security in Practice: The Politics of NATO–Russia Diplomacy*. Cambridge; New York, Cambridge University Press.

Pugh, Jonathan, Clive Gabay and Alison Williams (2013). 'Beyond the Securitisation of Development: The Limits of Intervention, Developmentisation of Security and Repositioning of Purpose in the UK Coalition Government's Policy Agenda', *Geoforum* 44: 193–201.

Ranis, Gustav (2004). 'The Evolution of Development Thinking: Theory and Policy', *Centre Discussion Paper No. 886*. New Haven, Economic Growth Centre, Yale University.

28 *A critical analysis of the nexus*

Reimers, Fernando and Luis Tiburcio (1993). *Education, Adjustment and Reconstruction: Options for Change. Education on the Move*. Paris, UNESCO.

Reisman, Michael (2003). 'Assessing Claims to Revise the Laws of War: Editorial Comment', *American Journal of International Law* 97(1): 82–90.

Richmond, Oliver (2007). 'Emancipatory Forms of Human Security and Liberal Peace-building', *International Journal* 62(3): 458–77.

Rogers, Paul (2002). *Losing Control: Global Security in the Twenty-First Century*. London, Pluto.

Salter, Mark (2013). 'The Practice Turn: Introduction', in Mark Salter and Can E. Mutlu (eds), *Research Methods in Critical Security Studies: An Introduction*. London; New York, Routledge.

Salter, Mark and Can E. Mutlu (eds) (2013). *Research Methods in Critical Security Studies: An Introduction*. London; New York, Routledge.

Samoff, Joel (1994). *Coping With Crisis: Austerity, Adjustment and Human Resources*. London, Casell.

Sen, Amartya (1999). *Development as Freedom*. Oxford, Oxford University Press.

Sisk, Timothy (2009). 'Conclusion: Confronting the Contradictions', in Roland Paris and Timothy Sisk (eds), *The Dilemmas of Statebuilding: Confronting the Contradictions of Postwar Peace Operations*. London, Routledge.

Smilie, Ian (1995). *The Alms Bazaar: Altruism Under Fire – Non Profit Organizations and International Development*. London, Intermediate Technology Publications.

Stamnes, Eli (2004). 'Critical Security Studies and the United Nations Preventive Deployment in Macedonia', *International Peacekeeping* 11(1): 161–81.

Stern, Maria and Joakim Ojendal (2010). 'Mapping the Security Development Nexus: Conflict, Complexity, Cacophony, Convergence?' *Security Dialogue* 41(1): 5–30.

Streeten, Paul (1979). 'From Growth to Basic Needs', *Finance and Development* 16(3): 28–31.

Stromquist, Nelly (1999). 'The Impact of Structural Adjustment Programmes in Africa and Latin America', in Christine Heward and Sheila Bunwaree (eds), *Gender, Education and Development: Beyond Access to Empowerment*. London, Zed Books.

Tadjbakhsh, Shahrbanou (2014). 'In Defense of the Broad View of Human Security', in Mary Martin and Taylor Owen (eds), *Handbook of Human Security*. New York; London, Routledge.

Tadjbakhsh, Shahrbanou and Anuradha Chenoy (2007). *Human Security: Concepts and Implications*. Oxford; New York, Routledge.

Tschirgi, Necla, Michael Lund and Francesco Mancini (2010a). 'The Security–Development Nexus', in Necla Tshirgi, Michael Lund and Francesco Mancini (eds), *Security and Development: Searching for Critical Connections*. Boulder, CO, Lynne Rienner.

Tschirgi, Necla, Michael Lund and Francesco Mancini (2010b). 'Conclusion', in Necla Tshirgi, Michael Lund and Francesco Mancini (eds), *Security and Development: Searching for Critical Connections*. Boulder, CO, Lynne Rienner.

UN (1998). *Report of the Secretary-General on the Work of the Organization*. New York, United Nations.

UNDP (UN Development Programme) (1990). *Human Development Report: Concept and Measurement of Human Development*. New York, United Nations Development Programme.

UNDP (UN Development Programme) (1994). *Human Development Report: New Dimensions of Human Security*. New York; Oxford, Oxford University Press.

Uvin, Peter (2002). 'The Development/Peacebuilding Nexus: A Typology and History of Changing Paradigms', *Journal of Peacebuilding and Development* 1(1): 1–20.

Wæver, Ole (2008). 'Peace and Security: Two Evolving Concepts and their Changing Relationship', in Hans Gunter Brauch, Ursula O. Spring and Czeslaw Mesjasz (eds), *Globalization and Environmental Challenges: Reconceptualizing Security in the 21st Century*. Berlin, Springer.

Watt, Nicholas (2010). 'Protests as UK Security Put at Heart of Government's Aid Policy', *Guardian*, 30 August: 1.

Williams, Michael C. (2007). *Culture and Security: Symbolic Power and the Politics of International Security*. London; New York, Routledge.

Williams, Michael and Keith Krause (eds) (1997). *Critical Security Studies: Concepts and Cases. Borderlines*. Minneapolis, University of Minnesota Press.

Woodward, Susan (2003). *On War and Peacebuilding: Unfinished Legacy of the 1990s*. New York, City University of New York.

World Bank (2001). *World Development Report 2000/2001: Attacking Poverty*. Washington DC, World Bank.

Wyn-Jones, Richard (2005). 'Emancipation in the Critical Security Studies Project', in Ken Booth (ed.), *Critical Security Studies and World Politics*. Boulder, CO; London, Lynne Rienner.

2 Tensions in the security–development nexus

For external actors, adoption of the security–development nexus is expected to achieve a new and comprehensive approach. For example, Schnabel (2011: 44) points to their 'mutually supportive coexistence'. There have been numerous calls to integrate the two concepts into a comprehensive approach (see for example UN 2004a). However, as noted earlier the nexus has been critiqued for its asymmetry, suggesting that either security or development dominates. The focus of critics on the asymmetry of the security–development nexus suggests that rather than a mutually supportive relationship, the linkage between security and development is uneasy – attempts at integration raise a series of conflicts and contradictions that are not easily resolved.

With the expectation that the integration of development with security would ensure the activities of external actors shift away from a traditional security approach, the spectrum between traditional security approaches and emancipation provides a useful analytical tool. Different elements of external engagement can be mapped along this spectrum to identify what inhibits the integration of security and development. The adoption of the security–development nexus does not imply a complete shift towards emancipation, but the integration of security and development would result in some movement away from traditional security.

Hypotheses have been developed of four tensions that influence the integration of security and development. In their study on post-conflict reconstruction, Paris and Sisk (2009: 1) define the tensions as 'competing (and sometimes contradictory) imperatives facing those who attempt to reconstitute effective and legitimate governmental structures in war-torn states'. These competing imperatives become 'vexing policy dilemmas – that is, multiple imperatives where there are no obvious solutions' (Paris and Sisk 2007: 1). This research contends that conceptual, causal, institutional and motivational tension influences the integration of security and development.

The integration of security and development into a nexus that shifts interventions from a traditional security approach to something more emancipatory relies on specific understandings of security and development. Conceptual tension, which arises from the different understandings of security and development, influences what is integrated with what and thus the type of nexus that emerges.

Similarly, an emancipatory nexus relies on a particular understanding of the relationship between security and development – how they influence each other to achieve a particular outcome. The causal tension, which arises from different perspectives on how security and development are applied and the linkages between them, influences the form of integration between the two concepts.

Even when there is a concerted effort to achieve an emancipatory nexus, the actors and institutions involved influence the balance between security and development. This institutional tension influences the extent of the integration between the two concepts. Although the security–development nexus is a new trend to ensure that post-conflict reconstruction becomes more effective and sustainable, this is driven by different motivations, from containing problems to enhancing the security and wellbeing of individuals. This motivational tension reveals the reasons why security and development are being integrated and thus the prioritisation of each concept within the nexus.

The analysis of each tension investigates specific elements of external engagement through the two case studies, mapping them along the spectrum from traditional security approaches to emancipation in order to identify what inhibits the integration of security and development.

Conceptual tension

Security and development are difficult concepts to pin down. There are numerous different understandings and they are not always clearly articulated. Shifts in the two concepts since the end of the Cold War suggest that they are becoming closely related and interconnected, making their integration into a comprehensive approach that aligns with human security appear to be a natural evolution. However, other understandings of security and development have also emerged, including a resurgence of more traditional state- or economic-centred perspectives.

A full discussion of the evolution of security and development is beyond the scope of this book. However, Rothschild (1995) argues that security has extended from the Cold War preoccupation with existential threats and sovereignty in four ways: downwards from national to individual levels and upwards from the national to the global level to recognise a broader range of referent objects to be secured; horizontally to recognise many more security threats; and the range of actors responsible for providing security has expanded to account for these new areas.

A similar analysis can be applied to development. Development has also shifted downwards from the national to individual level through human development. The recognition that development problems are not geographically isolated, as pressures such as climate change and economic decline are not contained within state borders, has shifted development to be considered within a global context. The variables that impact on development have broadened to include migration, water, trade, culture, democracy, technology, human rights, globalisation, consumption, gender and participation. As a result, the actors

32 *Tensions in the security–development nexus*

tasked with providing development has expanded. As well as official governmental aid agencies, NGOs and intergovernmental agencies, the private sector is also increasingly participating in development (Donahue and Zeckhauser 2011).

Rather than a linear evolution, both security and development have broadened into many areas. Human security and human development approaches have continued to gain prominence. Although there are conflicting perspectives on human security, with a division between 'freedom from fear' and 'freedom from want', the main premise behind human security is the emphasis on people's security (Kaldor 2007). Similarly, human development also emphasises the wellbeing of people rather than economic performance (Jahan 2002). Drawing on Sen's capabilities approach, the aims of both human security and human development is to enable individuals to shape their future (Sen 1999).

Despite the increasing focus on human security and human development, the practice of some actors continues to fit within a traditional understanding of hard security and economic development approaches. Williams (2011: 164) argues that development is directly informed by the 'prevailing international order'. Given the recent changes in international order – from the terrorist attacks of September 11, 2001, the invasion of Iraq and Afghanistan, the rise of the BRICS and the global financial crisis – development is in a state of flux (Williams and Harmon 2013). This argument can be applied to international politics more broadly, having implications for security policy also. For example, the terrorist attacks in September 2001 resulted in a rethinking of security policy by the US in particular, with the result that underdevelopment was considered a threat in the 2002 and 2004 National Security Strategy (National Security Council 2002; National Security Council 2004).

Although the US National Security Strategy has included development as a key element, this is driven by concerns over the survival of the state and preservation of sovereignty. The 2002 US National Security Strategy recognised that 'the events of September 11, 2001 have taught us that weak states like Afghanistan can pose as great a danger to our national interest as strong states' (National Security Council 2002: 4). While this statement recognises underdevelopment as a threat to security, the security under threat is not that of the Afghan people but of the US state. As such, development is being used as a strategy to ensure state security, an approach that adheres to realist understandings of security and the securitisation of development.

Similarly, while development has become increasingly framed in human development terms, neoliberal economic perspectives continue to influence some actors. Craig and Porter (2003) argue that 'sharp neoliberal economism' continues to influence the World Bank and IMF despite their adopting human development principles. Private sector involvement adds another dimension as a number of organisations now seek to profit from development funding.

While these perspectives can be considered opposite to human security and human development, with the focus on the state or economy rather than individuals, there are blurred boundaries between them with new understandings of security and development emerging in between. Human security and human

Tensions in the security–development nexus 33

development depend on bottom-up approaches that directly engage with individuals to achieve human-centred outcomes. However, other approaches emphasise human-centred outcomes but address problems from the top-down. The Millennium Development Goals (MDGs), which seek to improve development outcomes for individuals, employ top-down strategies that are implemented at the state level through strategies such as privatisation of public services (Bond 2006). Antrobus (2003) critiques the MDGs over their quantifiable indicators and their abstraction from the social, political and economic context. While the MDGs aim to improve conditions for individuals, they are indicative of an approach to development that fits in between human development, and neoliberal economism.

Debates regarding resilience also assume a position between the two dominant approaches. Strategies to ensure resilience are focused at the individual or community level to enhance self-reliance to cope with security and development challenges. Chandler (2012a: 213) argues that ensuring resilience has the effect of 'facilitating or developing the self-securing agency ... of those held to be the most vulnerable'. While these strategies are implemented at the local level, they are designed to protect international security. As Duffield (2007: viii) argues, 'the benevolence with which development cloaks itself – its constant invocation of rights, freedom and the people – conceals a stubborn will to manage and contain disorder rather than resolve it'. The result is practices to contain problems in order to support international interests.

These four perspectives on security and development differ in their referent object. Buzan *et al.* (1998) define the referent object of security as the object identified as being existentially threatened with a legitimate claim to survival which justifies extraordinary measures. Although development does not address claims to survival, an analysis of the referent object still reveals the priorities of external actors, specifically what they seek to achieve and for whom. The moral claims of development can also be viewed as extraordinary measures as they are 'actions outside the normal bounds of political procedure' (Buzan *et al.* 1998: 24). Rather than being governed by the state, development often bypasses beneficiary governments or takes on state responsibilities. For example, Duffield and Waddell (2006) refer to NGOs tendering for contracts to run government departments in Afghanistan.

For external actors addressing organised crime after conflict, there are a range of referent objects that reflect the perspectives on security and development discussed above. Human security and human development, as well as top-down but human-centred approaches, focus on the sub-state level, identifying individuals, groups and people as the referent object. In contrast, realist and containment perspectives focus on the regime, state and international level as the referent object. Another layer of analysis is required to further distinguish between these different understandings. The locus of external initiatives, whether initiatives are implemented at the state or local level, distinguishes between top-down and bottom-up approaches, revealing the nuances in the different approaches (see Figure 2.1).

34 *Tensions in the security–development nexus*

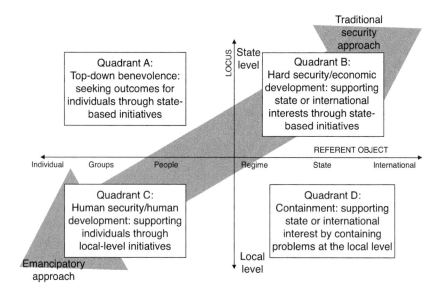

Figure 2.1 Understandings of security and development by referent object and locus.

These different approaches align with the spectrum, from traditional security approaches to emancipation with the trade-offs in between (Quadrants A and D). The individual end of the axis of referent objects may refer to the promotion of agency and bottom-up processes to address organised crime, drawing on Sen's (1999) work on capabilities. Chandler (2012b: 116) notes that 'the individualised understanding of development takes a rational-choice view of the individual, or an "agent-orientated view" in which development is about enabling individuals to make effective choices by increasing their capabilities'. However, the focus on individuals does not necessarily imply agent-centred approaches. Sorenson and Soderbaum (2012) argue that the safety of individuals is often provided from above, and individual-focused approaches may entail biometric techniques and racial profiling.

While an individual referent object may be agent centred, it requires initiatives directed at the local level to be agent oriented. The Human Security Study Group (2007: 4) contends that a bottom-up approach is necessary 'to enable vulnerable communities to create the conditions for peace and stability themselves'. The result, as set out in Quadrant C of Figure 2.1, is a human security or human development approach that supports individuals. This aligns with an emancipatory approach to post-conflict reconstruction. While Sen (1999) recognises that the state has a supporting role in enabling individuals, initiatives implemented at the state level result in top-down benevolence (Quadrant A). Liberal peacebuilding literature argues that top-down approaches 'provide the answers on how to build peace before the questions have even been asked about how it constitutes a

Tensions in the security–development nexus 35

local, more locally sustainable, fitting form of peace' (Richmond 2010: 5). As a result, initiatives are imposed even though they seek positive outcomes for individuals (Kaldor and Salmon 2006).

Further along the spectrum, groups include self-organised social, economic or political units such as interest groups, ethnic groups, tribes, networks or villages (Bueger and Vennesson 2009). 'People' considers the population as a whole. 'People' and 'individual' appear in line with a human-centred approach, and proponents of human security regularly use 'individuals' and 'people' interchangeably when discussing human-centred approaches (see for example Haq 1994; Newman 2001). However, there is a risk that individuals become disembodied, stripped of their political and social life, with their agency reduced to 'bare life' (Agamben 1998). When individuals are removed from their social and political interests and grouped together, they cannot be empowered to create the necessary conditions themselves. Shani (2011: 65) argues that grouping peoples together 'divests the individual of dignity and identity – rendering her/him "mute and absolutely alone"'. The result is a top-down approach as it seeks to improve the conditions for the group as a whole, without acknowledging their different interests.

Quadrant D includes a different trade-off. Duffield (2005) argues that hard security approaches have increasingly shifted to focus on securing populations. As a result, initiatives that seek to address the state–international referent object can also be implemented at the local level (Quadrant D). Programmes that seek to foster resilience through local-level capacity building adhere to this perspective. However, the primary aim of local resilience to insecurity and underdevelopment is to contain problems locally to prevent international spill over, rather than enhancing security and development at the local level (Duffield 2005). As such, these approaches are not human centred despite implementation at the local level.

The trade-offs point to the site of integration between security and development, which allows an analysis of the relationship between the two concepts and what inhibits their integration.

Causal tension

As noted earlier, proponents of the security–development nexus regularly assert that security and development are 'intrinsically linked' or that 'there will be no security without development and no development without security'. These and similar statements have become so widespread that they are referred to as a mantra. They present the relationship between security and development as common sense and beyond debate. However, the practice of external actors points to different understandings of the cause and effect between security and development.

The policy mantra that security and development are 'intrinsically linked' points to a circular causal relationship where the achievement of security has a direct effect on development and vice versa. This is recognised as a 'virtuous'

36 *Tensions in the security–development nexus*

relationship, where success in one area has a direct positive influence on the other, 'with high levels of security leading to development and development further promoting security' (Stewart 2004: 19). This understanding justifies the integration of security and development into a nexus and suggests a positive relationship, where both development and security needs are addressed. Stewart (2004: 2) argues that in this context 'policies towards security may become one part of development policy because in so far as they enhance security, they will contribute to development; and policies towards development may become part of security policies because enhanced development increases security'.

Arguments suggesting a 'virtuous cycle' have been contested, however. Stewart herself acknowledges that this cycle

> can more readily be broken because it is easy to have relatively high levels of security without necessarily experiencing economic growth, or to have high levels of security and economic growth, but not inclusive growth so the potential for conflict remains.
>
> (Stewart 2004: 19)

Similarly, Denney (2011) finds that while there is evidence to support a negative correlation between security and development, it is much more difficult to prove a positive causal relationship. Denney (2011: 291) contends that 'there may be no natural, self-fulfilling correlation between security and development and that forging this link is an uphill struggle'.

Attempts to comprehend the relationship between conflict and development have resulted in varied and often conflicting arguments on the causal relationship between security and development. In the World Bank report *Breaking the Conflict Trap*, Collier *et al.* have identified a two-way relationship between development and the incidence of civil war: 'war retards development, but conversely, development retards war' (Collier *et al.* 2003: 1). Civil war has been acknowledged as detrimental to development, being labelled 'development in reverse' (Collier *et al.* 2003: ix). The report goes on to explore the social and economic costs of war. However, development is also recognised as a strategy that can mitigate and prevent civil war. 'Development can be an effective instrument for conflict prevention ... civil war thus reflects not just a problem for development, but a problem of development' (Collier *et al.* 2003: ix).

While it is now well established that violent conflicts have a negative impact on development, the converse argument has also been made, that underdevelopment and poverty increases the risk of insecurity. Schnabel and Farr (2011: 3) argue that 'repeated cycles of political and criminal violence cause human misery and disrupt development. Additionally, low levels of human development can contribute to instability and conflict.' Some scholars have also highlighted the role of misplaced development in increasing insecurity. Krause and Jutersonke (2005) argue that development programmes in Rwanda, which were viewed as successful, actually entrenched social cleavages and contributed to genocide.

Tensions in the security–development nexus 37

These relationships have been further developed by Menkhaus (2004). In contrast to the 'virtuous cycle', Menkhaus outlines the 'vicious circle' of the security–development nexus in Somalia: 'Endemic insecurity blocks progress in economic rehabilitation and recovery. The lack of employment opportunities in turn impedes demobilisation and reinforces criminality and armed conflict' (Menkhaus 2004: 149–50). Menkhaus argues that the 'vicious circle' metaphor is compelling because it explains the intractability of civil war, it acknowledges the complexity and mutually reinforcing causes of conflict and underdevelopment, and it fits in with political economy explanations of protracted conflict.

Similarly, Stewart (2004) contends there is a three-way connection between security and development: security/insecurity impacts on wellbeing; insecurity affects development and economic growth; and development affects security. These three connections primarily focus on the 'vicious' cycle, in that insecurity undermines development, economic growth and wellbeing, and underdevelopment contributes to insecurity. In particular, Stewart (2004) addresses the impact of horizontal inequalities in driving insecurity. However, as noted above, Stewart (2004) also highlights the potential for a 'virtuous' cycle.

The policy mantra that 'there will be no security without development and no development without security' obscures the lack of clarity on the causal relationship between security and development. However, external actors expect that the security–development nexus adheres to the 'virtuous' cycle. This assumes a particular causal relationship and conceals the tension in how the two concepts interact. As Waddell (2006: 531) argues, 'understanding the linkages between security and development must involve more than simply asserting that either one necessarily encompasses, requires or reinforces the other'.

The lack of clarity on how security and development are connected is heightened when they are applied to a particular problem, such as organised crime. The policy of external actors addressing organised crime in Sierra Leone and Bosnia reveals three different ways that the concepts are related to organised crime: security and development approaches are necessary to address organised crime; organised crime undermines security and development; and insecurity and underdevelopment are connected to a rise in organised crime. These perspectives embrace both the 'vicious' and 'virtuous' cycles of security and development. However, they create different interactions between security and development. As a result, the way that security and development influence each other remains unclear.

Two factors influence how the two concepts are integrated: how each concept is applied by external actors, and how the linkage between the two concepts is understood. Both of these factors can be mapped on the spectrum from traditional security approaches to an emancipatory approach.

The application of security and development

Security and development can be applied in different ways. Security and development can be considered as approaches or processes to achieve a beneficial end state, in this case the absence or reduction of organised crime. However, security

38 *Tensions in the security–development nexus*

and development may also refer to an end state, or the goal of external engagement. Tschirgi (2010a: 3) sums up this distinction as 'between security and development as societal goals and as policies to achieve these goals'. These different applications affect whether they are considered a cause or effect, with consequences for how the two concepts influence each other.

The argument that if security and development were in place it would be more difficult for organised crime to take root refers to security and development as an end state or condition, as does the argument that addressing organised crime will enhance security and development in Sierra Leone and Bosnia. In contrast, the argument that security and development approaches are necessary to address organised crime refers to security and development as processes. Although subtle, these differences influence whether organised crime is seen as a barrier to achieving security and development, or whether security and development are strategies to prevent and address organised crime. As such, the different applications have implications for how the two concepts are integrated, with an influence on the causal relationship between the two concepts.

Traditionally, security and development have been applied in different ways. Security has referred to an end state where the referent object, whether individuals, the state or international level, is secure. Luckham (2007: 683) refers to security as 'an abstract noun, describing a desirable existential state'. The focus on the end state is often connected to exit strategies, as security actors have traditionally been deployed to achieve certain objectives and withdraw. What that end state is can differ, from the absence of a particular threat, to capacity to solve problems, to human security (Baker and Weller 1998). While the changing global order has raised questions over what security is, whose security is at stake, how and from what threat, the application remains the same: achieving a desirable end state.

In contrast to security, the application of development has historically been more variable. Radical perspectives pose development as a grand strategy of social transformation. These perspectives stem from Sen's (1999) arguments that development is not about specific goals, but the provision of freedoms. Leal (2007: 546) contends that the primary goal of development is 'not to reform institutional development practice, but to transform society'. Cornwall (2007) also views development as a transformative process, informed by moral imperatives of what is possible. Rather than defining a particular end goal, these applications of development provide space for bottom-up engagement to define priorities and processes.

However, development has also been defined in terms of specific goals to be achieved. From the early attempts at modernisation via the Structural Adjustment Programmes of the 1980s to the current focus on Millennium Development Goals, development has attempted to achieve a particular end state. Such an approach is necessarily top-down as development is expressed in terms of predefined goals (Penska 2013).

Viewing security and development as a process aligns with the promise of emancipation. Engaging with the two concepts as processes identifies steps to address the needs of the referent object, acknowledging that this is not a static goal. For example, at an early stage of international engagement, if a community is asked what would make them secure and enhance their wellbeing, they identify X. Before X is achieved, they realise that Y would be beneficial. But this may not have been foreseeable from the initial standpoint, and the first stage was required to make Y an option. Such a perspective identifies concerns in partnership with those directly affected, suggesting a people-centred approach that engages with the full range of concerns. In contrast, understanding security and development as an end state or condition suggests that it is an achievable, identifiable goal. Such a perspective results in a top-down approach as there is no need to work in partnership with local actors to determine what needs to be achieved and how. This aligns more closely with a traditional security approach.

These different applications influence the causal relationship between security and development. As a process, security and development would be considered a cause contributing to an end state. In contrast, as an end state of external involvement, security and development become the effect. Applying the concepts in the same way may indicate a strong relationship between the concepts where they are mutually constitutive. However, they may remain separate. Different applications complicate the relationship. If one is understood as an approach or process while the other is an end state or condition, this could suggest a sequential relationship rather than one that is mutually constitutive. As such, the application of security and development has implications for how security and development influence each other.

The linkages between security and development

The causal tension is also evident in how external actors perceive the linkages between security and development. Although it is recognised that the two concepts are interconnected, these linkages can be placed into two categories: separate or integrated. As separate factors, both security and development are necessary to address organised crime. However, this linkage does not consider security and development to be dependent on each other. From this perspective there is no causal relationship between security and development: they are both important but require separate processes and will have separate outcomes. In contrast, some external actors perceive the linkage between security and development to be integrated. This implies a deeper relationship where one concept depends on the other in a sequential relationship. Alternatively, the integration of security and development may be interdependent, where both concepts need to be implemented simultaneously or there will be adverse consequences for both security and development.

In their review of the literature pertaining to the security–development nexus, Spear and Williams (2012) have identified additional categories to describe the linkages between security and development. Security and development can be defined in either-or terms (zero-sum) (Spear and Williams 2012). However, as this research engages with actors that are working within the framework of the security–development nexus, it is unlikely that this category will apply in relation to initiatives to address organised crime in Sierra Leone and Bosnia. Integration is further broken down. While Spear and Williams (2012) recognise the sequential approach to the security–development nexus, they add a new category – hierarchical – where development is employed to achieve security outcomes. As well as recognising a mutually reinforcing relationship, Spear and Williams (2012) also contend that security and development may be conceived as synonymous, where they entail the same thing, 'ensuring that the referent object can pursue its cherished values effectively'. Other categories also engage with specific contexts. Security and development may be selectively co-constitutive, where they are interconnected in complex and diverse ways, or sui generis, where the relationship is always context dependent.

These categories establish a spectrum from separate to integrated linkages (see Figure 2.2). While Spear and Williams (2012) consider sequential, hierarchical, mutually constitutive and synonymous linkages as integrated, the level of integration varies. For example, a sequential linkage does not imply integration. Security is believed to make space for development. While this points to a connection between the two, they remain separate. These categories establish an analytical framework that will be used to understand how external actors addressing organised crime in Sierra Leone and Bosnia perceive the linkages between security and development, and what this means for the causal relationship between security and development.

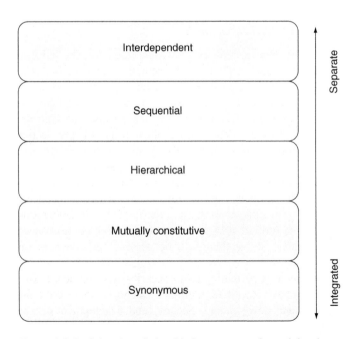

Figure 2.2 Defining the relationship between security and development.

Tensions in the security–development nexus   41

The two elements examined as part of the causal tension also deepen the analysis of whether the security–development nexus has resulted in a shift away from traditional security approaches. The application of security and development as goals links to a traditional security approach, whereas as a process interventions become more emancipatory. With the linkages, continued separation has parallels with a traditional security approach as security would not be influenced by the modalities of development, while increased integration allows for deepening comprehensiveness. As with the conceptual tension, identifying where these elements fit within the spectrum allows an analysis of what inhibits integration.

Institutional tension

Different actors and institutions have traditionally informed security and development approaches. Through the security–development nexus, attempts have been made to develop linkages between institutions associated with development and those associated with security. As mentioned earlier, the UK, US, EU and other governments have created new joined-up mechanisms that bring different elements of government together. However, Kent (2007: 129) argues that the relationship between security and development aspects of government remains difficult as 'the established organisational procedures and perspectives from one institution do not readily mix with those of others'. For example, the UK government established Conflict Prevention Pools, bringing together representatives of the Ministry of Defence, the Foreign and Commonwealth Office and DfID to share their expertise on conflict and post-conflict countries. However, there were difficulties in bringing the different bodies together. 'Though the cabinet officials expressed their will, they did not ultimately provide the structures or incentives that would facilitate the modification of organisational behaviour, patterns or attitudes' (Kent 2007: 133).

While the Conflict Prevention Pools may reach a compromise that satisfies all three bodies, this is difficult to translate into practice. Members of the Conflict Prevention Pools have reported distrust from their own departments. Kent noted that one official involved in a 'joined up' government approach on Sudan complained that membership in that unit 'meant they individually were ostracized by their own departments, "since they could no longer be trusted"' (Kent 2007: 133).

While external actors engaged in post-conflict reconstruction have been eager to merge security and development, the interface between the two areas remains problematic. Security and development actors have been informed by specific institutional drivers: they have emerged from different institutional architecture, they understand problems in different ways and thus their approach to problems differs. While the adoption of the security–development nexus seeks to bring the two areas together, there is a risk that these institutional differences will continue to influence the practices of external actors engaged in post-conflict reconstruction, affecting the balance between security and development and the extent of their integration.

42 Tensions in the security–development nexus

Institutions are 'organised, established procedures'; they are 'frameworks of programs or rules enabling identities and activity scripts for such identities' (Jepperson 1991: 143, 146). As such, institutions are self-reproducing to the point that they become taken for granted (Greenwood *et al.* 2008). For security and development approaches, particular practices have become associated with their institutional identity. These institutional underpinnings influence how the security–development nexus is implemented. As Przeworski (2004: 527) argues, ' "institutions matter": they influence norms, beliefs and actions, therefore they shape outcomes'. Meyer and Rowan (1977: 340–1) argue that these norms are nothing more than 'powerful myths', yet many organisations adopt them even when conformity 'conflicts sharply with efficiency criteria'.

Tolbert and Zucker (1983: 22) argue that organisations can be viewed as 'captives of the institutional environment in which they exist'. As a result, it is difficult for external actors to move beyond their institutional underpinnings. Numerous governments have created bodies to integrate security and development elements of post-conflict reconstruction. From the UK's Conflict, Security and Stability Fund to the EU's Instrument contributing to Stability and Peace, these mechanisms seek to combine security and development practices into a new and comprehensive approach. However, there is a risk that security and development practices will 'speak past each other' (Spear and Williams 2012: 10), with practices continuing to adhere to either security or development rather than integrating the two into a genuine nexus.

This suggests that the institutional underpinnings of security and development may continue to influence practices even when external actors seek to integrate the two through the security–development nexus.

Analysis of the institutional tension assesses whether institutions adhere to traditional security approaches or have become more emancipatory. As outlined in the discussion on the conceptual tension, there are multiple interpretations of security and development. As a result, it is necessary to construct a specific ideal type to operationalise the spectrum. To understand where institutional factors fit within the spectrum, security and development are taken at their most different to determine whether the adoption of the security–development nexus has influenced the practices of external actors. Drawing on the framework to examine the conceptual tension, the ideal type of security is linked to Quadrant B: Hard security, with the state as the referent object and a locus at the state level. This ideal type aligns with traditional approaches to organised crime which have adopted a hard security approach. For example, US agencies such as the Drug Enforcement Agency (DEA) and the Bureau for International Narcotics and Law Enforcement Affairs (INL) are heavily militarised. As Carrier and Klantschnig (2011: 3) argue, 'the USA has certainly been a prime mover in global drug policy, pushing an agenda of prohibition and harsh supply-reduction measures that in their militarised form truly resemble a war'. In contrast, the ideal type of development is linked to Quadrant C: Human development, with the referent object at the individual/people level and a locus at the local level. This ideal type aligns with emancipation as it supports individual needs through a bottom-up approach.

According to Gerhardt (1994), ideal-type analysis is effective when it focuses only on the elements deemed indispensable. Analysis addresses those elements that reveal insights on the institutional underpinnings of the actors addressing organised crime in Sierra Leone and Bosnia. This includes their institutional architecture, how they understand organised crime and how they approach organised crime. How the ideal types frame these three factors is outlined in the following section.

Institutional architecture

The institutional architecture of security and development actors differs as they are influenced by different contributors and donors. External actors engaged in post-conflict reconstruction do not exist in a vacuum. The inception and creation of initiatives to address organised crime in Sierra Leone and Bosnia were decided upon and planned in donor countries before the missions were deployed. These actors in headquarter locations played a key role in setting the mandate and objectives of the initiatives to address organised crime. As such, the background of these actors – whether they come from a security or development perspective – influences the approach of actors addressing organised crime in Sierra Leone and Bosnia.

Donors also influence the institutional architecture of external actors addressing organised crime. Donors often overlap with contributors. However, they play an ongoing role throughout the initiative and funding may be directed to activities deemed by donors to be the most important. As such, their background has a significant influence on the priority given to security and development elements. Analysis of the contributors and donors of external actors addressing organised crime in Sierra Leone and Bosnia will develop an understanding of the institutional architecture underpinning their engagement – whether it is security or development focused.

From the security ideal type aligned with Quadrant B, the primary contributor to post-conflict reconstruction is the state. The security ideal type is designed to achieve the objectives of government ministries or departments, which maintain direction and control. As a result, funding is also channelled through the state. This ensures that the donor retains some influence over the objectives of the programme. Carrier and Klantschnig (2012) assert that UNODC's reliance on law enforcement programmes is a result of the key priorities of its major donors. As such, the security ideal type is influenced by state priorities.

In contrast, the development ideal type is independent. The development ideal type continues to be guided by the humanitarian principles set forth by the Red Cross, such as independence, humanity, impartiality and neutrality. Neutrality has become less important; particularly as advocacy and issues related to justice and human rights have become a core feature of development engagement. The development ideal type is independent of governments in both their home and host countries. As such, the key contributors to the organisation's strategy and direction are internal, including the board of directors and staff. Local partners also influence the objectives of the development ideal type.

44 *Tensions in the security–development nexus*

Funding for the development ideal type comes from a variety of sources. The development ideal type receives grants from government development agencies, regional organisations such as the European Union, and the UN. These grants may be for specific projects or operational funding to support the organisation. Public donations, either through regular giving or appeals, also provide substantial funding. The diverse funding sources add to the independence of the development ideal type. While they are accountable to donors, whether individuals or governments, objectives are set by the organisation rather than donors.

Understanding of organised crime

Security and development actors also have a different understanding of problems. How problems are understood influences how they are addressed by external actors. Analysis will focus on how organised crime is understood and the language adopted by external actors to discuss organised crime, as this reveals how external actors are likely to address it. The language adopted to discuss the programme and organised crime also reveals the position of external actors. Buzan *et al.* (1998: 46) argue that 'a speech act is not only linguistic; it is also social and is dependent on the social position of the enunciator and thus in a wider sense is inscribed in a social field'. As such, these factors are analysed to determine how external actors understand problems.

For the security ideal type, organised crime is understood as a threat to the donor country. This includes security threats posed by organised crime networks, such as extortion, kidnapping and violence, plus the low-level crime and violence associated with the demand side of organised crime. As such, initiatives to address organised crime focus on the elements that pose the greatest threat to donors. Organised crime is treated as 'a political actor to be contained through reactive bargaining and coercion' (Cockayne 2011: 5).

The language employed by the security ideal type also reflects how organised crime is understood. The language of the security ideal type is technical and task oriented, referring to a situation that needs to be addressed before the organisation can withdraw. Terms such as 'interdiction', 'eradication' and 'demand reduction' reinforce the view of organised crime as a threat as they refer to specific goals and associated responses that are understood by all personnel. The technical nature of the terminology removes the human element of approaches to organised crime and focuses solely on the objectives of the operation. The technical language also distances security engagement from local civilians, invoking a requirement for experts. Security language heightens the urgency of a situation. A security speech act designates 'an existential threat requiring emergency action or special measures and the acceptance of that designation by a significant audience' (Buzan *et al.* 1998: 27). Donors often respond to such language by prioritising security.

The development ideal type understands organised crime in terms of its impact on individuals and communities. USAID (2013: 3) notes that organised crime 'threatens political, economic and social development: it can foster corruption and violence, undermine rule of law and good governance, jeopardise economic growth and pose potential public health risks'. As such, the focus is on the effect that organised crime has on affected countries and their population. This influences the activities development actors engage in as they seek to address the underlying factors that support the growth of organised crime, such as poverty, unemployment and weak institutional capacity. However, they also seek to directly address the impact of organised crime through the treatment of drug users and raising awareness of the dangers of organised crime. As such, organised crime is treated as 'a structural factor that should be addressed through structural transformation' (Cockayne 2011: 5).

As a result, the language of the development ideal type focuses on the agency of intended beneficiaries. The development ideal type seeks to 'work with' beneficiaries rather than do things for them. As such, the language is empowering and positive. Cornwall (2007: 471) contends that 'the language of development defines worlds-in-the-making, animating and justifying intervention in current worlds with fulsome promises of the possible'. Development language places itself as virtuous, moral and above criticism. For example, Toye (2007: 505) argues in relation to poverty reduction that it 'has a luminous obviousness to it, defying mere mortals to challenge its status as a moral imperative'. The development ideal type also has a tendency to employ technical language to carve out a role for itself. However, in contrast to the technical language of security actors, it remains focused on people-centred objectives.

Approach to organised crime

Security and development actors have also traditionally had a different approach to problems. Generally, security actors have sought to neutralise threats, while development actors have engaged in long-term strategies of social transformation. The approach to problems is intertwined with the structure of the organisation. Directly addressing a threat goes hand in hand with a hierarchical structure with a clear chain of command, whereas a focus on transformation is compatible with a collaborative approach. Security and development actors have also traditionally worked in partnership with different actors to achieve their aims, with benefits accruing to different referent objects. As such, analysis examines the approach of external actors, their structure, who they work with and who they seek to benefit.

The aim of the security ideal type is to achieve the designated objectives and withdraw. Operations are conducted in the most efficient way to neutralise the threat, often stopping the flow of illicit goods at its source. The approach is top-down, following directives issued at headquarters. While the security ideal type often works with local law enforcement in the country of deployment to build their capacity, this is rarely in partnership due to fears of corruption. Adhering to a militaristic approach, the personnel of the security ideal type are armed and trained to use force if necessary.

This approach is supported by a hierarchical structure. Guidance and directives are issued by government ministries and contributing organisations with

46 *Tensions in the security–development nexus*

frontline personnel following orders. There is a clear chain of command from the strategic, headquarter level to those carrying out initiatives. Objectives are pursued through 'operations' with clearly defined aims and activities. These objectives are carried out in partnership with actors at the state level to enhance state institutions.

The approach of the development ideal type is determined through internal consultation and external analysis. Programmes respond to the situation on the basis of advice from partners rather than strategies developed at headquarters. The development ideal type works in partnership with local organisations, supporting them to make change. As such, the approach is bottom-up and context specific. Decision making within the development ideal type is collaborative, involving the board and staff members. The development ideal type has offices in many countries which results in long-term engagement and embedded staff, many of whom are local. The experiences of ground staff are incorporated into strategy and programming. There is also a strong emphasis on partnership with local organisations. As the development ideal type is based in countries for long periods, plans, strategies and relationships are long term and focus on a range of issues that change over time depending on the country context. The development ideal type works at the local level in partnership with civil society and community-based organisations to ensure positive outcomes for individuals (see for example Blagescu and Young 2005).

Figure 2.3 outlines the three factors of analysis across the ideal types, which parallel the spectrum from traditional security approaches to an emancipatory approach. Of course, approaches to security and development exist across this spectrum. However, the ideal types are a useful tool to establish whether the institutional underpinnings of external actors addressing organised crime adhere to security or development, or whether they have integrated the two into a new and comprehensive approach. Analysis also draws out whether particular institutional underpinnings are a barrier to the integration of security and development.

Motivational tension

Although donors, policymakers and practitioners have enthusiastically adopted the security–development nexus as a new trend to enhance the effectiveness and sustainability of post-conflict reconstruction, this is driven by different motives. From a critical security studies perspective, it can be assumed that the adoption of the security–development nexus will refocus attention on individual security and human development. However, the motivational drivers of donor governments may still be framed by concerns over their own economic and state security. As such, donor governments can use the security–development nexus in self-interest. This creates a tension in the security–development nexus as external actors can implement initiatives according to human security and emancipatory principles while being driven by motives based on state and economic security. The motivational tension influences why security and development are being integrated and the prioritisation of each concept within the nexus.

Tensions in the security–development nexus 47

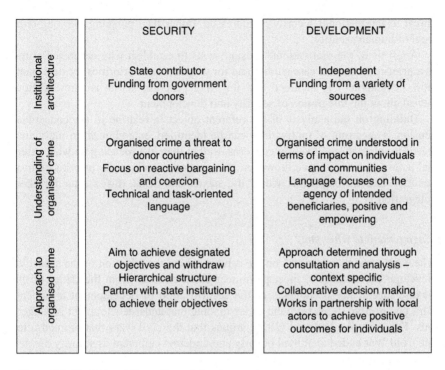

Figure 2.3 Ideal types of security and development.

Proponents of human security have connected the human security of individuals in conflict-affected countries to the human security of individuals in donor countries (Kaldor 2009). The *Barcelona Report of the Study Group on Europe's Security Capabilities* called for 'enlightened self-interest' as 'Europeans cannot be secure while others in the world live in severe insecurity' (Human Security Study Group 2004: 10). The *Madrid Report of the Human Security Study Group* (Human Security Study Group 2007) argues that human security augments national security. Similarly, Axworthy (2004) argues that human security and national security are two sides of the same coin. However, this argumentation does not align with the emancipatory view of human security. With the continued interest of states in their own security and economic growth, the needs of individuals in conflict-affected states are likely to take second place.

Rather than security challenges such as internal wars, failed states, terrorism and crime becoming a priority because of their impact on civilians, the interest of many donors is derived from the threat they pose to international security. As Duffield (2007: 1) has argued, underdevelopment is now seen as dangerous as its effects are not contained by borders but have the potential to 'inundate and destabilise Western society'. Even when international involvement is connected

48 *Tensions in the security–development nexus*

to human security, there is a risk that external actors will withdraw once the threat to international security is addressed, rather than pursuing the long-term goal of human security.

Analysis of the motivational tension seeks to establish why organised crime is a priority in the two case studies and for whom; whose priorities are dominant; how development is included and for what purpose; and what these factors reveal about the integration of security and development.

Building on the analysis of the referent object in relation to the conceptual tension, a spectrum of motivations can be identified, extending from individual needs to international security concerns. Rather than just focusing on what external actors seek to achieve, however, this tension examines the prioritisation of security and development within the nexus and what this means for their integration.

Engagement to what end?

There are varying arguments on the drivers behind the adoption of the security–development nexus. The most prominent claim emerges from the critics of the nexus, specifically proponents of the securitisation of development argument. This perspective stems from the understanding that underdevelopment is dangerous. For example, Duffield (2001) argues that the civil wars that erupted after the Cold War ended identified poverty and underdevelopment as security threats. This understanding has emerged from concerns raised by scholars such as Fukuyama (2004) about the inability of weak and underdeveloped states to control security problems such as terrorism and organised crime as they often have weak law enforcement and poorly guarded borders. In this context, the security–development nexus seeks to address poverty and underdevelopment to achieve Western security interests. While a comprehensive approach that addresses the underlying factors of insecurity, such as poverty and unemployment, is valuable, the preference is for a minimal approach that seeks to contain problems within the developing world before they affect international security (see for example Duffield 2007).

Governments and international organisations have driven these concerns, particularly after the terrorist attacks in September 2001. In 2004, Kofi Annan recognised that 'chaos can no longer be contained by frontiers. It tends to spread, whether in the form of refugee flows, terrorism or illicit trafficking in drugs, weapons or even human beings' (Annan 2004: A20). As such, the UN notes the importance of development in protecting against these threats.

> Development has to be the first line of defence for a collective security system that takes prevention seriously. Combating poverty will not only save millions of lives, but will also strengthen states' capacities to combat terrorism, organised crime and proliferation. Development makes everyone more secure.
>
> (UN 2004a: 2)

Tensions in the security–development nexus 49

The argument that weak states are breeding grounds for security threats such as terrorism and organised crime has been challenged. Newman (2007) in particular argues that terrorist groups emerge from strong, stable states as well as weak states, and from many different government systems from authoritarian to democratic. Moreover, Newman notes that most weak states are not a base for terrorist groups: 'most of the "weakest" and poorest African states, for example, are not associated with terrorism, whereas more relatively stable and prosperous states in the Middle East clearly are' (Newman 2007: 464). However, development is increasingly posed as a strategy to address security threats. For example, the 2005 annual report of Denmark's development agency, DANIDA, states that 'development assistance is useful, if necessary for our own security' (DANIDA 2005: 15). Scholars have also taken on board the threats to international security. Picciotto *et al.* (2007: 98) argue that the growth in intra-state war, increasing global interconnectedness and the rise of frail and fragile states demands the merging of security and development to ensure international stability and prosperity.

These arguments can result in the comprehensive approach attributed to the security–development nexus. In relation to EU engagement in global security, Penska and Ginsberg (2012: 233) argue that the EU 'will yield a far larger security dividend than it does at present if it can harness the so-called three Ds – diplomacy, development and defence/security into a strategic decision-making system'. The UK's former Secretary of State for International Development, Hilary Benn, noted that 'in today's interdependent world – this small and fragile planet – our self-interest and our mutual interests are inextricably woven together. Our personal security depends on international security' (Benn 2004: 8). While this supports a comprehensive approach based on 'enlightened self-interest', there is a risk that international security will be an overriding concern with the result that the development needs of individuals and communities receive less attention.

From the securitisation of development perspective, the security–development nexus has emerged from growing concerns that underdevelopment poses risks to international security, from intra-state conflict – with its potential for spill over to neighbouring states, refugee flows and a need for international involvement to end conflict and maintain peace – to organised crime and terrorism. Accordingly, ensuring the most effective processes for individuals and communities in post-conflict states is given less priority than addressing the security threats. As Ayangafac and Cilliers (2011: 124) argue, 'rather than focusing on improved security for the population, subsequent assistance provided is focused on bolstering measures and systems geared towards countering threats to Western interests/ countries and the international system'. Ioannides and Collantes-Celador (2011: 415) argue that this has been the case with EU engagement in the Western Balkans, where initiatives 'respond primarily to internal security needs rather than functional imperatives or local realities'.

The result is an attempt to contain problems before they spread internationally. This defensive approach does not seek to overcome problems, but rather

50   Tensions in the security–development nexus

aims to ensure problems in fragile and conflict-affected states do not affect donor countries or international security. Chandler (2012a) contends that the emphasis on containment is evident in the way Western powers and international institutions are distancing themselves from taking responsibility for development. The result is an approach that addresses the symptoms rather than the causes of problems in fragile and conflict-affected states. As a result, they will never be resolved, just managed. This approach is evident in traditional law-enforcement approaches to organised crime. Cockayne (2011: 6) argues that the focus of these initiatives 'are not, as a rule, to transform local interdiction capacity, but rather to contain the impacts of criminal activity in that country on the interests of the home jurisdiction'.

On the other end of the spectrum, however, the security–development nexus is employed for different motives. While many development agencies have engaged with the security–development nexus because of security concerns, others have become involved in security programmes to create a suitable environment for development. As Glasius (2008: 47) notes, 'projects aimed at long-term solutions but with a higher risk of going wrong – such as repairing infrastructure, putting people back in education or employment, or overtly political projects – are put on hold until circumstances allow'. As a result, development actors have participated in security programmes, particularly security sector reform (SSR), to provide space for development. This was the rationale behind DfID's SSR programme in Sierra Leone (UK Government 2004). While this represents self-interest, as development agencies are pursuing security reforms to enable their own programmes, the end result is ultimately focused on individuals within the post-conflict country rather than the donor country.

This perspective aligns with an emancipatory view of the security–development nexus. From this viewpoint, the security–development nexus is understood as an integrated approach to address the overlapping development and security challenges present in post-conflict countries. As Tschirgi (2010b: 5) argues, 'the nexus emerged in response to the complex and interlocking humanitarian, human rights, security and development crises that confronted international policy-makers in the immediate aftermath of the Cold War'. This poses the security–development nexus as a necessary innovation to address contemporary challenges more effectively. This also aligns with the understanding of a 'virtuous' relationship between security and development by seeking to achieve more inclusive development (Stewart 2004). This suggests that the security–development nexus seeks improvements for individuals in fragile and conflict-affected states. Such a perspective draws on the shift of both security and development approaches away from a focus on the state and economic development to acknowledge the needs of individuals.

These different perspectives highlight a spectrum of motivations, from the needs of individuals in beneficiary countries to international security concerns (see Figure 2.4). As such, evaluation of the motivational tension builds on the analysis of the referent object in relation to the conceptual tension. While analysis of the conceptual tension identifies the object threatened by organised

Figure 2.4 Spectrum of motivations.

crime, analysis of the motivational tension examines why this referent object is prioritised to identify the drivers of external actors.

These different motivations create a tension in the security–development nexus as they result in the prioritisation of different elements. An approach driven by concerns of international security will engage with development to the extent that it contributes to international security, rather than addressing the needs of individuals in the country of focus. When international involvement is centred on individual needs, the result is likely to be more comprehensive as insecurity and underdevelopment both need to be addressed. These differences have implications for the balance between security and development, and thus how they are integrated.

To establish the motivations of external actors addressing organised crime and the influence of these motivations on the integration of security and development, the research examines three interlinked but separate issues: which actors are addressing organised crime and why, how this affects their practices and how development is included.

Prioritising organised crime

Organised crime by its nature extends beyond borders as trafficking, money laundering and transnational networks bring unwanted security threats into otherwise secure countries. The threat to international security posed by organised crime has been a growing concern for international actors. In 2004, the UN High-level Panel on Threats, Challenges and Change noted that 'organised criminal activities undermine peacebuilding efforts and fuel many civil wars through illicit trade in conflict commodities and small arms' (UN 2004b: 16). In 2009, a special debate of the UN Security Council focused on drug trafficking as a threat to international security (UN Security Council 2009). In 2010, the UN Security Council recognised the 'serious threat posed in some cases by drug trafficking and transnational organised crime to international security in different regions of the world' (UN Security Council 2010: 1). And a special meeting in 2012 recognised illicit cross-border trafficking and movement as a threat to international peace and security (UN Security Council 2012). As such, organised crime is a particularly salient example of self-interest. To determine whether organised crime is prioritised solely because of the threat it poses to international security, or because of the impact it has locally, analysis will examine which actors are engaged in initiatives to address organised crime and why.

52 *Tensions in the security–development nexus*

Practices

Even when international security is identified as the motivational driver of international involvement, it does not necessarily undermine the integration of security and development into a nexus. The security–development nexus may be adopted as it is understood to contribute to more effective outcomes in terms of international security. As a result, development can be used to enhance international security. Analysis of the motivational tension and its impact on the integration of security and development needs to go deeper to examine how the interests of external actors affects their practices. Engaging with local priorities aligns with an emancipatory perspective but also contributes to international security by addressing organised crime at its source. However, a continued focus on international priorities in the target country adheres to a traditional security approach, suggesting that the security–development nexus has not altered the practices of external actors.

In a study on local ownership in statebuilding, Martin *et al.* (2012) evaluate tensions between the security needs and agendas of international and local actors. 'Internationals tend to focus on state and institution building, whereas local priorities centre much more on the need for socio-economic reconstruction, including improved job prospects' (Martin *et al.* 2012: 3). This division is common across many areas of international engagement as the security threats that affect locals differ from those of concern to internationals. Referring to piracy in the Gulf of Guinea, Ayangafac and Cilliers (2011: 122) note that it is of 'immense importance to the West'. However, within the region, 'the principal security threats posed by the lack of capacity to monitor territorial waters are illegal fishing and the exploitation of natural resources' (Ayangafac and Cilliers 2011: 122). A similar disjuncture can be seen in approaches to organised crime. Schroeder and Friesendorf (2009: 151) argue that 'current counter-crime programmes have reflected the interests of international actors and their ways of fighting crime rather than local conditions or the needs of the local population'. To understand what impact the motivational drivers of external actors has on the integration of security and development, analysis will establish whether practices address international or local priorities.

Inclusion of development

As noted previously, the merging of security and development into a nexus came out of attempts to enhance post-conflict reconstruction to ensure more effective outcomes. Within the framework of the security–development nexus it is understood that for organised crime to be addressed effectively, negating the potential threat to international security, approaches need to move beyond a security approach. A traditional security approach, such as arresting known criminals, does not address the root causes of the problem. These strategies are unlikely to be effective and may even have negative unintended consequences. Glenny (2008) discusses the case of Viktor Kulivar 'Karabas', a well-respected criminal

Tensions in the security–development nexus   53

leader in Odessa, Ukraine. When 'Karabas' was assassinated in 1997, his death resulted in a power struggle between other criminal groups, initiating open violence and instability. Similarly, Felbab-Brown (2010) argues that standard law enforcement programmes can have unintended consequences: 'the weakest criminal groups can be eliminated through such an approach, with law enforcement inadvertently increasing the efficiency, lethality and coercive and corruptive power of the remaining criminal groups.' Comparatively, the arrest of key individuals can empower other groups to take their place.

As such, development can enhance approaches to organised crime, resulting in a more sustainable response. However, the inclusion of development also engages with local needs, moving beyond a focus solely on international priorities to align with emancipation. Analysis of the motivational tension investigates the inclusion of development through the security–development nexus, assessing how it is integrated with security. This will determine whether the inclusion of development aligns with an emancipatory approach or whether it adheres to a traditional security approach.

Conclusion to Chapter 2

Although the security–development nexus is expected to achieve a new and comprehensive approach to post-conflict reconstruction, the critiques suggest that the relationship between the two concepts is not straightforward. This research investigates the relationship between security and development in more detail, examining how the four hypothesised tensions influence the integration of security and development into a nexus. Based on the positive standpoint of the Welsh School of Critical Security Studies, the hypothesised tensions emerged from an analysis of what might limit the shift away from a traditional security approach. This chapter has set out the parameters of these four hypothesised tensions: the basis and assumptions behind each tension, as well as the analytical tools that will be used to investigate the influence of each tension in relation to initiatives to address organised crime in Sierra Leone and Bosnia. These four tensions will be examined in Chapters 3, 4 and 5 through the two selected case studies: initiatives to address organised crime in Sierra Leone and Bosnia.

References

Agamben, Giorgio (1998). *Homo Sacer: Sovereign Power and Bare Life*. Stanford, Stanford University Press.

Annan, Kofi (2004). 'In Haiti for the Long Haul', *Wall Street Journal*, 16 March: A20.

Antrobus, Peggy (2003). 'Presentation to the Working Group on the MDGs and Gender Equality', *UNDP Caribbean Regional Millennium Development Goals Conference*. Barbados.

Axworthy, Lloyd (2004). 'A New Scientific Field and Policy Lens', *Security Dialogue* 35(3): 348–349.

Ayangafac, Chrysantus and Jakkie Cilliers (2011). 'African Solutions to African Problems: Assessing the Capacity of African Peace and Security Architecture', in Chester

54 Tensions in the security–development nexus

Crocker, Fen Osler Hampson and Pamela Aall (eds), *Rewiring Regional Security in A Fragmented World*. Washington DC, United States Institute of Peace.

Baker, Pauline H. and Angeli E. Weller (1998). *An Analytical Model of Internal Conflict and State Collapse: Manual for Practitioners*. Washington DC, Fund for Peace.

Benn, Hilary (2004). *A Shared Challenge: Promoting Development and Human Security in Weak States*. Washington DC, Center for Global Development.

Blagescu, Monica and John Young (2005). *Partnerships and Accountability: Current Thinking and Approaches among Agencies Supporting Civil Society Organisations*. Working Paper 225. London, Overseas Development Institute.

Bond, Patrick (2006). 'Global Governance Campaigning and MDGs: From Top-Down to Bottom-Up Anti-Poverty Work', *Third World Quarterly* 27(2): 339–54.

Bueger, Christian and Pascal Vennesson (2009). *Security, Development and the EU's Development Policy*. Florence, European University Institute.

Buzan, Barry, Ole Wæver and Jaap de Wilde (1998). *Security: A New Framework for Analysis*. Boulder, CO, Lynne Rienner.

Carrier, Neil and Gernot Klantschnig (2012). *Africa and the War on Drugs*. London; New York, Zed Books.

Chandler, David (2012a). 'Resilience and Human Security: The Post-Interventionist Paradigm', *Security Dialogue* 43(3): 213–29.

Chandler, David (2012b). 'Development as Freedom? From Colonialism to Countering Climate Change', *Development Dialogue* 58: 116–29.

Cockayne, James (2011). *State Fragility, Organised Crime and Peacebuilding: Towards a More Strategic Approach*. Oslo, NOREF.

Collier, Paul, Lani Elliot, Havard Hegre, Anke Hoeffler, Marta Reynal-Querol and Nicholas Sambanis (2003). *Breaking the Conflict Trap: Civil War and Development Policy*. Washington DC, World Bank.

Cornwall, Andrea (2007). 'Buzzwords and Fuzzwords: Deconstructing Development Discourse', *Development in Practice* 17(4–5): 474–84.

Craig, David and Doug Porter (2003). 'Poverty Reduction Strategy Papers: A New Convergence', *World Development* 31(1): 53–69.

DANIDA (2005). *DANIDA's Annual Report 2005*. Copenhagen, Ministry of Foreign Affairs of Denmark.

Denney, Lisa (2011). 'Reducing Poverty with Teargas and Batons: The Security–Development Nexus in Sierra Leone', *African Affairs* 110(439): 1–20.

Donahue, John D. and Richard J. Zeckhauser (2011). *Collaborative Governance: Private Roles for Public Goals in Turbulent Times*. Princeton, Princeton University Press.

Duffield, Mark (2001). *Global Governance and the New Wars: The Merging of Security and Development*. London, Zed Books.

Duffield, Mark (2005). 'Getting Savages to Fight Barbarians: Development, Security and the Colonial Present', *Conflict, Security & Development* 5(2): 141–59.

Duffield, Mark (2007). *Development, Security and Unending War: Governing the World of Peoples*. Cambridge, Polity Press.

Duffield, Mark and Nicholas Waddell (2006). 'Securing Humans in a Dangerous World', *International Politics* 43(1): 1–23.

Felbab-Brown, Vanda (2010). 'The Design and Resourcing of Supply-Side Counternarcotics Policies', www.brookings.edu/research/testimony/2010/04/14-drug-funding-felbabbrown accessed 19 May 2013.

Fukuyama, Francis (2004). *Statebuilding: Governance and World Order in the 21st Century*. Ithaca, NY, Cornell University Press.

Gerhardt, Uta (1994). 'The Use of Weberian Ideal-type Methodology in Qualitative Data Interpretation: An Outline for Ideal-type Analysis', *Bulletin de Méthodologie Sociologique* 45(1): 74–126.

Glasius, Marlies (2008). 'Human Security from Paradigm Shift to Operationalization: Job Description for a Human Security Worker', *Security Dialogue* 39(1): 31–54.

Glenny, Misha (2008). *McMafia: A Journey through the Global Criminal Underworld*. New York, Alfred A. Knopf.

Greenwood, Royston, Christine Oliver, Kerstin Sahlin and Roy Suddaby (2008). 'Introduction', in Royston Greenwood, Christine Oliver, Kerstin Sahlin and Roy Suddaby (eds), *The Sage Handbook of Organisational Institutionalism*. London; Los Angeles, Sage.

Haq, Mahbub ul (1994). 'New Imperatives of Human Security'. *RGICS Paper No. 7*. New Delhi, Rajiv Gandhi Foundation.

Human Security Study Group (2004). *A Human Security Doctrine for Europe: The Barcelona Report of the Study Group on Europe's Security Capabilities*. Barcelona, LSE Global Governance.

Human Security Study Group (2007). *A European Way of Security: The Madrid Report of the Human Security Study Group*. Madrid, LSE Global Governance.

Ioannides, Isabelle and Gemma Collantes-Celador (2011). 'The Internal–External Security Nexus and EU Police/Rule of Law Missions in the Western Balkans', *Conflict, Security & Development* 11(4): 415–45.

Jahan, Selim (2002). *Measuring Human Development: Evolution of the Human Development Index*. New York, UNDP.

Jepperson, Ronald (1991). 'Institutions, Institutional Effects and Institutionalism', in Walter Powell and Paul Dimaggio (eds), *The New Institutionalism in Organizational Analysis*. Chicago, University of Chicago Press.

Kaldor, Mary (2007). *Human Security: Reflections on Globalization and Intervention*. Cambridge, Polity Press.

Kaldor, Mary (2009). 'The Reconstruction of Political Authority in a Global Era', in Denisa Kostovicova and Vesna Bojicic-Dzelilovic (eds), *Persistent State Weakness in the Global Age*. London, Ashgate.

Kaldor, Mary and Andrew Salmon (2006). 'Military Force and European Strategy', *Survival* 48(1): 19–34.

Kent, Randolph (2007). 'The Governance of Global Security and Development: Convergence, Divergence and Coherence', *Conflict, Security & Development* 7(1): 125–65.

Krause, Keith and Oliver Jutersonke (2005). 'Peace, Security and Development in Post-Conflict Environments', *Security Dialogue* 36(4): 447–62.

Leal, Pablo Alejandro (2007). 'Participation: The Ascendancy of a Buzzword in the Neo-Liberal Era', *Development in Practice* 17(4–5): 539–48.

Luckham, Robin (2007). 'The Discordant Voices of "Security"', *Development in Practice* 17(4–5): 682–90.

Martin, Mary, Vesna Bojicic-Dzelilovic, Denisa Kostovicova, Anne Wittman and Stefanie Moser (2012). *Exiting Conflict, Owning the Peace: Local Ownership in International Peace Operations*. Berlin, Friedrich Eberty Stiftung.

Menkhaus, Ken (2004). 'Vicious Circles and the Security Development Nexus in Somalia', *Conflict, Security & Development* 4(2): 149–65.

Meyer, John and Brian Rowan (1977). 'Institutionalized Organizations: Formal Structures as Myth and Ceremony', *American Journal of Sociology* 83(2): 340–63.

National Security Council (2002). *The National Security Strategy of the United States of America*. Washington DC, National Security Council.

56 Tensions in the security–development nexus

National Security Council (2004). *The National Security Strategy of the United States of America.* Washington DC, National Security Council.

Newman, Edward (2001). 'Human Security and Constructivism', *International Studies Perspectives* 2(3): 238–51.

Newman, Edward (2007). 'Weak States, State Failure and Terrorism', *Terrorism and Political Violence* 19(4): 463–88.

Paris, Roland and Timothy Sisk (2007). 'Managing Contradictions: The Inherent Dilemmas of Postwar Statebuilding'. *Research Partnership on Postwar Statebuilding.* International Peace Academy.

Paris, Roland and Timothy D. Sisk (2009). 'Introduction: Understanding the Contradictions of Postwar Statebuilding', in Roland Paris and Timothy Sisk (eds), *The Dilemmas of Statebuilding: Confronting the Contradictions of Postwar Peace Operations.* London, Routledge.

Penska, Susan (2013). 'Measuring Impact: Specific Achievements and Outcomes', in Tobias Flessenkemper and Damien Helly (eds), *Ten Years After: Lessons from the EUPM in Bosnia and Herzegovina 2002–2012.* Paris, EU Institute for Security Studies.

Penska, Susan and Roy Ginsberg (2012). *The European Union in Global Security: The Politics of Impact.* London; New York, Palgrave Macmillan.

Picciotto, Robert, Funmi Olonisakin and Michael Clarke (2007). *Global Development and Human Security.* New Brunswick, NJ, Transaction Publishers.

Przeworski, Adam (2004). 'Institutions Matter?' *Government and Opposition* 39(4): 527–40.

Richmond, Oliver (2010). 'Becoming Liberal, Unbecoming Liberalism: The Everyday, Empathy and Post-Liberal Peacebuilding', *Working Paper: Liberal Peace and the Ethics of Peacebuilding.* St Andrews, University of St Andrews.

Rothschild, Emma (1995). 'What is Security?' *Daedalus* 124(3): 53–90.

Schnabel, Albrecht (2011). 'The Security–Development Discourse and the Role of SSR as a Development Instrument', in Albrecht Schnabel and Vanessa Farr (eds), *Back to the Roots: Security Sector Reform and Development.* Geneva, Centre for the Democratic Control of Armed Forces.

Schnabel, Albrecht and Vanessa Farr (2011). 'Returning to the Development Roots of Security Sector Reform', in Albrecht Schnabel and Vanessa Farr (eds), *Back to the Roots: Security Sector Reform and Development.* Geneva, Centre for the Democratic Control of Armed Forces.

Schroeder, Ursula and Cornelius Friesendorf (2009). 'Statebuilding and Organised Crime: Implementing the International Law Enforcement Agenda in Bosnia', *Journal of International Relations and Development* 12(2): 137–67.

Sen, Amartya (1999). *Development as Freedom.* Oxford, Oxford University Press.

Shani, Giorgio (2011). 'Securitising "Bare Life": Critical Perspectives on Human Security Discourse', in David Chandler and Nik Hynek (eds), *Critical Perspectives on Human Security: Rethinking Emancipation and Power in International Relations.* Abingdon; New York, Routledge.

Sorenson, Jens Stilhoff and Fredrik Soderbaum (2012). 'Introduction – The End of the Development–Security Nexus?' *Development Dialogue* 58: 8–19.

Spear, Joanna and Paul D. Williams (2012). 'Conceptualizing the Security–Development Relationship', in Joanna Spear and Paul D. Williams (eds), *Security and Development in Global Politics: A Critical Comparison.* Washington DC, Georgetown University Press.

Stewart, Frances (2004). *Development and Security.* Oxford, Centre for Research on Inequality, Human Security and Ethnicity (CRISE).

Tolbert, Pamela and Lynne Zucker (1983). 'Institutional Sources of Change in the Formal Structure of Organization: The Diffusion of Civil Service Reform, 1880–1935', *Administrative Science Quarterly* 28(1): 22–39.

Toye, John (2007). 'Poverty Reduction', *Development in Practice* 17(4–5): 505–10.

Tschirgi, Necla, Michael Lund and Francesco Mancini (2010a). 'The Security–Development Nexus', in Necla Tshirgi, Michael Lund and Francesco Mancini (eds), *Security and Development: Searching for Critical Connections.* Boulder, CO, Lynne Rienner.

Tschirgi, Necla, Michael Lund and Francesco Mancini (2010a). 'The security–development nexus', in Necla Tshirgi, Michael Lund and Francesco Mancini (eds), *Security and Development: Searching for Critical Connections.* Boulder, CO, Lynne Rienner.

Tschirgi, Necla, Michael Lund and Francesco Mancini (2010b). 'Conclusion', in Necla Tshirgi, Michael Lund and Francesco Mancini (eds), *Security and Development: Searching for Critical Connections.* Boulder, CO, Lynne Rienner.

UK Government (2004). *Security Sector Reform Strategy: GCPP SSR Strategy 2004–2005.* London, MoD, FCO, DfID.

UN (2004a). *A More Secure World: Our Shared Responsibility. Report of the Secretary-General's High-level Panel on Threats, Challenges and Change.* New York, United Nations.

UN (2004b). *A More Secure World: Our Shared Responsibility, Executive Summary. Report of the High-level Panel on Threats, Challenges and Change.* New York, UN.

UN Security Council (2009). *Statement by the President of the Security Council.* S/PRST/2009/32. New York, UN Security Council.

UN Security Council (2010). *Statement by the President of the Security Council.* S/PRST/2010/4. New York, UN Security Council.

UN Security Council (2012). *6760th Meeting.* S/PV.6760. New York, UN Security Council.

USAID (US Agency for International Development) (2013). *The Development Response to Drug Trafficking in Africa: A Programming Guide.* Washington DC, USAID.

Waddell, Nicholas (2006). 'Ties that Bind: DfID and the Emerging Security and Development Agenda', *Conflict, Security & Development* 6(4): 531–55.

Williams, David (2011). *International Development and Global Politics: History, Theory and Practice.* London, Routledge.

Williams, David and Sophie Harmon (2013). *Governing the World? Cases in Global Governance.* London; New York, Routledge.

3 Addressing organised crime through the security–development nexus in Sierra Leone and Bosnia

The tensions in the security–development nexus will be investigated by analysing how the nexus is implemented by external actors addressing organised crime in Sierra Leone and Bosnia. As discussed in previous chapters, organised crime was addressed in Sierra Leone through the West Africa Coast Initiative (WACI), which brought together in a collaborative approach the UN Office on Drugs and Crime (UNODC), the UN Peacebuilding Mission in Sierra Leone (UNIPSIL), the Economic Community of West African States (ECOWAS) and other bodies. In Bosnia, organised crime was addressed through the EU Police Mission (EUPM). In both case studies, initiatives to address organised crime were framed by the security–development nexus. Organised crime was also identified as a significant factor in the post-conflict period that needed to be addressed through external involvement in both Sierra Leone and Bosnia. Programmatically this provides a comparability not found across many cases of post-conflict reconstruction. As such, the two case studies provide a strong basis to investigate what in practice inhibits the integration of security and development.

This chapter sets out the rationale for focusing on organised crime as a site of inquiry on the security–development nexus, and it then examines the selected case studies in more detail. The comparability of the two case studies is outlined, identifying both their similarities and differences. Each case is then explored in more depth, setting out the presence of organised crime in each country, how the security–development nexus is invoked and what this means in practice. This sets up the framework for the analysis of the tensions within the two case studies.

Initiatives to address organised crime as a site of inquiry

Post-conflict reconstruction can mean many things. It has been used synonymously with statebuilding and peacebuilding, it has been used to refer to physical reconstruction, it has also been used to refer to social reconstruction such as reconciliation (Ramsbotham *et al.* 2005; Paris and Sisk 2007; Roberts 2008). Post-conflict reconstruction can include all of these areas, as it has become a multifaceted process that aims to rebuild states, societies and communities through a shift from a conflict shattered shell towards a vibrant, sustainable and

Addressing organised crime through the nexus 59

democratic state that meets the needs of its citizens (Darby and MacGinty 2008). As an object of study, post-conflict reconstruction is too large to generate detailed insight into the security–development nexus. As a result, initiatives to address organised crime have been selected as one element of post-conflict reconstruction that can provide insight into the implementation of the security–development nexus.

The study of organised crime has been dominated by criminology. From this perspective, the focus has been on understanding particular forms of organised crime, the actors involved, and the methods and routes employed. This strategy has also been adopted by the policy literature, such as threat assessments produced by UNODC and other law-enforcement bodies. Consequently, much of the literature takes a positivist or objectivist stance.

There is a growing body of critical literature on organised crime covering a wide spectrum of issues. Beare (2003: xviii) compiled a collection of articles to outline 'the exploitable nature of the concepts we are discussing; the non-empirical basis for many of the media, police and political responses; and the unintended consequences that can result from well-intentioned initiatives'. Critical scholars have examined the social construction of crime, identifying it as behaviour that threatens the interests of the powerful (see for example Quinney 2001). This has been particularly prevalent in contemporary debates on drug policy. Critical scholars have also been exploring areas that are often 'off limits' in conventional organised crime literature. In relation to conflict-affected states, this includes the potential for criminal groups to play a stabilising role in the post-conflict period because of their role in governance, the economy and the provision of livelihoods and services for people (see for example Reno 2011). Such a perspective generates very different responses to law enforcement, including bringing criminal actors into political settlements.

While this research uses responses to organised crime as a site of enquiry, it does not engage with debates in the organised crime literature. Rather the focus is on how the security–development nexus is understood and implemented. How external actors engaged in post-conflict reconstruction engage with organised crime is taken as the starting point. As such, this section outlines how policy-makers understand the presence of organised crime in the post-conflict period, and how this shapes their response.

The role of organised crime in post-conflict countries has increasingly been recognised. As Kemp *et al.* (2013: 8) note, 'look at a map showing the location of UN peace operations and superimpose a map of major crime-affected regions and there is a clear overlap'. Many armed groups rely on illicit economies to fund their activities and they are unlikely to disengage once violent conflict ends. The post-conflict context also provides a 'site of competitive advantage' for organised crime networks because of 'their ready pools of unemployed labour, populations inured to violence and weakened state capacity' (Cockayne 2011: 1). As a result, organised crime poses significant challenges and it has become a key element of post-conflict reconstruction in many countries. As such, initiatives to address organised crime provide a microcosm of post-conflict

60 *Addressing organised crime through the nexus*

reconstruction. These initiatives are part of a broader programme of international engagement, they are implemented by actors engaged in other aspects of post-conflict reconstruction, and they interact and overlap with other initiatives.

The presence of organised crime has an impact on both development and security in post-conflict countries. During post-conflict reconstruction, governments are only beginning to regain control over the economy, security forces and rule of law. With incomes that dwarf official revenue, organised crime has the potential to undermine state capacity to control security threats and leverage government officials. The Organisation for Economic Co-operation and Development (OECD) estimates that drug trafficking profits alone are around $125 billion US dollars, giving organised crime groups significant economic power in contrast to governments emerging from conflict (FES 2013). Miraglia *et al.* (2012) argue that organised crime erodes the state's capability to deliver public goods, harms the state's legitimacy and affects the peace process. Similarly, van Dijk (2007) notes that the most significant effect is on the quality of governance. Writing on US engagement in Iraq, Williams (2011: 115) notes that 'criminal enterprises, criminal activities and corruption have had profoundly debilitating effects on US efforts to impose political and military stability as well as on its reconstruction efforts'. The World Bank estimates that the impact on development from organised crime is similar to that of violent conflict – both result in 20 per cent less development performance (World Bank 2011).

These factors highlight that organised crime is not just a security problem; it also has consequences for development, governance, rule of law, corruption and state legitimacy. As a result, the need for a comprehensive approach to organised crime that engages with both security and development is gaining wider acceptance. Felbab-Brown (2013) calls for a multifaceted approach that addresses 'all the complex reasons that populations turn to illegality, including law enforcement deficiencies and physical insecurity, poor rule of law, suppression of human rights, economic poverty and social marginalisation'. Cockayne and Lupel (2009a: 4) note that 'the threat posed by organised crime to international and human security has become a matter of considerable strategic concern for national and international decision-makers'. The connection between organised crime and development has increasingly been recognised by international actors. The 66th session of the General Assembly Thematic Debate focused on drugs and crime as a threat to development. As a result, external actors addressing organised crime after conflict are readily engaging with the security–development nexus.

Although often posed as a security problem, the financial motives behind organised crime impact on development as well as security. Illicit trade in goods undermines the economic security of the state as it can 'undermine competition and investment, hollow out production capacity and fuel inflation, fatally weakening state revenues' (Cockayne and Lupel 2009b: 153). The presence of organised crime can also encourage individuals to seek out opportunities in the illicit economy, which detracts resources from the development of small- and medium-sized enterprises. Cockayne and Lupel (2009b: 153) argue that 'organised crime

Addressing organised crime through the nexus 61

can offer survival strategies or even sustainable livelihoods, creating a ladder of opportunity and upward mobility for communities with few other economic prospects'. The development challenges posed by organised crime are more pronounced in post-conflict states. The UN Office on Drugs and Crime (UNODC 2008a: 1) notes that 'they risk becoming shell-states: sovereign in name but hollowed out from the inside by criminals in collusion with corrupt officials in the government and security services. This not only jeopardises their survival, it poses a serious threat to regional security because of the transnational nature of the crimes.' As a result, organised crime cannot be addressed solely through security strategies but requires an integrated approach.

Despite the wider implications of organised crime, it has traditionally been addressed as a security problem. For example, the 1961 Single Convention on Narcotic Drugs emphasised law enforcement strategies 'at the cost of alternative methods from the medical, educational and development fields' (Carrier and Klantschnig 2012: 4). The US government's 'war on drugs' further securitised this approach to drug control and many governments have adopted similar tactics. Laws have been passed in Honduras, and Bolivia is discussing similar legislation, allowing the air force to shoot down suspected drug planes (Cawley 2014). The reliance on security approaches also extends to other forms of organised crime. Responses to organised crime have frequently relied upon security strategies, using military and police in order to reduce avenues available to organised criminals and punish individuals involved (Cockayne and Pfister 2008).

The adoption of the security–development nexus to address organised crime represents a significant change in approach. However, the need for a broader response to organised crime has gained increasing recognition. In 1998, at a special session on drug control, the UN General Assembly recognised that existing security approaches were inadequate. The UN noted that drug problems are often connected to underdevelopment and called for a more balanced approach.

> Despite the adoption of international conventions promoting the prohibition of illicit drug crops, the problem of the illicit cultivation of the opium poppy, the coca bush and the cannabis plant continues at alarming levels. History has shown that there is no single response to reducing and eliminating the cultivation and production of illicit drugs. Balanced approaches are likely to result in more efficient strategies and successful outcomes.
>
> (UN General Assembly 1998: 17)

The balanced approach included alternative development strategies to prevent and eliminate cultivation of illicit crops, rural development measures, economic growth and sustainable development (UN General Assembly 1998). While these strategies adhere to the argument on the securitisation of development, as development is merely a strategy to address the security threat posed by drug trafficking, the impact of organised crime on civilians has also been recognised.

62 *Addressing organised crime through the nexus*

While initially focused on drug control, the call for a more balanced approach has expanded to other forms of organised crime. The 2004 UN Convention against Transnational Organised Crime considers economic development and technical assistance to be one method of implementation, calling on state parties to take 'into account the negative effects of organised crime on society in general, in particular on sustainable development' (UN 2004: 32). The Convention also recognises the impact underdevelopment can have on organised crime. The Protocol to Prevent, Suppress and Punish Trafficking in Persons calls on state parties to 'take or strengthen measures, including through bilateral or multilateral cooperation, to alleviate the factors that make persons, especially women and children, vulnerable to trafficking, such as poverty, underdevelopment and lack of equal opportunity' (UN 2004: 46). These changes contribute to a shift towards an emancipatory approach as the impact of organised crime on individuals and communities is recognised, resulting in attempts to address the human side of security.

The shift towards an emancipatory approach is evident in the policy of initiatives to address organised crime through the integration of development. UNODC has increasingly recognised the linkages between security and development in their approach to organised crime. In 2005, UNODC recognised the linkage between underdevelopment and a crime-prone environment (see for example UNODC 2005). More recent reports on organised crime in West Africa cite the level of development with reference to the Human Development Index (HDI), claiming that poor countries 'are unable to control their coasts and airspace' (UNODC 2008a: 1). UNODC also recognised that 'the Millennium Development Goals (MDGs) are the most effective antidote to crime, while crime prevention helps to reach the MDGs' (UNODC 2010a: iii). UNODC also contributed to discussions to formulate the new Sustainable Development Goals, resulting in a focus on organised crime in Goal 16. While some of these statements invoke development as a strategy to achieve security, there is an increasing recognition that development is an important objective and tool in addressing organised crime independent of security.

As a result, UNODC policy has become increasingly focused on development. UNODC has included alternative development programmes alongside rule of law and trend analysis, as 'drugs, crime, corruption and terrorism affect the lives of individuals and are major obstacles to sustainable development' (UNODC 2008b: 13). UNODC also aimed to place strategies to address organised crime within national development strategies (UNODC 2012). The 2010 report *Crime and Instability* recognises the importance of UN agencies working together and 'making use of the full range of military, development and crime prevention tools available' (UNODC 2010b: 55).

Rather than just achieve security for countries and regions affected by organised crime, UNODC's policy seeks to achieve both security and development. Organised crime is recognised as an impediment to development but underdevelopment is also acknowledged as a factor that allows organised crime to flourish. As a result, organised crime is recognised as a much broader problem that

Addressing organised crime through the nexus 63

requires a range of strategies beyond policing and military tactics. The focus of UNODC policy extends beyond the state to consider underdevelopment as a factor in encouraging organised crime. As such, the inclusion of development in policy shifts initiatives to address organised crime away from military and policing strategies and a preoccupation with the state.

The adoption of the security–development nexus to frame approaches to organised crime provides an effective site of enquiry to assess what in practice inhibits the integration of security and development into a nexus. As a microcosm of post-conflict reconstruction, it also allows insight into these factors in relation to post-conflict reconstruction more broadly. Accordingly, two case studies of post-conflict reconstruction that focused on organised crime have been selected to investigate the security–development nexus.

Comparability of the case studies

Although sparked by different factors, the wars that preceded post-conflict reconstruction in Sierra Leone and Bosnia had many similarities, resulting in a comparable response from external actors. The conflicts in Sierra Leone and Bosnia had high levels of civilian casualties and both conflicts were ended through forceful international intervention. Both conflicts were regional in nature. The Bosnian war was one of a series of wars of secession from Yugoslavia. The Sierra Leone war was linked to the war in Liberia, with rebel leaders supported by Charles Taylor.

In both countries, post-conflict initiatives commenced at a similar time: 1995 in Bosnia and 1997 in Sierra Leone.[1] As a result, post-conflict reconstruction was based on the same principles of good practice and followed similar approaches. Elections were held early in the post-conflict phase in both countries. Each country had a justice mechanism to address war crimes and crimes against humanity: the hybrid Special Court for Sierra Leone and the International Criminal Tribunal for the former Yugoslavia in Bosnia. As the security sector played a violent role in both conflicts, SSR was a key aspect in both post-conflict reconstruction operations. Initiatives to address organised crime became a core element in both cases. These elements ensure that the two cases are comparable. However, there are also several key differences to provide insight into the practice of the security–development nexus in two different contexts.

Bosnia was formed following a referendum to secede from the post-communist Yugoslavia. The legacy of the communist state structured around nationalities was utilised by leaders, resulting in a war fought on ethnic lines. Although the international community understood the war to be based on 'ancient rivalries', Kaldor (2006: 128) quotes Bosnians that say 'the war had to be so bloody ... because we did not hate each other; we had to be taught to hate each other'. The conflict was ended by an intervention led by the North Atlantic Treaty Organisation (NATO). Despite the presence of UN peacekeepers on the ground, US reluctance to engage ground troops ensured that the intervention was primarily carried out through air strikes, which endangered civilians (Wheeler

64 *Addressing organised crime through the nexus*

2000). The Dayton Peace Agreement, which ended the war in 1995, divided Bosnia into two entities, the primarily Serb Republika Srpska, and the Croat and Muslim Federation of Bosnia and Herzegovina.

The Dayton agreement also set out much of the agenda for post-conflict reconstruction, leaving little room for local input. The reconstruction effort evolved from the provision of assistance to a quasi-protectorate with an internationally imposed High Representative able to remove public officials and pass legislation (Belloni 2007). However, the High Representative justified these practices on the basis of local ownership. Successive High Representatives purported to 'really speak for the people, while the three [political] parties just got in the way' (Cox 2001). As a result, many initiatives, particularly SSR, were delivered through a top-down imposed process. Chandler (2006) labels this approach 'empire in denial', where international actors deny accountability for the exercise of their power by placing the onus on local actors through a focus on local ownership. In relation to Bosnia, Chandler (2006) notes that power was transferred to Brussels through the EU's engagement but the EU distanced itself from this power.

Bosnia had the added difficulty of a non-functional state. The divisions between the entities drawn up in the Dayton Peace Agreement created a continued divide between ethnic groups that affects many areas. Governance is provided through a rotating presidency, which stalls many decisions. Although the SSR process aimed to integrate the various police bodies, the result was a continued division between the entities. Although there are some institutions at the state level – such as the State Investigation and Protection Agency (SIPA), the Border Police and the Ministry of Interior – each entity has its own police force. Within the Federation of Bosnia and Herzegovina, this is further divided with each of the ten cantons having their own police department. This creates difficulties for addressing organised crime as the different police bodies are reluctant to share information and records.

A former British colony, Sierra Leone was a destination for slaves freed by the British armed forces. The capital, Freetown, and the rest of the country were developed separately and unequally, with different legal systems (SLTRC 2004). As the capital was primarily inhabited by the descendants of freed slaves, 'the divide between the two entities bred deep ethnic and regional resentment and destabilised the traditional system of chieftaincy' (SLTRC 2004: 9). This was exacerbated by multi-party democracy with parties divided along ethnic lines. However, the primary basis of the war was not ethnic tensions but frustration over governance failures, corruption, nepotism, fiscal mismanagement and poverty (Human Rights Watch 2003; SLTRC 2004). After several attempts at peace, conflict finally ended in 2002 through a British intervention. The intervention was a last-minute effort after British troops had been deployed to free UN peacekeepers that had been taken hostage.

Following the intervention, three UK government ministers pushed the urgency of reconstruction in Sierra Leone and signed a ten-year Memorandum of Understanding with the Sierra Leone government (Grant 2005). DfID took a

Addressing organised crime through the nexus 65

lead role in post-conflict reconstruction. Because of limited resources, local actors were given responsibility for many aspects of post-conflict reconstruction. As a result, Sierra Leone is widely cited as a success story of bottom-up practices (White 2008).

The different approach of external actors in the two case studies allows analysis of the tensions in the security–development nexus in two different contexts. The top-down approach of external actors in Bosnia aligns with a traditional security approach. However, this approach was justified on the basis of local ownership and local needs, which suggests a shift away from traditional approaches. In contrast, external actors in Sierra Leone engaged in a bottom-up approach. However, this was driven by a lack of resources rather than an interest in the local context. While the methods shift away from a traditional security approach, the rationale does not.

The current context of the two cases also differs. Sierra Leone remains a 'less developed country', continuing to occupy a low position on the Human Development Index (HDI). In contrast, although Bosnia's Gross Domestic Product (GDP) remains low compared to Western European states, the country is ranked within the 'high' human development band of the HDI[2] and the World Bank classes Bosnia as an upper middle-income country (World Bank 2016). This may influence the role of development in the two case studies. Sierra Leone was considered a 'less-developed country' before and after the war. As such, it has a long history of engagement from development actors. However, prior to the war, in Bosnia development engagement was rare because of the political situation in Yugoslavia. While development actors have been engaged in Bosnia since the war ended, their presence is still recent and not always viewed positively by locals who do not consider the country in need of development assistance.[3]

In both of these case studies, organised crime has become a significant problem in the post-conflict context. How organised crime is addressed through post-conflict reconstruction raises another key difference between the two case studies. In Sierra Leone, initiatives to address organised crime were part of a multi-agency programme. The WACI was developed and implemented by ECOWAS, UNODC, UNDPA, Interpol and UNIPSIL. In contrast, initiatives in Bosnia were driven by a single actor, the EU Police Mission (EUPM).

Overall, the two case studies have adequate similarities to be comparable. The differences in context, and also initiatives to address organised crime discussed above, will be considered throughout the analysis to determine whether they produce salient differences in how security and development come together and how the security–development nexus is implemented. Drawing on within-case analysis, the case study chapters will analyse how each tension affects the integration of security and development in Sierra Leone and Bosnia separately, before drawing the findings together.

As mentioned previously, the most important element of comparability between the two case studies arises from the presence of organised crime and the use of the security–development nexus as a framework for initiatives to address it. Although organised crime manifests differently in both cases, it has become a

66 *Addressing organised crime through the nexus*

key element of post-conflict reconstruction. The following sections will outline the presence of organised crime in Sierra Leone and Bosnia and how the strategies to address it fit within the framework of the security–development nexus.

Organised crime in Sierra Leone

West Africa became recognised as a drug trafficking hub in December 2007 following the release of a UNODC report *Cocaine Trafficking in West Africa: The Threat to Stability and Development.* However, Ellis details the key role that West Africa has played in drug trafficking since the 1950s, when the region was first used by Lebanese smugglers transporting heroin to the US (Ellis 2009). The 1960s saw a boom in marijuana trafficking to Europe, primarily by Nigerian and Ghanaian smugglers (Ellis 2009). Nigerian and Ghanaian smugglers then expanded into cocaine and to some extent heroin (Ellis 2009). Nigeria in particular has a deep history of organised crime, with heavy involvement in drug trafficking, oil bunkering and financial crimes, such as advance fee fraud (Ellis 2015). The networks set up by Nigerian organised crime were crucial in the rise of the region as a valuable transit hub for cocaine (Glenny 2008). The increased sophistication of financial infrastructure in Nigeria and Ghana, and increasingly other countries in the region, has also played a key role (Ellis 2009).

As the pace of cocaine trafficking has increased in West Africa, Mazzitelli (2007) has documented three different and complementary trafficking operations in the region. The first model is most closely linked to traditional organised crime structures. Latin American organisations have set up branches in some West African countries and coordinate the transit of cocaine through them (Mazzitelli 2011). This model also allegedly has links to the Sicilian mafia, as mafia boss Giovanni Bonomo was arrested for drug trafficking at Dakar airport, Senegal (Berticelli 2007). As local operators 'have developed a stronger capacity for taking over a more ambitious and lucrative role in the business as transporters, partners and final buyers', the cocaine trade is increasingly becoming controlled locally (Mazzitelli 2011: 5). This has given rise to the second form of organised crime, where local trafficking networks are paid in kind for logistics or purchase consignments directly from the traffickers for onward transportation into Europe (Mazzitelli 2007). In many cases this results in multinational trafficking networks. For example, in 2008 a network was dismantled in Togo with members from Colombia, Costa Rica, Mexico, South Africa, Ghana and Togo (Mazzitelli 2011). The increasing availability of wholesale cocaine has also fostered a third model, where 'freelance' traffickers buy a few kilograms of cocaine and transport it independently to Europe (Mazzitelli 2007). These models differ from those employed by 'classic' organised crime, such as Italian, Russian, Japanese and Chinese organised crime networks. Mazzitelli (2011: 33) argues that it 'represents a new challenging and successful model of an organised crime network'.

Sierra Leone is not the most significant transit country for cocaine trafficking. Ghana and Nigeria have maintained their status as a destination for drug traffickers and Guinea-Bissau and Mali have received significant flows, with

Guinea-Bissau regularly labelled Africa's first narco-state (see for example Shaw and Reitano 2013). However, Sierra Leone has witnessed significant interdictions. In June 2007, 2.5 tonnes of cocaine were seized in Venezuela on a plane bound for Sierra Leone (UNODC 2008a). In July 2008, 700 kg of cocaine was seized at Lungi airport in Freetown (UNODC 2008a). With limited capacity to patrol territorial waters, there are concerns that much more has passed through the country undetected. Illicit trade also played a significant role during the Sierra Leonean war. Diamond smuggling funded the operations of the Revolutionary United Front (RUF) and the group smuggled weapons into Sierra Leone, as well as drugs to control child soldiers (SLTRC 2004). While trafficking is not a new phenomenon for Sierra Leone, its obscurity in the larger scheme of drug trafficking means that the structures are not as well understood as those in Nigeria or even Guinea-Bissau. Given the country's history, drug trafficking could have a destabilising effect. As Walker and Buchert (2013: 165) note, 'observers have been quick to forewarn that widespread organised crime could bring recovery in Sierra Leone to an abrupt halt'. This has only been heightened by the downturn brought about by the Ebola epidemic from mid-2014.

Cocaine is entering Sierra Leone through shipping containers and by air via Lungi airport and unmarked airstrips throughout the country. Increasing numbers of flights to London, Paris and Brussels have also created a gateway to Europe for cocaine traffickers, although there has been a preference to move drugs overland or by sea to Guinea for onward shipment (Wikileaks 2009a). Between January and October 2008 there were 17 drug seizures in Sierra Leone, totalling 743.5 kg of cocaine and 10,602 kg of cannabis (Wikileaks 2009a). Sierra Leone has also had a number of successful prosecutions. Following the 2008 interdiction at Lungi airport, 17 narcotics cases were pursued in the High Court with 15 convictions, including two police officers and one officer from the Office of National Security (ONS) (Wikileaks 2009a). In April 2009, a number of West African narco-traffickers were extradited to the US for prosecution, including the high-profile Sierra Leonean Gibrilla Kumara who had allegedly been active in the recruitment of South American organisations (Wikileaks 2009b).

At present, 'West Africa has not witnessed the high levels of violence associated with the drug trade in Latin America, or the high levels of consumption in Europe and Latin America' (NYU CIC 2012). However, there are reports that local consumption is rising. In 2015, the West Africa Commission on Drugs released a report detailing local use, arguing that drugs were no longer just in transit (WACD 2015). For some time Sierra Leonean elites have been purchasing cocaine, while crack cocaine has been traded on the street (Boas and Hatloy 2005). There were also allegations of politicians using drugs to recruit youth to intimidate opposition supporters in the lead up to the 2012 election (Saidu 2011). While locals view exploitative trafficking practices in Sierra Leone – such as diamond smuggling and illegal logging – negatively, drug smuggling is not seen the same way. Organised criminals are seen to be 'providing a service' (Mazzitelli 2007: 1085). As Sierra Leone has primarily been a transit country, there is a common perception that locals should benefit from the trade.[4] However, as

68 *Addressing organised crime through the nexus*

local consumption rises, there is potential for this to change. As drug trafficking in the region becomes better understood, concerns are also being raised about increasing violence. In a letter to the Security Council ahead of a discussion on organised crime, the Togolese President expressed concern over the potential for inter-cartel violence similar to Mexico (UN Security Council 2012). These concerns contributed to the development of the WACI to address organised crime in Sierra Leone and the West Africa region.

The adoption of the security–development nexus

Although it is not one of the primary trafficking hubs, addressing organised crime in Sierra Leone became a priority due to its potentially destabilising influence. Along with Liberia, Guinea-Bissau and Côte d'Ivoire, Sierra Leone was one of the pilot countries for the WACI. A multi-agency initiative to address organised crime, the WACI adopted the security–development nexus as a framework. Based on the ECOWAS Political Declaration on Drug Trafficking and Other Organised Crimes in West Africa and its associated regional action plan, the WACI was developed by UNODC. UNODC recognises a two-way relationship between development and organised crime in West Africa: organised crime 'constitutes a major threat to peace and security and an impediment to development' and 'state fragility and poor governance have opened the way for criminal networks' (UNODC 2008c).

As a result, the WACI project document that sets out the strategy, objectives, outputs and indicators of the project in Sierra Leone acknowledged that poverty, weak institutions, high youth unemployment and Sierra Leone's low position on the HDI provide ideal conditions for organised crime (UNODC 2010c). The document also recognised that

> a post-conflict environment, fragile political and state institutions, coupled with increased drug abuse, a growing crime rate and weak law enforcement agencies all combine to have the potential to derail Sierra Leone's tentative steps toward recovery and development after decades of political instability and violent conflict.
>
> (UNODC 2010c: 2)

These statements highlight how the WACI aimed to integrate security and development as organised crime raises many concerns beyond the state. Various strategies were invoked to address organised crime. For example, development was employed as a strategy to address its impact.

Youth were a particular focus of the policy approach to organised crime in Sierra Leone. The WACI was linked with Priority One of the UN Joint Vision for Sierra Leone, which aimed to consolidate peace and stability, as well as Priority Three, which focused on the economic and social integration of youth (UNODC 2010c). The focus on youth is particularly important. Rather than just addressing how organised crime affects the state, in line with a security

Addressing organised crime through the nexus   69

approach, the role of youth – and in particular unemployed youth – is recognised. Youth unemployment provides an entry point for organised crime as many young people are willing to take the risks associated with drug trafficking in order to make money. Unemployed youth are also the most likely to be negatively affected through the increased availability of drugs in Sierra Leone. The focus of policymakers on youth clearly highlights the integration of security and development in their approach to organised crime, as it overcomes the preoccupation with the state and engages with the impact of organised crime on individuals.

Within the WACI organised crime was understood as a threat to development, thus recognising the impact of organised crime on individuals and communities. Underdevelopment was also viewed as a factor conducive to organised crime. This suggests that underdevelopment needs to be addressed in order to prevent organised crime. Poverty, weak institutions and high youth unemployment were viewed as particular problems that encourage organised crime. This perspective supports the assumption that the security–development nexus integrates security and development into a new and comprehensive approach to organised crime that engages with the human dimension.

The security–development nexus in practice

Although the security–development nexus framed the policy of external actors addressing organised crime in Sierra Leone, the integration of security and development in practice was less clear.

External actors addressing organised crime in Sierra Leone recognised the need to address development problems, particularly youth unemployment. As noted previously, the WACI was linked to social and economic integration of youth as set out in the UN Joint Vision (UNODC 2010c). The Office of National Security (ONS) also recognised the importance of youth. The key to addressing organised crime is 'to make the youth, who is the key courier for organised crime to be better catered for, in terms of employment, in terms of even scholarships to university and other welfare issues, to make sure they turn their attention to something that is legal'.[5] While the importance of development issues such as youth unemployment were recognised in the WACI and by local law enforcement, the implementation of the WACI did not match.

Many of the processes of the WACI remained security focused. One of the key processes to reduce drug trafficking and organised crime in Sierra Leone was the establishment of the Transnational Organised Crime Unit (TOCU) to ensure effective cooperation among all law enforcement agencies in Sierra Leone (UNODC 2008c). The unit brought together all law enforcement agencies that address organised crime, as well as the ports authority, the maritime agency and airport control. The WACI also aimed to adopt and upgrade legislation on money laundering and build the capacity of the Bank of Sierra Leone to conduct financial investigations. There was also a broader focus on capacity building. International actors aimed to build capacity in the areas of law enforcement

70 *Addressing organised crime through the nexus*

including drug interdiction, forensics, intelligence, border management, money laundering and criminal justice (UNODC 2010c). These elements continue to adhere to a traditional security approach.

External actors also sought to build the capacity of security agencies to reduce illegal activities in Sierra Leone's territorial waters through patrol activities (UNODC 2010c). Similarly, anti-trafficking and anti-organised crime activities at Lungi airport were enhanced. A subsequent element of the WACI, launched in January 2012, aimed to improve border control, address illicit drugs and organised crime, and further enhance airport security (UNDP 2012a). Strengthening border control was achieved by providing technical equipment and training for immigration staff. International initiatives to address illicit drugs and organised crime directly funded the operations of TOCU, but also improved intelligence gathering and processing by working on practical case investigations and real-time field operations. Airport security was enhanced by improving security standards and engaging in an awareness-raising campaign to deter organised crime. These processes focused on the technical aspects of addressing organised crime, including intelligence collection and analysis, surveillance, investigations, tactical operations and international coordination, which maintained a security focus.

The WACI did, however, move beyond a traditional security approach. Goudsmid *et al.* (2011: 164) argue that, as well as the security elements, 'development initiatives have been attached to the programme to support local communities and reverse the vicious cycle of crime, insecurity and underdevelopment'. This was particularly evident through the anti-drugs programme. An anti-drugs officer based at UNIPSIL developed a drug users register and used radio campaigns to raise awareness of the dangers of drug use.[6] UNIPSIL also worked in collaboration with local NGOs to provide sensitisations on drug use to communities.[7] In line with a development approach, these programmes shift the focus to individuals affected by drug trafficking. However, they also have elements of a security approach.

> When we intend to engage at the community level firstly it is to get them to understand drug abuse, what the law prohibits and the negative health effects and how it increases criminality … on three fronts: drug abuse can impede health, can impede agricultural security and it can add to criminality. If we can get them to understand that, we could get their cooperation.[8]

The external actors addressing organised crime in Sierra Leone perceived their processes to be connected to development. The initiatives to improve border control were prioritised because 'the situation has particularly adverse effects on the country's social and economic development agenda' (UNDP 2012b: 5). Furthermore, the project aimed 'to contribute to the strengthening of the security sector governance, institutional build up of the department of immigration, fight against organised crime and development agenda' (UNDP 2012a: 4). Organised crime was prioritised because of the risk it places on 'governance structures and the stability of the country and the sub-region' (UNDP 2012a: 8). These statements suggest that addressing organised crime will create space for development. Goudsmid *et al.* (2011) contend that the success of the WACI contributed to an enhanced economic environment, citing rising capital investment and interest from Chinese and European companies. However, this does not constitute a shift towards emancipation. Security processes are seen to create space for development rather than development processes adding useful tools to address organised crime.

Some elements of the WACI were more closely aligned to development processes. For instance, Goudsmid *et al.* (2011: 161) argue that 'awareness and knowledge of illicit drugs among certain groups of youngsters have been increased, fostering a better sense of community and shared concerns about threats of development'. While raising awareness is a viable strategy, when economic opportunities particularly for youth continue to be lacking it is unlikely to have a significant impact. Dr Edward Nahim, who works on drugs and mental health issues in Freetown, states that drug use 'is more common amongst the unemployed vagrants because they don't have any work to do' (Trenchard 2013). Reports also suggest that drug use among youth, particularly in Freetown, is increasing (Lupick 2013). However, there was no connection between initiatives to address organised crime and programmes that address youth unemployment.[9]

The processes employed to address organised crime in Sierra Leone appear to be one sided as they primarily focus on law enforcement, which is linked to traditional security approaches. Rather than contributing to an integrated approach, elements of development were 'attached' to security approaches to organised crime, such as the anti-drugs programme. Within the WACI, security- and development-focused initiatives did coexist but there was limited coordination as they were understood to address different areas of organised crime. Beyond the anti-drugs project which engaged with local NGOs, there was no engagement with other actors engaged in development programmes connected to organised crime, such as UNDP's work on youth unemployment. One UNIPSIL officer noted that 'where I rub shoulders with them [UNDP] is on elections'[10] and that UNDP didn't view their programme in connection with organised crime.[11] However, the WACI programme document specifically identified youth unemployment as a problem. This suggests that processes followed a traditional security approach, with elements of development added on.

Although the project document that informed the WACI recognised the importance of both security and development to address organised crime in Sierra Leone, this does not appear to have translated into practice. This gap between policy and practice will be examined in the next chapter, assessing the influence of the four tensions.

Organised crime in Bosnia

Organised crime formed a key element of the Bosnian war, including the smuggling and trafficking of people, arms, drugs, timber, fuel and cigarettes

72 *Addressing organised crime through the nexus*

(Friesendorf *et al.* 2010). Andreas (2004: 38) notes that 'the outbreak, persistence, termination and aftermath of the 1992–1995 war cannot be explained without taking into account the critical role of smuggling practices and quasi-private criminal combatants'. In part, smuggling networks were formed out of necessity as trade sanctions placed a strain on the survival of civilians and combatants. There were also economic functions as smugglers supplied all sides of the conflict (Andreas 2004). Criminal gangs were also involved in the war militarily, initially because they had the best weapons and ammunition. The varied roles of criminal actors meant that they 'robbed and abused those they were supposed to be defending.... The sheer diversity of actors and activities involved in the smuggling economy suggests there were many shades of grey blurring the distinctions between patriots and profiteers' (Andreas 2010: 186–7).

The end of the war did not mark the end of organised crime; rather it provided new opportunities. In 1996, Bosnian newspaper *Oslobođenje* noted that 'before our eyes, the new class is being born in this war, the class of those who got rich overnight, all former "marginals"' (cited in Alibabic 1996: 73). These 'nouveau riche' are connected to figures in government and political parties, converting their criminal capital into political capital (Andreas 2004: 44). Wartime smuggling networks and their close ties to political actors has left an 'expansive postwar smuggling economy based on political protections and informal trading networks' (Andreas 2004: 31).

War was not the only influencing factor on the growth of organised crime in Bosnia, or the Western Balkans region as a whole. As communism gave way to open markets individuals began to rely increasingly on personal networks, which bolstered organised crime.

> Suddenly people who have been guaranteed security from the cradle to the grave are forced to negotiate an unfamiliar jungle of inflation, unemployment, loss of pension rights and the like. At such junctures, those personal networks from the Communist period become very important.
>
> (Glenny 2008: 74)

In many post-communist states, organised crime has taken over the patronage networks of the party. This has made organised crime a major challenge for the Western Balkans region (European Commission 2008).

The Western Balkans region is a 'crucial crossroads for criminal networks spanning the four continents of Europe, Asia, Africa and the Americas' (Montanaro-Jankovski 2005: 9). The region is also marked by criminal groups that operate across borders (Montanaro-Jankovski 2005). The *Southeast European Times* reports that 'in international police circles, Bosnia and Herzegovina (BiH) is recognised as one of the most important links in the narcotics smuggling chain that leads from Afghanistan and Turkey to the European Union' (Dragojlovic 2013).

Organised crime groups operating in the Western Balkans can be roughly divided into three levels.[12] The first are based on the 'old Yugoslav mafia style,

Addressing organised crime through the nexus 73

they tend to be violent', and involved in drug trafficking, extortion rackets and theft.[13] These groups do not have strong political connections, and 'if they do something too stupid they get arrested'.[14] One example is Joca Amsterdam, who was arrested after allegedly arranging the murder of journalist Ivo Pukaniæ.[15] The second level are sophisticated drug dealers and money launderers. 'They have deals with high-level oligarchs and they have a lot of money ... so they have less problems, but they're more high profile, so people know they're out there'.[16] The third level is political organised crime, i.e. well-known political or business figures connected to organised crime but not directly involved.[17]

While Bosnia is not as significant a case for organised crime as some of its neighbours, in particular Montenegro, Serbia and Kosovo, it continues to be a conduit for illicit goods. Bosnia remains part of the 'Balkan route' for heroin entering Europe from Afghanistan and increasingly for precursor chemicals and cocaine travelling in the other direction (EUROPOL 2005). Bosnia has also become known for economic crimes including the smuggling of high-excise goods such as cigarettes, fuel and alcohol, document counterfeiting, customs fraud, tax evasion, money laundering and fraudulent privatisation (Friesendorf *et al.* 2010).

Structural factors make Bosnia an enticing country for organised crime networks. The country is a major crossroads in the region with numerous border crossings. The Organised Crime and Corruption Reporting Project (OCCRP) reports that smuggling 'is so robust that criminals have built their own private roads around border crossings' (OCCRP 2008). Continuing divisions between the two entities – Republika Srpska and the Federation of Bosnia and Herzegovina – mean that police networks rarely share information, making investigation of organised crime difficult as it rarely stays in one entity.[18] Similarly, Republika Srpska and the Federation have different penalties for organised crime (Anastasijevic 2010). Corruption is high and links to political actors reduces the rate of prosecution. Bosnia also has a primarily cash base and unregulated economy, which is advantageous for organised criminals (Montanaro-Jankovski 2005).

Diverse criminal activities continue to occur in Bosnia. Accurately measuring organised crime remains difficult, as the more effective criminals are the less identifiable they become (see van Duyne *et al.* 2004; van Dijk 2007). As a result, evidence remains anecdotal and based on cases that have actually been pursued by law enforcement. There have been several high-profile cases pursued in Bosnia. Between 2004 and 2007, the State Court convicted 19 people for involvement in organised crime (Friesendorf *et al.* 2010). In 2005, a group of 30 people were arrested in Republika Srpska for involvement in the theft and trafficking of stolen vehicles (Friesendorf *et al.* 2010). In January 2008 Muhamed Ali Gasi, known as 'the capo of the Albanian mafia in Bosnia', was arrested with four associates (Sarjanen 2008; Hopkins 2012). And in late 2011 Zoran Æopiæ and two Bosnian associates were arrested in Republika Srpska in connection to money laundering for Montenegrin drug lord Darko Šariæ (OCCRP 2012).

An ongoing operation, Operation Lutka, intended to target Nasser Kelmendi,[19] resulted in a number of arrests, including 32 indictments in August 2013 for

74   *Addressing organised crime through the nexus*

gang members accused of murder and armed robbery (Sito-Sucic 2013). In September 2013, several high-ranking customs officials were arrested accused of tax evasion, customs evasion, accepting bribes and money laundering. A number of prosecutions were also made in 2013. Gang leader Zijad Turkovic and four accomplices received prison sentences for murder, attempted murder, narcotics trafficking, weapons trafficking, extortion, theft and money laundering (Jukic 2013).

Initially, organised crime was not a priority for post-conflict reconstruction in Bosnia. However, it quickly became recognised as 'one of the major obstacles to the establishment of a stable, peaceful and democratic Bosnia' (Friesendorf *et al.* 2010: 266). Not everyone agrees that organised crime is the most pressing police problem in Bosnia (see Ioannides and Collantes-Celador 2011). One EUPM official noted that the focus on organised crime was not just about tackling the problem: 'looking at it from a technical point of view, if you are able to conduct an investigation into organised crime, which is the most complex, then you are capable of any other kind of investigation'.[20] In contrast, the EUFOR Commander David Leakey claimed that organised crime was the 'main impediment to security and democracy in Bosnia' (cited in Friesendorf *et al.* 2010: 271). Despite debates over the size of the problem, it is clear that organised crime is present in Bosnia and it has continued to be a key focus for external actors.

The adoption of the security–development nexus

Addressing organised crime and corruption became the main priority of the EU Police Mission (EUPM) in its final two phases. As the integration of security and development has become a firm priority of EU policy, initiatives to address organised crime were implemented under the framework of the security–development nexus. The EU's report on Policy Coherence for Development (European Commission 2005) states:

> no one questions anymore the importance of security for development and the role that development plays for preventing conflicts, ensuring durable exits from conflicts and for accompanying crisis management through protective, confidence-building and crisis-alleviating measures. The security–development nexus has been firmly established in the EU's political priorities.

The Council Conclusions on Security and Development (EU 2007) state that 'the EU is addressing insecurity, and conflicts and their root causes, through a wide range of instruments. Inter-linkage between security and development should be seen as an integral part of the ongoing EU efforts'. As such, the security–development nexus has been established as a framework to guide external engagement in EU policy.

Organised crime is recognised as an aspect of broader SSR programmes within EU policy. In Bosnia, the police were seen to protect criminal networks

Addressing organised crime through the nexus 75

and, with organised crime viewed as a serious threat to future peace in the country, reform of the security sector was a strategy to address organised crime (Muehlmann 2008). Despite early resistance from European development mechanisms, it is perceived that within the EU 'SSR embodies the nexus between security and development' (Muguruza 2008: 107). Albrecht *et al.* (2010) consider EU engagement through the security–development nexus as the 'developmentalisation of security': 'Characterised as "holistic" in scope and "politically sensitive" in approach, SSR is ultimately developmental, focusing on the governability of a country's internal and external security institutions and democratic accountability' (Albrecht *et al.* 2010: 75).

Addressing organised crime is also specifically acknowledged as a security and development issue. The 2005 Enlargement Strategy for Bosnia considered organised crime to be 'a major threat for Bosnia and Herzegovina's stability and overall socio-economic development' (Commission of the European Communities 2005: 20). The EUPM acknowledged that 'organised crime is holding back BiH by preventing foreign investment, economic growth and slowing down European integration (Osmanović-Vukelić 2012: 44). The Croat member of the Bosnian Presidency from 2006 referred to organised crime as the biggest obstacle in Bosnia's development (Osmanović-Vukelić 2012). He also noted that 'the work of security agencies in BiH and the bodies that support their work, one of which is the EU Police Mission, is of key importance for the future progress and development of Bosnia and Herzegovina' (Osmanović-Vukelić 2012: 100). Accordingly, the EUPM was a cross-pillar instrument which brought together a focus on long-term development, short-term security, and justice and home affairs (Juncos 2007). Identifying organised crime as a threat to development in policy ensured that it was not understood merely as a security threat to the state, but also has implications for individuals and communities.

The EUPM was influenced by EU policy on the security–development nexus where 'inter-linkage between security and development should be seen as an integral part of the ongoing EU efforts' (EU 2007). As in Sierra Leone, organised crime was understood as a threat to development. As such, the impact of organised crime on individuals and communities was also acknowledged. This suggests that the integration of security and development through the security–development nexus was expected to achieve a new and comprehensive approach to organised crime in Bosnia.

The security–development nexus in practice

As with Sierra Leone, the adoption of the security–development nexus to frame approaches to organised crime in Bosnia was more evident in policy than practice.

Although the EU has a detailed policy on the security–development nexus and the EUPM had a strong mandate that combined security, development and organised crime, processes tended to prioritise security elements. The primary focus of initiatives to address organised crime in Bosnia focused on law enforcement and

76 *Addressing organised crime through the nexus*

criminal liability. As Stephen Goddard (2009: 138), the chief of the Anti-Organised Crime Department noted, 'with the fragmented and confusing structure that exists in Bosnia and Herzegovina this is one of the main problem areas that the international community is assisting the law enforcement and judicial agencies to improve'. The key tasks of the EUPM included:

- the strengthening of operational capacity and joint capability of the law enforcement agencies engaged in the fight against organised crime and corruption;
- assisting and supporting the planning and conduct of investigations in the fight against organised crime and corruption;
- assisting and promoting the development of criminal investigative capacities;
- enhancing police–prosecutor cooperation and police–penitentiary cooperation;
- and ensuring a suitable level of accountability (EU 2012).

In the final two phases of the EUPM, when the focus was solely on organised crime and corruption, the processes of the mission fell into five priority areas: capability, capacity, coordination, cooperation and communication.

The EUPM's first priority focused on improving capability 'to assist to improve operational efficiency as well as build increased capability to identify, investigate and dismantle organised crime networks within an enhanced legal framework' (EUPM 2010a: 1). The processes focused on assisting law enforcement to enhance capabilities in specific areas, such as organisational structures and systems, linking IT systems, information gathering, recording and sharing, intelligence analysis, investigative methods, and the identification of legal deficiencies requiring reform or harmonisation (EUPM 2010b). These activities were undertaken in partnership with local law enforcement by conducting a needs analysis as cases were being pursued.[21] However, at times the EU provided expert advice.

The second priority was improving capacity. The aim was 'to assist in building an increased ability to plan and implement measures that are designed to fight organised crime and corruption within corruption resistant organisational structures' (EUPM 2010a: 1). The focus of these processes was to assist local law enforcement in implementing strategies to address organised crime and corruption. This included the implementation of national strategies as well as the production and implementation of strategies within their own organisation or jurisdiction to address organised crime and corruption (EUPM 2010b). The EUPM also assisted their local counterparts to use intelligence to inform the development of strategies and ensure they had adequate resources and capacity for effective implementation.

The third priority addressed coordination, 'to assist in the further development of strategic and tactical coordination mechanisms in the fight of organised crime and corruption' (EUPM 2010a: 1). To do this, the EUPM assisted local

Addressing organised crime through the nexus   77

counterparts to improve cooperation by improving their ability to work together to plan and implement effective joint investigations and operations, and developing strategic coordination mechanisms (EUPM 2010b).

The fourth priority focused on cooperation, seeking to 'facilitate greater collaboration to improve the efficacy of the overall competence to disrupt the activities of organised criminals' (EUPM 2010a: 1). The EUPM aimed to improve cooperation at a range of levels, between national and international law enforcement and judicial cooperation, regional cooperation initiatives and operations as well as operational agreement with EUROPOL (EUPM 2010b). The mission also sought to enhance the sharing of intelligence, links and best practice.

The final priority was communication. The EUPM aimed 'to assist in the establishment of functional information exchange mechanisms to identify and progress organised crime and corruption investigations' (EUPM 2010a: 1). The EUPM worked with local counterparts to ensure that formal communication channels were established to facilitate information exchange, cooperation and coordination, as well as improving the flow of information and intelligence (EUPM 2010b). These strategies sought to overcome distrust (particularly between entity bodies) and to enhance organised crime investigations.

> Where successes have been gained it's been an informality of exchanging data. So they're prepared to do that when they can see the initial reward of exchanging data, but just having a silo of information that they have no control over once they give it in, there is serious distrust.[22]

The processes of the EUPM were innovative and locally centred. EUPM officers were co-located with counterparts allowing them to monitor, mentor and advise at all levels, including local entity and state bodies (EU 2012). However, the processes were very security focused as they sought to enhance law enforcement. Ioannides and Collantes-Celador (2011) raise concerns that the security focus detracts from the development oriented benefits: 'The overreliance on the transfer of skills and technologies to fight organised crime and corruption also bring to the fore questions over EUPM's commitment to local ownership and sustainability, two of its identified goals as early as 2003' (Ioannides and Collantes-Celador 2011: 432). Activities such as specialist training, the implementation of effective technology to record and share information, and expert assistance for intelligence analysis and covert evidence gathering techniques enhance technical aspects of approaches to organised crime but not developmental elements. While security and development were integrated in some areas, the processes overwhelmingly adhered to a traditional security approach that prioritised law enforcement.

The EUPM did engage in other areas that go beyond law enforcement. The mission had a strong focus on gender. Local police were trained on gender equality and the role of women in the police was promoted (EUPM 2010b). However, this was not directly linked with initiatives to address organised crime. The EUPM also engaged in public information campaigns to raise awareness of

78 *Addressing organised crime through the nexus*

organised crime and corruption, a crime hotline was set up, and the public were surveyed on their opinion of organised crime and corruption (EUPM 2010b). While these initiatives were focused directly on organised crime and corruption, they were not included in the five key priorities of the mission. As one EUPM official noted, the mission engaged in activities that focused on 'gender, human rights activities, outreach, public information, but that's rather horizontal and marginal to what the activity is'.[23] While the EUPM did engage in a diverse range of activities, the main processes to address organised crime were security oriented.

The focus on law enforcement in Bosnia suggests that the EUPM adhered to a security approach in practice. However, the mission did engage in other areas, such as gender. Despite the top-down approach of EU engagement, EUPM personnel worked in partnership with their local counterparts, encouraging the development of local solutions. Local law enforcement were treated as agents in the fight against organised crime. However, they were expected to adhere to EU policy. While local personnel were empowered to contribute to the programme, it was within boundaries set by the EU. This indicates the beginnings of a shift away from traditional security approaches. However, law enforcement remained the priority. This research investigates what inhibits the full integration of security and development. However, it also assesses where integration has taken place.

The primacy of law enforcement

In both Sierra Leone and Bosnia, initiatives to address organised crime have prioritised law enforcement approaches. Law enforcement can be linked to some conceptualisations of the security–development nexus, which view security as a precondition for development. This is often one of the arguments behind SSR. Schnabel and Farr (2011: 45) contend that

> if SSR assures that security providers are prepared to meet security threats and do not themselves compromise the security of the population, or societies' ability to meet their own welfare and development needs, it makes a critical contribution to building and consolidating a stable, just, inclusive, secure and well-to-do societies.

The fact that law-enforcement approaches prioritise security over development suggests that the two concepts are not integrated in practice.

Shaw and Reitano (2013: 17) argue that law enforcement is 'woefully inadequate' as it is merely responding to the problem of organised crime rather than the factors that encourage organised crime. Cockayne (2011) also argues that law enforcement does not address the problem but shifts it elsewhere. This is supported by law-enforcement professionals: 'if it doesn't pay and constantly gets disrupted, you give up and go somewhere else.'[24] Cockayne (2011: 3) notes that 'efforts to control cocaine production and trafficking in Central America and

Addressing organised crime through the nexus 79

the Caribbean have led to significant "balloon" effects … displacing major cocaine flows to West Africa'.

It is these criticisms of law enforcement that have led to calls for a more comprehensive approach to address organised crime. Naim (2012: 108) argues that 'fighting transnational crime must mean more than curbing the traffic of counterfeit goods, drugs, weapons and people; it must also involve preventing and reversing the criminalisation of governments'. Felbab-Brown (2010) advocates for the inclusion of socio-economic elements. In policy, initiatives to address organised crime are framed by the security–development nexus, emphasising corruption, unemployment and weak governance as important contributing factors that need to be addressed. However, practices on the ground continued to adhere to a security approach.

In both Sierra Leone and Bosnia there was a lack of concerted engagement with development aspects of responses to organised crime. In Sierra Leone there is potential for organised crime to become more of a problem than it is currently. Young people on the streets of Freetown selling mobile phone credit and exchanging money are eager to engage in drug trafficking to earn a higher income.[25] However, the WACI did not engage with this aspect of organised crime. Internationals supported the pursuit of drug smugglers. However, when a long line of unemployed youth is willing to engage in drug trafficking, the risk of arrest is not a deterrent. UNDP delivered programmes to address youth unemployment but they were not connected to strategies to address organised crime.

While the EUPM did engage in activities to address corruption in Bosnia, it didn't extend into broader attempts to address weak governance, which allows organised crime to take root. Cox argued in 2001 that 'unless significant institutional development takes place, breaking the hold of nationalist parties will not lead to better governance' (Cox 2001: 8). Governance remains a serious problem. Between October 2010 and December 2011 the country suffered from political stagnation as there was no national government (USAID 2012). In 2012 Bosnia was ranked in the bottom 20 per cent of countries in terms of government effectiveness (UNDP 2012b). As a result, political and business elites have capitalised on weak governance to engage in illicit practices. Pugh (2005) argues that privatisation within Bosnia became a criminalised process. Domm (2011: 62) contends that 'the politico-criminal nexus that took root in the 1990s has given rise to a generation of business and political elites who see their economic interests threatened by a rationalised, effective legal and institutional state framework'. By adhering to a security approach, the EUPM's approach to organised crime is reactive, responding to the problems created by weak governance but not addressing weak governance directly.

Although initiatives to address organised crime in Sierra Leone and Bosnia are framed by the security–development nexus in policy, this hasn't been accompanied by a significant shift in practice. Through immanent critique, this research seeks to understand why the security–development nexus does not fulfil its potential – it examines what inhibits the integration of security and development into a nexus. While the discussion of the case studies points to the continued dominance of

80 *Addressing organised crime through the nexus*

security, it also indicates the beginning of a shift away from a traditional security approach, with development playing a more active role. As such, analysis of the tensions also identifies where integration has taken place and why.

Notes

1 A further outbreak of violence in Sierra Leone in 1999 brought a halt to these initiatives. Reconstruction recommenced in 2002.
2 Out of 188 countries, Sierra Leone is ranked 181st and Bosnia is ranked 85th in terms of human development (UNDP 2015).
3 Interview, Sarajevo, October 2011.
4 Interviews, Freetown, January 2012.
5 Interview, Freetown, January 2012.
6 Interview, Freetown, January 2012.
7 Interview, Freetown, January 2012.
8 Interview, Freetown, January 2012.
9 Communication with UNDP, Sierra Leone.
10 Interview, Freetown, January 2012.
11 Communication with UNDP, Sierra Leone.
12 Interview, Sarajevo, March 2012.
13 Interview, Sarajevo, March 2012.
14 Interview, Sarajevo, March 2012.
15 Interview, Sarajevo, March 2012.
16 Interview, Sarajevo, March 2012.
17 Interview, Sarajevo, March 2012.
18 Interview, Sarajevo, March 2012.
19 Kelmendi was arrested in May 2013 in Kosovo.
20 Interview, Sarajevo, March 2012.
21 Interview, Sarajevo, March 2012.
22 Interview, Sarajevo, March 2012.
23 Interview, Sarajevo, October 2011.
24 Interview, Freetown, January 2012.
25 Interview, Freetown, January 2012.

References

Albrecht, Peter, Finn Stepputat and Louise Andersen (2010). 'Security Sector Reform, the European Way', in Mark Sedra (ed.), *The Future of Security Sector Reform.* Waterloo, ON, Centre for International Governance and Innovation.

Alibabic, Munir (1996). *Bosna u Kandzma (Bosnia in the Claws of KOS).* Sarajevo, NIP Behar.

Anastasijevic, Dejan (2010). 'Getting Better? A Map of Organised Crime in the Western Balkans', in Wolfgang Benedek, Christopher Daase, Voijin Dimitrijevic and Petrus van Duyne (eds), *Transnational Terrorism, Organised Crime and Peace-Building: Human Security in the Western Balkans.* Basingstoke; New York, Palgrave Macmillan.

Andreas, Peter (2004). 'The Clandestine Political Economy of War and Peace in Bosnia', *International Studies Quarterly* 48(1): 29–51.

Andreas, Peter (2010). 'The Longest Siege: Humanitarians and Profiteers in the Battle for Sarajevo', in Wolfgang Benedek, Christopher Daase, Voijin Dimitrijevic and Petrus van Duyne (eds), *Transnational Terrorism, Organised Crime and Peace-Building: Human Security in the Western Balkans.* Basingstoke; New York, Palgrave Macmillan.

Addressing organised crime through the nexus 81

Beare, Margaret (ed.) (2003). *Critical Reflections on Transnational Organised Crime, Money Laundering and Corruption.* Toronto, Toronto University Press.

Belloni, Roberto (2007). *State Building and International Intervention in Bosnia.* London, Routledge.

Berticelli, Alberto (2007). 'Scoperta a Milano la centrale della mafia calabrese', http://archiviostorico.corriere.it/2007/maggio/04/Scoperta_Milano_centrale_della_mafia_co_7_070504015.shtml accessed 3 August 2012.

Boas, Morten and Anne Hatloy (2005). *Alcohol and Drug Consumption in Post War Sierra Leone: An Exploration.* Oslo, Fafo.

Carrier, Neil and Gernot Klantschnig (2012). *Africa and the War on Drugs.* London; New York, Zed Books.

Cawley, Marguerite (2014). 'Honduras Approves Drug Plane Shoot-Down Law, Bolvia Set to Follow', www.insightcrime.org/news-briefs/honduras-approves-drug-plane-shoot-down-law-bolivia-set-to-follow accessed 20 January 2014.

Chandler, David (2006). *Empire in Denial: The Politics of State-building.* London; Ann Arbor, MI, Pluto Press.

Cockayne, James (2011). *State Fragility, Organised Crime and Peacebuilding: Towards a More Strategic Approach.* Oslo, NOREF.

Cockayne, James and Adam Lupel (2009a). 'Introduction: Rethinking the Relationship Between Peace Operations and Organised Crime', *International Peacekeeping* 16(1): 4–19.

Cockayne, James and Adam Lupel (2009b). 'Conclusion: From Iron Fist to Invisible Hand – Peace Operations, Organised Crime and Intelligent International Law Enforcement', *International Peacekeeping* 16(1): 151–68.

Cockayne, James and Daniel Pfister (2008). *Peace Operations and Organised Crime.* Geneva, Geneva Centre for Security Policy and International Peace Institute.

Commission of the European Communities (2005). *2005 Enlargement Strategy Paper.* Brussels, Commission of the European Communities.

Cox, Marcus (2001). *State Building and Post-Conflict Reconstruction: Lessons from Bosnia. The Rehabilitation of War-torn Societies.* Geneva, Centre for Applied Studies in International Negotations.

Darby, John and Roger MacGinty (2008). 'Introduction: What Peace? What Process?' in John Darby and Roger MacGinty (eds), *Contemporary Peacemaking: Conflict, Peace Processes and Post-War Reconstruction.* New York, Palgrave Macmillan.

Domm, Rory (2011). 'Next Steps on Bosnia-Herzegovina: Key Elements to a Revised EU Strategy', *Southeast European and Black Sea Studies* 11(1): 53–67.

Dragojlovic, Mladen (2013). 'BiH an Important Link in the Narcotics Smuggling Chain', www.setimes.com/cocoon/setimes/xhtml/en_GB/features/setimes/features/2013/08/30/feature-02 accessed 2 September 2013.

Ellis, Stephen (2009). 'West Africa's International Drug Trade', *African Affairs* 108(431): 171–196.

Ellis, Stephen (2015). *This Present Darkness: A History of Nigerian Organised Crime.* London, Hurst Publishers.

EU (2007). *Council Conclusions on Security and Development: 2831st External Relations Council Meeting 19–20 November 2007.* Brussels, EU.

EU (2012). *European Union Police Mission Bosnia and Herzegovina (EUPM) Factsheet.* Brussels, EU.

EUPM (European Union Police Mission) (2010a). *EUPM Strategic Objectives 2010/11.* Sarajevo, EUPM.

82 *Addressing organised crime through the nexus*

EUPM (European Union Police Mission) (2010b). *EUPM Mission Implementation Plan 2010*. Sarajevo, EUPM.

European Commission (2005). *Policy Coherence for Development: Accelerating Progress Towards Attaining the Millennium Development Goals*. Brussels, EU.

European Commission (2008). *Enlargement Strategy and Main Challenges 2008–2009*. Brussels, European Commission.

EUROPOL (2005). *2005 EU Organised Crime Report*. The Hague, EUROPOL.

Felbab-Brown, Vanda (2010). 'The Design and Resourcing of Supply-Side Counternarcotics Policies', www.brookings.edu/research/testimony/2010/04/14-drug-funding-felbabbrown accessed 19 May 2013.

Felbab-Brown, Vanda (2013). 'A State-building Approach to the Drug Trade Problem', www.brookings.edu/research/opinions/2013/07/18-state-building-drug-trade-problem-felbabbrown accessed 30 August 2013.

FES (Friedrich-Ebert-Stiftung) (2013). 'Interview: Organised Crime is a Development Challenge', *Being Tough is Not Enough: Curbing Transnational Organised Crime: Conference Report.* Friedrich-Ebert-Stiftung. Berlin, Friedrich-Ebert-Stiftung.

Friesendorf, Cornelius, Ursula Schroeder and Irma Deljkic (2010). 'Bosnia and the Art of Policy Implementation: Obstacles to International Counter-Crime Strategies', in Wolfgang Benedek, Christopher Daase, Vojin Dimitrijevic and Petrus van Duyne (eds), *Transnational Terrorism, Organised Crime and Peace-building: Human Security in the Western Balkans*. Basingstoke; New York, Palgrave Macmillan.

Glenny, Misha (2008). *McMafia: A Journey through the Global Criminal Underworld*. New York, Alfred A. Knopf.

Goddard, Stephen (2009). 'Recent Developments in Fighting Organized Crime in Bosnia-Herzegovina', in Ernst M. Felberbauer, Predrag Jurekovic and Frederic Labarre (eds), *Supporting Bosnia and Herzegovina: The Challenge of Reaching Self-Sustainability in a Post-War Environment*. Vienna, Austrian National Defence Academy.

Goudsmid, Tim, Andrea Mancini and Andres Vanegas Canosa (2011). 'Security Sector Reform, Crime and Regional Development in West Africa', in Albrecht Schnavel and Vanessa Farr (eds), *Back to the Roots: Security Sector Reform and Development*. Geneva, DCAF.

Grant, J. Andrew (2005). 'Diamonds, Foreign Aid and the Uncertain Prospects for Post-Conflict Reconstruction in Sierra Leone', *The Round Table* 94(381): 443–57.

Hopkins, Valerie (2012). 'US Blacklists Balkan Businessman Naser Kelmendi', www.reportingproject.net/occrp/index.php/en/ccwatch/cc-watch-indepth/1539-us-blacklists-balkan-businessman-naser-kelmendi accessed 12 August 2012.

Human Rights Watch (2003). *'We'll Kill You if You Cry': Sexual Violence in the Sierra Leone Conflict.* Washington DC, Human Rights Watch.

Ioannides, Isabelle and Gemma Collantes-Celador (2011). 'The Internal–External Security Nexus and EU Police/Rule of Law Missions in the Western Balkans', *Conflict, Security & Development* 11(4): 415–45.

Jukic, Elvira (2013). 'Bosnia Jails Top Crime Gang for 100 Years', www.balkaninsight.com/en/article/bosnia-jails-criminal-group-for-100-years accessed 17 January 2014.

Juncos, Ana E. (2007). 'Police Mission in Bosnia and Herzegovina', in Michael Emerson and Eva Gross (eds), *Evaluating the EU's Crisis Missions in the Balkans*. Brussels, Centre for European Policy Studies.

Kaldor, Mary (2006). *New Wars and Old Wars: Organised Violence in a Global Era*. Cambridge, Polity.

Addressing organised crime through the nexus 83

Kemp, Walter, Mark Shaw and Arthur Boutellis (2013). *The Elephant in the Room: How Can Peace Operations Deal with Organized Crime?* New York, International Peace Institute.

Lupick, Travis (2013). 'Drug Traffic Fuels Addiction in Sierra Leone', www.aljazeera.com/indepth/features/2013/01/2013121105523716213.html accessed 28 February 2013.

Mazzitelli, Antonio (2007). 'Transnational Organised Crime in West Africa: The Additional Challenge', *International Affairs* 83(6): 1071–90.

Mazzitelli, Antonio (2011). *The New Transatlantic Bonanza: Cocaine on Highway 10.* Miami, WHEMSAC.

Miraglia, Paula, Rolando Ochoa and Ivan Briscoe (2012). *Transnational Organised Crime and Fragile States.* Paris, OECD.

Montanaro-Jankovski, Lucia (2005). *Good Cops, Bad Mobs? EU Policies to Fight Transnational Organised Crime in the Western Balkans.* Brussels, European Policy Centre.

Muehlmann, Thomas (2008). 'Police Restructuring in Bosnia-Herzegovina: Problems of Internationally-led Security Sector Reform', *Journal of Intervention and Statebuilding* 2(1): 1–22.

Muguruza, Cristina Churruca (2008). *European Union Support for Security Sector Reform: The Added Value of the EU as a Global Security Actor.* Madrid, Ministerio de Defensa.

Naim, Moises (2012). 'Mafia States: Organised Crime Takes Office', *Foreign Affairs* 91(3): 100–11.

NYU CIC (New York University Centre for International Cooperation) (2012). *Background Paper: The Impact of Organised Crime and Drug Trafficking on Governance, Development and Security in West Africa.* New York, NYU Centre for International Cooperation.

OCCRP (Organised Crime and Corruption Reporting Project) (2008). 'Smuggling in Bosnia', www.reportingproject.net/occrp/index.php/en/projects/tobacco-project/32-bosnia-and-herzegovina/60-smuggling-in-bosnia accessed 20 August 2013.

OCCRP (Organised Crime and Corruption Reporting Project) (2012). 'Bosnia: Zoran Copic Convicted for Laundering Drug Money', www.reportingproject.net/occrp/index.php/en/ccwatch/cc-watch-briefs/1610-bosnia-zoran-copic-convicted-for-laundering-drug-money accessed 20 August 2013.

Osmanović-Vukelić, Sanela (2012). *10 Years of EU Police Mission in Bosnia and Herzegovina: The Story of the EU Police Mission in Bosnia and Herzegovina.* Sarajevo, EUPM.

Paris, Roland and Timothy Sisk (2007). 'Managing Contradictions: The Inherent Dilemmas of Postwar Statebuilding'. *Research Partnership on Postwar Statebuilding.* International Peace Academy.

Pugh, Michael (2005). 'Transformation in the Political Economy of Bosnia Since Dayton', *International Peacekeeping* 12(3): 448–62.

Quinney, Richard (2001). *The Social Reality of Crime.* New Brunswick, NJ, Transaction.

Ramsbotham, Oliver, Tom Woodhouse and Hugh Miall (2005). *Contemporary Conflict Resolution: The Prevention and Management of Deadly Conflicts.* Cambridge, Polity Press.

Reno, William (2011). 'Understanding Criminality in West African Conflicts', in James Cockayne and Adam Lupel (eds), *Peace Operations and Organised Crime.* London, Routledge.

Roberts, David (2008). 'Post-Conflict Statebuilding and State Legitmacy: From Negative to Positive Peace?' *Development and Change* 39(4): 537–555.

84 *Addressing organised crime through the nexus*

Saidu, Hindowa (2011). 'No Drugs for Votes!' www.crisp-berlin.org/index.php?id= 14&no_cache=1&tx_ttnews%5Bpointer%5D=2&tx_ttnews%5BbackPid%5D=15&tx_ ttnews%5Btt_news%5D=22 accessed 1 March 2012.

Sarjanen, Ari (2008). 'Interdependency: Key to Fight Against Organised Crime', *Mission Mag* 55: 4–5.

Schnabel, Albrecht (2011). 'The Security–Development Discourse and the Role of SSR as a Development Instrument', in Albrecht Schnabel and Vanessa Farr (eds), *Back to the Roots: Security Sector Reform and Development.* Geneva, Centre for the Democratic Control of Armed Forces.

Schnabel, Albrecht and Vanessa Farr (2011). 'Returning to the Development Roots of Security Sector Reform', in Albrecht Schnabel and Vanessa Farr (eds), *Back to the Roots: Security Sector Reform and Development.* Geneva, Centre for the Democratic Control of Armed Forces.

Shaw, Mark and Tuesday Reitano (2013). *The Evolution of Organised Crime in Africa.* Pretoria, Institute for Security Studies.

Sito-Sucic, Daria (2013). 'Dozens Indicted in Bosnia in One of Biggest Post-war Crime Busts', http://uk.reuters.com/article/2013/08/28/uk-bosnia-crime-idUKBRE97R0JR20 130828 accessed 17 January 2014.

SLTRC (Sierra Leone Truth and Reconciliation Commission) (2004). *Witness to Truth: Report of the Sierra Leone Truth and Reconciliation Commission.* Accra, Graphic Packaging.

Trenchard, Tommy (2013). 'Unemployed Youth Turn to Drugs', www.ipsnews. net/2013/01/unemployed-youth-turn-to-drugs/ accessed 28 February 2013.

UN (2004). *United Nations Convention Against Transnational Organised Crime and the Protocols Thereto.* New York, UN.

UN General Assembly (1998). *Measures to Enhance International Cooperation to Counter the World Drug Problem.* New York, UN.

UN Security Council (2012). *Letter dated 8 February 2012 from the Permanent Representative of Togo to the United Nations addressed to the Secretary-General.* S/2012/83. New York, UN.

UNDP (UN Development Programme) (2012a). *Sierra Leone MDTF.* Freetown, UNDP.

UNDP (UN Development Programme) (2012b). 'Bosnia and Herzegovina: Democratic Governance', www.undp.ba/index.aspx?PID=25&RID=27 accessed 3 March 2013.

UNDP (UN Development Programme) (2015). *Human Development Report 2015: Work for Human Development.* New York, UNDP.

UNODC (UN Office on Drugs and Crime (2005). *Transnational Organised Crime in the West Africa Region.* Vienna, UNODC.

UNODC (UN Office on Drugs and Crime) (2008a). *Drug Trafficking as a Security Threat in West Africa.* Vienna, UNODC.

UNODC (UN Office on Drugs and Crime) (2008b). *UNODC Strategy 2008–2011: Towards Security and Justice for All: Making the World Safer from Crime, Drugs and Terrorism.* Vienna, UNODC.

UNODC (UN Office on Drugs and Crime) (2008c). *An Integrated Response to Organised Crime and Illicit Drug Trafficking: West Africa Coast Initiative.* Dakar, UNODC.

UNODC (UN Office on Drugs and Crime) (2010a). *The Globalization of Crime: A Transnational Organized Crime Threat Assessment.* Vienna, UNODC.

UNODC (UN Office on Drugs and Crime) (2010b). *Crime and Instability: Case Studies of Transnational Threats.* Vienna, UNODC.

UNODC (UN Office on Drugs and Crime) (2010c). *Project Document: Building Institutional Capacity to Respond to the Threat Posed by Illicit Drug Trafficking and Organised Crime in Sierra Leone*. Dakar, UNODC Regional Office for West and Central Africa.

UNODC (UN Office on Drugs and Crime) (2012). *Regional Programme for West Africa 2010–2014*. Vienna, UNODC.

USAID (US Agency for International Development) (2012). *Country Development Cooperation Strategy for Bosnia and Herzegovina 2012–2016*. Washington DC, USAID.

van Dijk, Jan (2007). 'Mafia Makers: Assessing Organised Crime and its Impact on Socieities', *Trends in Organised Crime* 10(4): 39–56.

van Duyne, Petrus, Matjaž Jager, Klaus von Lampe and James Newell (eds) (2004). *Threats and Phantoms of Organised Crime, Corruption and Terrorism: Critical European Perspectives*. Nijmegen, Wolf Legal Publishers.

WACD (West Africa Commission on Drugs) (2015). *Not Just in Transit: Drugs, the State and Society in West Africa*. Geneva, Kofi Annan Foundation.

Walker, Summer and Elisa Buchert (2013). 'A Desk Study of Sierra Leone', in Camino Kavanagh (ed.), *Getting Smart and Scaling Up: Responding to the Impact of Organized Crime on Governance in Developing Countries*. New York, NYU Centre on International Cooperation.

Wheeler, Nicholas (2000). *Saving Strangers: Humanitarian Intervention in International Society*. Oxford, Oxford University Press.

White, Mark (2008). 'The Security and Development Nexus: A Case Study of Sierra Leone 2004–2006', in Peter Albrecht and Paul Jackson (eds), *Security System Transformation in Sierra Leone, 1997–2007*. London, SSR Network.

Wikileaks (2009a). 'Sierra Leone International Narcotics Control Strategy Report: US Embassy Sierra Leone Cable', http://leaks.hohesc.us/?view=09FREETOWN430 accessed 1 March 2012.

Wikileaks (2009b). 'Coke, Tokes and Inept Folks: Can SL Stay Tough on Drugs? US Embassy Sierra Leone Cable', www.cablegatesearch.net/cable.php?id=09FREETOWN 270 accessed 1 March 2012.

Williams, Phil (2011). 'Organised Crime and Corruption in Iraq', in James Cockayne and Adam Lupel (eds), *Peace Operations and Organised Crime: Enemies or Allies?* New York, Routledge.

World Bank (2011). *World Development Report: Conflict, Security, and Development*. Washington DC, World Bank.

World Bank (2016). 'Data: Country and Lending Groups', http://data.worldbank.org/about/country-and-lending-groups accessed 21 May 2016.

4 Tensions in the security–development nexus: Sierra Leone

In Sierra Leone, organised crime was addressed as a multi-agency initiative through the West Africa Coast Initiative (WACI). The project document that defined the project was framed by the security–development nexus. However, as outlined previously in this book, the implementation of the project was very security focused. Drawing on empirical evidence from interviews conducted in Sierra Leone and official documentation of external actors addressing organised crime, this chapter examines in detail how the four hypothesised tensions influence the integration of security and development within initiatives to address organised crime in Sierra Leone. It analyses how the key external actors – the UN Office on Drugs and Crime (UNODC), the UN Peacebuilding Mission in Sierra Leone (UNIPSIL) and the Economic Community of West African States (ECOWAS) – understand security and development, how security and development are applied, and the linkages between them, the institutional underpinnings of the WACI and the motivations of the external actors involved.

Conceptual tension

The security–development nexus brings together two highly contested concepts. Although it can be argued that security and development have become closely related through parallel shifts towards human security and human development, there are many other, potentially conflicting understandings of security and development that influence the type of nexus that emerges. By bringing together the plethora of actors active in West Africa – from ECOWAS, the UN Office for West Africa (UNOWA) and Interpol – with the key implementing agencies in Sierra Leone – UNODC and UNIPSIL – the WACI instituted a multi-stakeholder approach. This approach combined expertise to address the 'scope and complexity of increasing threats to security and stability in West Africa posed by transnational organised crime' (UNODC 2008a: 1). However, the involvement of different actors raised the potential for diverse and contradictory understandings of security and development. This section examines how the three key actors, ECOWAS, UNODC and UNIPSIL, understood security and development, mapping them on the diagram from Chapter 2 (Figure 2.1).

Security

ECOWAS

The foundations of the WACI were derived from the ECOWAS Political Declaration on the Prevention of Drug Abuse, Illicit Drug Trafficking and Organised Crime in West Africa and its accompanying regional action plan. These documents therefore had a strong influence on how the WACI was implemented. They recognise organised crime as a problem for both security and development, but they also reveal a tension in ECOWAS's engagement with the security–development nexus.

Some sections of the ECOWAS Political Declaration have a strong focus on the security of member states, which points to the state as the referent object. For example: 'illicit drug trafficking ... and other organised crime are serious threats to the regional and national security ... of member states' (ECOWAS 2008a: 1). Similarly, the regional action plan seeks to redefine 'the drugs problem and all related organised crime facing the region as threats to regional and national security' (ECOWAS 2008b).

Other sections of the Political Declaration focus on the security of individuals, suggesting a referent object at the other end of the spectrum. The declaration recognises the 'right of citizens of the community to live in safety and security without the threats posed by drug abuse and trafficking and other organised crime' (ECOWAS 2008a). The focus on regional and national security is also closely linked to public health. While this can be connected to state-based concerns, as the risk to public health would pose a significant burden on the state, it also addresses the effect of drug trafficking on the population, which points to the individual as the referent object. The focus on individual needs within these documents is connected to a broader shift within ECOWAS. Aning (2004: 533) notes that 'ECOWAS, through its increasing involvement in sub-regional security, seeks to shift emphasis away from traditional regime centred security to more people-centred approaches'. This suggests that understandings of security within ECOWAS follow the trajectory from traditional security to human security.

When it comes to translating the Political Declaration and Regional Action Plan into action through the WACI, the interests of member states played a much stronger role though. The perspectives of member states are outlined in the WACI Freetown Commitment drafted in 2010. The Freetown Commitment was signed by the four countries participating in the WACI, Sierra Leone, Liberia, Cote d'Ivoire and Guinea-Bissau, restating the goals of the initiative and reiterating their dedication. Illicit drug trafficking and organised crime are recognised for their contribution to corruption, money laundering and the movement of small arms. The document also recognises that drug trafficking and organised crime 'undermine the rule of law, democratic institutions and governance in our states' and are an 'impediment to economic development' (ECOWAS 2010: 3).

88 *Tensions in the nexus: Sierra Leone*

The effect of drug trafficking and organised crime on rule of law, democratic institutions, governance and economic development has an impact on individuals. The WACI Freetown Commitment also recognises the 'harmful effects of illicit drugs and organised crime on our respective population' (ECOWAS 2010: 5). For instance, corruption undermines democratic governance as politicians benefitting from organised crime have the means to stay in power even when they do not represent the needs of their constituents. The impact of organised crime on rule of law, democratic institutions and governance affects citizens by limiting access to justice and other services provided by the state. However, these factors also have a significant impact on the stability and security of the state. Money laundering undermines the stability of the economy, corruption undermines the stability of the regime, and the movement of small arms can foster conflict. The effect of organised crime on the rule of law, democratic institutions and governance also threatens the stability of the regime, and in post-conflict states can contribute to renewed conflict. Within the WACI Freetown Commitment, the threat organised crime poses to state stability and security was the key focus, as strategies focused on 'the threat posed to our states by the scourge of drugs and crime' (ECOWAS 2010: 5). For member states, the state was the referent object.

Although ECOWAS sought to shift towards a people-centred approach, member states remained preoccupied with state-level security. As such, there is inconsistency within ECOWAS regarding the understandings of security. At the Commission level, where the Political Declaration and regional action plan were drafted, drug trafficking and organised crime can be considered in a more abstract way, as commissioners are required to put their state interest to one side and consider how issues affect the region as a whole. As a result, the focus is on individuals and people as the referent object. The focus on individuals is also connected to a push within the Commission to become more people centred. When it comes to implementation, the concerns of member states and their own security come to the forefront. The emphasis on state security will be examined in more detail in the discussion on the motivational tension, as it suggests that state security is the primary objective, with the expectation that this will benefit individuals within the state. In contrast to the ECOWAS Commission, the focus on state security points to the state as the referent object.

Within ECOWAS there are different perspectives on the referent object but the locus of initiatives still remains the same. Within the regional action plan the focus is institutional reform addressing rule of law. The WACI Freetown Agreement also emphasises institutional reform. As such, initiatives are implemented at the state level. As a result, understandings of security within ECOWAS straddle the divide between Quadrant A: Top-down benevolence and Quadrant B: Hard security/economic development, with the interests of the Commission and member states pulling in different directions.

UNODC

The ECOWAS Regional Action Plan has been translated into practice by UNODC through the WACI. The WACI Project was initially part of UNODC's 2008–2011 strategy on rule of law. Rule of law is prioritised as it 'is the basis for providing justice and security for all' (UNODC 2008b: 10). The attention given to rule of law suggests a focus on the needs of individuals. However, organised crime is also understood as a threat to national security. While UNODC recognises that it is rare for organised criminals to overthrow governments or make areas ungovernable, it is considered more likely in West Africa (UNODC 2008c). As such, 'the security implications … go to the core of the state's ability to maintain its sovereignty and integrity' (UNODC 2007a: 1).

UNODC's focus on rule of law also reinforces the emphasis on national security. Without rule of law there is potential for lawlessness and chaos to ensue. While this affects individuals, it also threatens the regime in power and the stability of the state, with implications extending regionally and internationally. The concern for regional and international spill over is reiterated as UNODC seeks 'solutions to threats that do not respect borders' (UNODC 2008b: iii). Combined with the concern for national security already highlighted, rule of law programming points to the state as the referent object of security. Building on the regional action plan, UNODC seeks to address organised crime through institution building, placing the locus of initiatives at the state level. This situates UNODC's understanding of security within Quadrant B: Hard security/economic development.

UNIPSIL

Within Sierra Leone, the UN Peacebuilding Mission, UNIPSIL, was the driving force behind the WACI. UNODC had staff members located within the UNIPSIL compound, working in partnership with UNIPSIL's senior police advisor. UNIPSIL's police and security unit aimed to support the Sierra Leonean government in national security through capacity building, training, mentoring and monitoring the Sierra Leone police. This focus on national security ensured that the primary referent object of security was the state. However, there was also an interest in regional and international security. UNIPSIL noted that 'strengthening Sierra Leone's security forces in facing the threat of international organised crime has both a capacity building as well as a wider political aspect' (UN 2009: 5). This is connected to the interest of particular countries, specifically those affected by drug trafficking through West Africa, in addressing organised crime in Sierra Leone. As a result, initiatives to address organised crime targeted state institutions to prevent spill over to the regional and international level. The locus of UNIPSIL's initiatives were at the state level as they worked through the Transnational Organised Crime Unit (TOCU), which brings together police, the Office of National Security (ONS), the National Drug and Law Enforcement Agency (NDLEA) and other state bodies connected to organised crime. This

90 *Tensions in the nexus: Sierra Leone*

places the understanding of security within Quadrant B: Hard security/economic development.

Although there is inconsistency in how ECOWAS understands security, UNODC and UNIPSIL have a similar understanding, both fitting within Quadrant B. By focusing on state and international security, and with a locus at the state level, these understandings adhere to a traditional security approach. As a result, the inclusion of development within the security–development nexus has not influenced how security is understood.

Development

While development plays a key role in initiatives to address organised crime for ECOWAS, UNODC and UNIPSIL, there is no consensus on how it is understood.

ECOWAS

Within ECOWAS there is a strong emphasis on the development aspects of organised crime. Throughout the Political Declaration and the regional action plan, the impact of drug trafficking and organised crime on development is recognised alongside the security threat. The final communiqué of the ECOWAS Commission Heads of State Meeting considered initiatives to address organised crime within the context of human development (ECOWAS Commission 2008). This implies that initiatives to address organised crime focus on individuals as the referent object. However, the preamble of the Political Declaration emphasises the 'need to promote, foster and accelerate the economic and social development of our states in order to improve the living standards of our peoples' (ECOWAS 2008a). This denotes a top-down approach as development at the state level is expected to have benefits that flow down to individuals.

A top-down approach that has benefits for individuals points to primary and secondary referent objects. The state is the primary referent object, with benefits expected to accrue to individuals as the secondary referent object. However, there is no guarantee that the needs of individuals will be met by the state, particularly as 'trickle down' approaches have been widely criticised (see Stiglitz 1998). Furthermore, placing individuals as a secondary referent object assumes that all individuals will benefit equally from state-level development, disregarding the potential for unequal distribution. As a result, this understanding of development fits within Quadrant B: Hard security/economic development, as it is disconnected from individuals and communities.

ECOWAS's understanding of development has parallels with the perspective of member states. Although the WACI Freetown Commitment engages with issues that affect individuals, such as the impact of organised crime on rule of law, democratic institutions and governance, the primary focus is on economic development. However, as with security, the ECOWAS Commission seeks to shift understandings of development into Quadrant A: Top-down benevolence.

Through the Vision 2020 long-term development agenda, the President of ECOWAS seeks to transform the organisation from an 'ECOWAS of States' to an 'ECOWAS of Peoples' (Gbeho 2011; ECOWAS 2012). As a result, understandings of development also straddle the divide between Quadrants A and B, with different interests from the ECOWAS Commission and member states pulling in different directions. As with security, the Commission seeks to ensure that strategies are more people centred. However, when it comes to implementation, member states are more concerned about their own development, which is expected to benefit their own citizens.

UNODC

Development is also a key element of UNODC's response to organised crime. UNODC recognises that addressing drug trafficking and organised crime 'requires a comprehensive and engaged development strategy with economic support' (UNODC 2010a: 3). However, UNODC primarily engages in alternative development strategies that seek to 'reduce opportunities and incentives for illicit activities and gains' (UNODC 2008b: 3). Some of these strategies are focused at the community level. For example, UNODC seeks to engage in community-centred prevention, assistance to victims, juvenile justice, treatment and rehabilitation, and HIV/AIDS prevention and care. While this approach addresses health issues connected to drug users, it targets the community level to prevent further threats to the state. 'The overall Programme objective is to contribute and support the efforts of the Member states in West Africa, as well as those of regional organisations and civil society to respond to evolving health and security threats' (UNODC 2012a: 5). These strategies seek to prevent individuals from engaging in organised crime, rather than protecting individuals from the impact of organised crime. This places UNODC's understanding of development in Quadrant D: Containment.

UNIPSIL

The development aspect of UNIPSIL's response to organised crime had parallels to UNODC's understanding of development. UNIPSIL focused on drug demand-reduction, treatment, prevention and rehabilitation. As with UNODC's approach, while this appears to address the needs of individuals, the primary referent object is the state as the aim was 'to respond to the threat posed by illicit drug trafficking and organised crime in Sierra Leone' (UNIPSIL 2012a). However, these initiatives were located at the local level through engagement with civil society and NGOs, seeking to encourage a local response. While engagement at the local level suggests a locally centred understanding of development, the emphasis on the state as reference object indicates that locally based initiatives were implemented to contain security problems. As such, the understanding of development fit within Quadrant D: Containment. Drug demand-reduction, treatment, prevention and rehabilitation contain problems connected to drug trafficking in order to

92 *Tensions in the nexus: Sierra Leone*

ensure state security and limit international spill over. In this instance, development was employed to achieve security outcomes.

Among actors addressing organised crime in Sierra Leone, the security and development aspects of organised crime are acknowledged. While this ensures that the WACI is implemented within the framework of the security–development nexus, conceptual tension emerges from the different perspectives on what this means. Figure 4.1 plots how the three key actors addressing organised crime in Sierra Leone understand security and development.

As already noted, the propensity for understandings of security, in what is supposed to be the security–development nexus, to fit within Quadrant B suggests that the nexus does not result in a shift away from a traditional security approach. Quadrant B aligns with a state-centric worldview based on the primacy of military power (Newman 2010). The conceptual tension reveals the difficulty of a shift towards a comprehensive approach that engages with human security when security is understood in these terms.

The adherence to a traditional security approach is reinforced by understandings of development. Understandings of development point to an approach that is designed to support security, rather than enhance the wellbeing of individuals. The ECOWAS Commission has embraced principles of people-centred development but this is held in check by member states that maintain an interest in economic development and the wellbeing of the state. UNODC and UNIPSIL have incorporated community-level strategies to address organised crime through demand reduction, treatment, prevention and rehabilitation. While this appears to engage with individual needs, it merely seeks to ensure state security and limit the effect on international security. This is far from the transformative approach to development elaborated by Sen (1999) and Cornwall (2007). From this

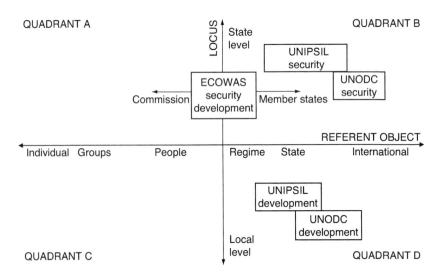

Figure 4.1 Understandings of security and development in Sierra Leone.

perspective, development does not bring a 'humanising' influence to the security–development nexus as it is employed to achieve security outcomes.

These understandings influence the type of nexus that emerges. Rather than a comprehensive approach that shifts away from a preoccupation with the state to also acknowledge the needs of individuals, a security–development nexus based on the understandings of security and development outlined in this section still focuses on state and international needs. However, the inclusion of development does result in a shift in how organised crime is approached. UNODC and UNIPSIL initiatives at the community level, although contributing to international security, also engage with the needs of individuals.

The different understandings of security and development among actors addressing organised crime also ensures there is no consistency within the WACI. With referent objects and the loci of initiatives spanning three quadrants, the security–development nexus has different meanings for the different actors involved. However, the WACI seeks to benefit from an inter-agency approach to operationalise the objectives put forward by ECOWAS. While all of the actors involved can discuss their initiatives within the framework of the security–development nexus, they are referring to different referent objects and loci. This has implications for the comprehensiveness of the approach as activities implemented by different actors do not necessarily contribute to the same overarching vision.

Causal tension

A second tension arises from the divergent understandings of the causal relationship between security and development; in short, how they influence each other. As with understandings of security and development, questions regarding cause and effect are rarely answered explicitly beyond stating that security needs development, and development needs security. As a result, the International Peace Institute argues that there is a 'panoply of theory, policy, and practice on the interplay between security and development' (IPA 2006: 2). This section examines how security and development are applied in Sierra Leone – whether they are an end state or a process to achieve a desired end state. It also examines how the linkage between security and development is perceived – whether the relationship is separate or integrated. This reveals how external actors understand the causal relationship between security and development, and the form of the integration between security and development.

Application

Traditionally, security has referred to an end state where the referent object is secure. External actors addressing organised crime in Sierra Leone all perceive security as an end state. The Political Declaration that informs the WACI notes the consequences of organised crime on peace and security and the 'negative impact on the security of member states' (ECOWAS 2008a). This perspective

94 *Tensions in the nexus: Sierra Leone*

views security as a tangible state that is negatively affected by organised crime. As a result, security is considered to be an end state, not a process to achieve a desired end state. The threat of organised crime is also applied to 'citizens' ability to live in safety and security' (ECOWAS 2008a). Although addressing different referent objects, these references engage with security as an achievable condition that is negatively affected by organised crime.

For UNODC, the threat that organised crime poses to security is mentioned regularly (UNODC 2009; UNODC 2010b; UNODC 2012a). For example, the Regional Programme for West Africa states that 'the criminal behaviour and corruption that travel alongside the cocaine are seriously affecting the security of countries in the region' (UNODC 2010a: viii). UNODC also views approaches to address organised crime as designed to 'ensure internal and sub-regional security' (UNODC 2010b: 3). As a condition that is threatened by organised crime, security is viewed as an end state that needs to be protected, rather than a process to address organised crime.

Similarly, UNIPSIL acknowledges that 'the arrival of illicit drugs in West Africa, particularly cocaine, poses a serious threat to the youth and ultimately the security of the nation' (UN 2009: 5). UNIPSIL's mandate is to establish national security and the UN Joint Vision discusses 'access to security' and 'maintaining security' (UN 2009: 10–11). These references all refer to security as a condition experienced by the state and individuals. In particular, the focus on achieving national security directly implies that security is an end state that can be achieved through international engagement. The emphasis on threats also refers to security as a condition that can be undermined by organised crime. However, UNIPSIL recognises that security is not evenly distributed; access to security for some still needs to be provided. As such, security is an end state or condition that needs to be restored, put in place or protected; it is not a process to address organised crime.

In contrast to security, the application of development has been more variable. It has been perceived as a process that responds to local needs, or the desired end state of international involvement. In Sierra Leone, the Political Declaration discusses the 'need to promote, foster and accelerate economic and social development of our states' (ECOWAS 2008a). This reference can be taken to mean the need to promote, foster and accelerate progress towards the end goal of development, or it may refer to the process of achieving social and economic progress. When the aims of the Political Declaration were reiterated by member states in the WACI Freetown Commitment, organised crime was seen as an 'impediment to economic development' (ECOWAS 2010: 3). Viewing organised crime as an impediment suggests that the application of development is perceived in the same way as security: as a condition that is undermined by organised crime. The focus on economic development also points to a specific end state. However, this statement could also refer to the threat organised crime poses to ongoing economic development. The WACI Freetown Commitment also refers to 'the need to encourage and accelerate the economic and social development of our states in order to improve the living standards of our people' (ECOWAS 2010: 3). Within ECOWAS the application of development is not clearly defined as either process or end state.

This lack of clarity continues with UNODC and UNIPSIL. UNODC views development as both a condition and a process. UNODC notes that organised crime has 'the potential to derail Sierra Leone's tentative steps towards recovery and development' (UNODC 2010b: 2). This implies that development is an end state that Sierra Leone is working towards. However, there are also references to the implementation of 'robust development strategies' (UNODC 2010b: 3). Perhaps because UNIPSIL is tasked with supporting the Sierra Leone government, development is viewed primarily as a process. The mandate of UNIPSIL includes the promotion of development, and the UN Joint Vision on Sierra Leone discusses 'development programmes' and the promotion of sustainable development (UN 2009: 1, 8; Gbeho 2011). However, the 2013 mandate renewal is more ambiguous, referring to long-term development but also to 'development priorities' and 'goals' (Biondo *et al.* 2013). As such, development is not clearly articulated as a process or end state in relation to approaches to organised crime in Sierra Leone.

In terms of how security and development are applied in Sierra Leone, security continues to adhere to the traditional perspective where it is considered to be an end state. This undermines a shift towards an emancipatory approach, as the end state can be predetermined by external actors rather than defined in collaboration with local actors. This likelihood is reinforced by the focus on the international level as referent object, outlined earlier in this book. The ambiguity of development fits in with the broader lack of consensus on how development is applied. As the application of development is not clearly articulated by any of the actors, it suggests that they are not familiar with development, which may imply that security is implemented through a security lens.[1]

The different applications also raise questions around the integration of security and development into a nexus. The ambiguity on the application of development suggests that it is easier to be integrated into a circuitous relationship where development processes directly contribute to security outcomes, while achieving development as a condition also enhances security. While the achievement of security as an end state can make space for development, it indicates a continued disconnect between the two concepts.

With security perceived as an end state and development as a process, this may imply that development processes seek to achieve conditions of security. As a process, development is expected to address organised crime, which will result in the end goal of security. These applications point to a one-sided nexus.

Linkages

External actors also have different perspectives on the linkages between security and development, which affects the causal relationship. As noted in Chapter 2, these different perspectives can be mapped on a spectrum from separate to integrated. Within this spectrum the linkages between security and development may

96 *Tensions in the nexus: Sierra Leone*

be interdependent, sequential, hierarchical, mutually constitutive or synonymous. These different linkages influence the form of integration between security and development and how the nexus is put into practice.

Within the ECOWAS Political Declaration, organised crime is viewed as a threat to both security and development. 'Illicit drug trafficking … and other organised crimes are serious threats to the regional and national security, political, economic and social development of Member states' (ECOWAS 2008a). This statement acknowledges that both security and development are threatened by organised crime. Accordingly, addressing organised crime would have benefits for security and development conditions. However, effectively addressing organised crime does not require an integrated response. This perspective suggests that if organised crime was effectively addressed through a security approach, there would be a positive outcome for both security and development in Sierra Leone.

Underdevelopment and insecurity are also viewed as factors that allow organised crime to flourish. 'Poverty, illiteracy, inadequate resources and limited law enforcement and criminal justice capacity contribute significantly to the region being used for transhipment of drugs' (ECOWAS 2008a). Viewing both underdevelopment and a lack of security as contributors to organised crime means these factors both need to be addressed to prevent the threat of organised crime to regional and national security, and to political, social and economic development. This indicates a closer relationship where both underdevelopment and insecurity need to be addressed to limit the threat of organised crime. However, these strategies still do not need to be integrated because they can be pursued separately. As a result, the ECOWAS Political Declaration perceives the linkage between security and development to be separate rather than integrated.

The WACI Freetown Commitment acknowledges the threat that organised crime poses to both security and development. While the document refers to economic development specifically, the threats are otherwise bundled together (ECOWAS 2010). The signatories acknowledge the 'threats posed by organised crime, illicit drug trafficking and drug abuse' (ECOWAS 2010: 3). By not separating these into threats to security or development, the document identifies a wide range of threats connected to both security and development. The document identifies the movement of small arms and light weapons, violence, money laundering, corruption, public health problems and other factors as threats. As such, security and development threats are closely related and perhaps indivisible. However, viewing organised crime as a threat to both security and development does not necessarily mean the two concepts are integrated. Rather the implication here is that if the 'threat' is effectively addressed it will have benefits for both security and development in Sierra Leone. This means that the linkages between security and development in the WACI Freetown Agreement fits within the separate category.

ECOWAS takes the linkages between security and development further. The 2000 *Protocol Relating to the Mechanism for Conflict Prevention, Management, Resolution, Peacekeeping and Security* recognises that 'economic and social development and the security of peoples and states are inextricably linked' (ECOWAS 2000: 4). This goes beyond the recognition that organised crime threatens both security and development to acknowledge a more connected relationship. These linkages are expanded in the 2008 ECOWAS Conflict Prevention Framework, which 'adopts a comprehensive approach to social, economic, political and security challenges in West Africa ... based on the perspective that addressing these issues simultaneously would help in preventing conflicts' (ECOWAS 2008c: 2).

Furthermore, definitions of security and development have become intertwined in ECOWAS policy. 'Human security refers to the creation of conditions to eliminate pervasive threats to peoples and individuals' rights, livelihoods, safety and life, the protection of human and democratic rights and the promotion of human development' (ECOWAS 2012: 7). While it appears as though this comprehensive approach seeks to prevent insecurity, ECOWAS recognises a two-way relationship between security and development. ECOWAS's long-term development strategy, Vision 2020, notes that 'peace and security as a transnational and cross-sector issue is both a prerequisite for realising the new vision and one of the long term benefits' (ECOWAS Commission 2008: 6). From this perspective, ECOWAS policy places the linkages between security and development in the mutually constitutive category.

UNODC's strategy to address organised crime is situated within the UN's efforts towards peace, security and development. Organised crime is recognised as a threat to both security and development: there is 'potential for transnational organised crime and illicit trafficking to undermine the stability and development of the West African region' (UNODC 2010a: vii). As with the ECOWAS Political Declaration, this does not point to an integrated approach as addressing organised crime would have benefits for security and development. However, the linkages between security and development expand beyond this as UNODC notes that 'organised crime plays a role in perpetuating both the poverty and the instability of the region, while poverty and instability provide optimum conditions for organised crime' (UNODC 2009: 9). Taking poverty and instability as features of underdevelopment and insecurity, UNODC perceives a two-way relationship of organised crime with security and development. While this implies that addressing insecurity and underdevelopment will address organised crime, it does not necessarily require an integrated approach.

When it comes to implementing the security–development nexus in Sierra Leone through the WACI, the linkage becomes clearer. The WACI project document notes that 'Sierra Leone needs the support of the international community to make security and justice the platforms of future development' (UNODC 2010b: 5). This does not imply integration. Rather this statement notes that security is a precondition for development. From this perspective, security and development are sequential, with security creating space for development.

The UN's Joint Vision for Sierra Leone, which seeks to improve coordination between all UN agencies, is the driver behind UNIPSIL's approach to organised crime. The UN Joint Vision effectively combines security and development

98 *Tensions in the nexus: Sierra Leone*

concerns. The five aims of the Joint Vision are to consolidate peace and stability; integrate rural areas into the national economy; economic and social integration of youth; equitable and affordable access to health; and accessible and credible public services (UN 2009). While all of the five aims, in particular equitable and affordable health, seek to address the development needs of individuals, the majority of the aims also seek to prevent renewed conflict. The consolidation of peace and security overtly seeks to prevent conflict. However, other goals also contribute to this aim. Integrating rural areas into the national economy seeks to address the 'deteriorating social climate' created by the gap between urban and rural communities through agriculture and economic development (UN 2009: 2). The economic and social integration of youth seeks to address the ongoing marginalisation of youth, which was a significant factor in the onset and continuation of violent conflict. Accessible and credible public services also seek to consolidate peace and security and 'lay the foundation for economic development' (UN 2009: 34). Security and development are integrated within UN policy in Sierra Leone, fitting within the mutually constitutive category.

Despite the strong linkages, there is still a disconnect between security and development in UNIPSIL's approach to organised crime in Sierra Leone. UNIPSIL had a political and development mandate. The political mandate of the mission can be equated to security as it involves 'providing political support to national and local efforts for identifying and resolving tension and threats of potential conflict' (UNIPSIL 2012b). The mission also focused on other political reforms to remove the threat of conflict and consolidate peace (UNIPSIL 2012b). While many of the factors set out in the Joint Vision are considered to have both development and political elements, organised crime does not. The UN Joint Vision notes that decentralisation and the integration of youth have developmental and political aspects (UN 2009). However, strengthening the security forces to address organised crime is viewed as a capacity-building and political aspect, removing the development focus (UN 2009). Although UNIPSIL has integrated many security and development issues, organised crime is viewed primarily as a security issue. While there are some interconnections, in relation to initiatives to address organised crime, security and development remain separate.

External actors addressing organised crime in Sierra Leone recognise some connection between security and development. However, there are varying perspectives on this relationship. For ECOWAS, security and development have become closely related but the implementation of the WACI is less integrated. While UNODC viewed the relationship as integrated, the relationship was sequential, where security is necessary in order to create space for development. A sequential relationship suggests that security is the cause but development is not necessarily the effect. As security merely makes space for development, it does not directly contribute to it. UNIPSIL's broader policy views security and development as integrated. However, when it comes to organised crime the two areas are interconnected but separate. Although not stated directly, this may align with UNODC's approach of creating space for development.

Local law enforcement has certainly adopted this perspective on the linkage between security and development. For example, the Transnational Organised Crime Unit (TOCU) believes that 'if we try and mitigate the level of organised crime it will open up ways for development to come into this country'.[2] Similarly the TOCU states that 'if we improve security measures, it is going to positively reflect development'.[3] Perhaps this approach has ensued from DfID's earlier approach to security sector reform within the framework of the security–development nexus. DfID followed a 'security first' approach based on the assumption that 'a democratically run, accountable, competent, effective and efficient security sector helps to reduce the risk of conflict and enhance the security of the citizens of the country, and in the process helps to create the necessary conditions for development' (UK Government 2004: 4). As DfID worked closely with local law enforcement, this perspective has translated into their practices too.

DfID's perspective points to a sequential or 'security first' relationship, where security creates space for development. Within Sierra Leone, external actors are attempting to address organised crime by strengthening security and law enforcement, a strategy that seeks to mitigate insecurity. This is based on the belief that successful prevention of further insecurity would limit negative effects on the current state of development. Local and external actors also believe that this will open the door for investment and thus economic development.

But external actors addressing organised crime do not actually engage with development. UNIPSIL does engage in anti-drugs programmes by funding local organisations, raising awareness of the health risk of drug use and providing support to drug users, but this only addresses the side effects of organised crime. Although UNODC identifies the social and economic integration of youth as a priority in its work on organised crime, problems such as youth unemployment are not directly confronted. UNDP and other development actors are addressing youth unemployment in Sierra Leone. However, this is not linked in to initiatives to address organised crime. Among the external actors engaged with organised crime in Sierra Leone, security and development are not understood to be mutually beneficial. Security is necessary for development but the reverse is not recognised. By not directly addressing underdevelopment and poverty, external engagement does not address the role of underdevelopment in creating an increased risk of insecurity.

Although there is no direct causal relationship between security and development, the relationship still reveals a shift in the approach of external actors. The sequential relationship highlights that creating space for development is now an objective of their engagement. Although this is not the same as directly engaging in development, it does indicate a shift away from a traditional security approach.

Institutional tension

Security and development actors have traditionally had different institutional architecture: they have understood problems in different ways and taken

100 *Tensions in the nexus: Sierra Leone*

different approaches to address them. Although these institutional factors are rarely articulated, they continue to influence the engagement of external actors pursuing joined-up approaches.

Institutional architecture

Key contributors and donors influence the inception and creation of initiatives to address organised crime in Sierra Leone. As a multi-agency initiative, there are a wide range of external contributors that influenced the inception and creation of the WACI. As previously outlined, the WACI was developed in response to the ECOWAS Political Declaration on Drug Trafficking and Other Organised Crimes in West Africa and its associated regional action plan, which was the outcome of a ministerial conference attended by 15 ECOWAS member states. The WACI Freetown Commitment, signed by participating governments, reiterated the key concerns set out in the regional action plan and confirmed the involvement of the four pilot countries, including Sierra Leone. As the contributors to the regional action plan and the WACI Freetown Commitment were also member states of ECOWAS, the WACI seeks to advance the concerns of member states arising from organised crime. For example, the WACI Freetown Commitment raises concerns over the potential for organised crime to 'undermine the rule of law, democratic institutions and governance'. Although these factors also influence citizens, Ayangafac and Cilliers (2011: 135) argue that the commitment of states often becomes 'premised on the quest for regime (not human) security', as their priority is often their own survival. As noted previously, the ECOWAS Commission seeks to shift the focus of the organisation towards human security; however, the concerns of member states over their own security has remained dominant.

UNODC's approach to drug trafficking involves technical projects to build the capacity of law enforcement agencies to counteract organised crime (UNODC 2007b). However, UNODC has also recognised the importance of development, and engaged in alternative development programmes and initiatives to address drug use (UNODC 2007b). In 1998, UNODC stated that

> alternative development programmes now aim at elimination or prevention of the production of illicit crops through a methodology encompassing a broader conception of rural development aimed at improving the overall quality of life of the target population by addressing not only income but also education, health, infrastructure and social services.
>
> (UNODC 1998: 1)

For example, in Colombia and Peru UNODC engaged in crop-replacement programmes, encouraging the production of coffee, palm oil and palm cabbage, which supported the livelihoods of thousands of households (UNODC 2005). As such, UNODC's contribution brings experience of combining security and development elements.

Tensions in the nexus: Sierra Leone 101

Although UNODC, UNOWA and Interpol are involved in the WACI, implementation of the project was managed by the UN's Department of Peacekeeping Operations (UNDPKO) through UNIPSIL. While the WACI is founded by UNODC, there were a number of difficulties in establishing a field office. Until UNIPSIL's mandate ended, UNODC officers were based in the mission's National Security Unit with support from the UNODC Regional Headquarters in Dakar, Senegal.[4] The mandate of UNIPSIL's National Security Unit was to support the Government of Sierra Leone in ensuring national security, suggesting that security influences dominate the implementation of the WACI.

The security perspective is amplified by the personnel engaged in implementation of the WACI. The UNIPSIL team responsible for the WACI came from a policing background. The head of the team was the senior police advisor. The senior police advisor who served the mission between 2006 and 2011 had previously been a police officer for 24½ years with the Austin Police Department, including as assistant chief of police (Boutellis 2008). While a skilled police officer, knowledgeable on policing and rule of law, he had no prior experience of peacebuilding or development, making it difficult to bring in a development perspective. This is compounded by a lack of training in development and post-conflict reconstruction. In an interview for Princeton's 'Innovation for Successful Societies' series, the former senior police advisor noted that

> this was my first mission ever. A lot of experience in policing, but this was the first time I ever worked for the UN in a mission. I only had three days – it was a whirlwind orientation. I can't say it was an induction training, it was just an orientation. When I arrived here in Sierra Leone you received just the check-in. There was no type of training. There was no real induction training whatsoever.
>
> (Boutellis 2008: 4)

The senior police advisor in post between 2011 and 2013 did have experience working internationally, bringing more direct experience of the post-conflict context.[5] However, these roles were also in policing and maintained a security focus.

Other staff engaged in the WACI also originated from a policing background, drawn from their national police forces or Interpol. The terms of reference for the national project officer for the WACI required a 'university degree in the fields of criminology, law, public administration or equivalent education from a recognised national police, customs or another staff learning college with specialisation in criminal justice, crime prevention or law enforcement' and 'at least five (5) years of relevant work experience ... in national and/or international law enforcement, investigation, police, drug control, judiciaries and/or crime prevention, including a sound knowledge of criminal intelligence processes' (UNODC 2010b). The WACI staff also included counter-narcotics advisors and an anti-drugs officer drawn from international and national police forces.[6] As staff were primarily derived from policing or law enforcement

102 *Tensions in the nexus: Sierra Leone*

backgrounds, it is difficult to bring elements of development into the programme.

As with the contributors, the donors to the WACI also influence which elements are prioritised. The WACI is completely funded by international donors. The government covers the expenses of the security agencies that make up the TOCU, but not programmatic expenses.

> Police have their own budget, ONS has its own budget, the ministry has its own budget, but that's for their day-to-day running. When it comes to TOCU, there is nothing government provided, unfortunately, so what is running TOCU is what the international partners are providing. We are trying to get government to own it, and of course it owns it as the agency, but we are trying to get it to own it in terms of providing more financial support for it.[7]

With funding primarily coming from international donors, there is a risk that priorities will focus on their interests, such as concerns over the drug market in their own country. This is evident in the focus on cocaine trafficking, rather than the increase in cannabis production within Sierra Leone.[8]

The majority of funding for the WACI is channelled through UNODC. As a result, UNODC maintains significant influence over the direction of the programme. Although the WACI sought to operationalise the ECOWAS Political Declaration and regional action plan, UNODC developed the mandate, objectives and activities of the programme. As such, the approach taken by the WACI may be informed by UNODC's strategic interests. Carrier and Klantschnig (2012) argue that UNODC's approach is influenced by its own donors – primarily the US, Sweden and Japan – who prioritise law enforcement over softer interventions. Despite UNODC's experience in alternative development programmes, the influence of the US, Sweden and Japan ensures that a law-enforcement approach is prioritised, which adheres to a traditional security approach.

Other donors also support the WACI through specific projects. The new headquarters of TOCU was funded by the US government.[9] The Netherlands government provided funds for the procurement of equipment for TOCU (UNODC 2011). There are also

> funds for equipment and training from the US Africa Command, funds for mobile border crossing inspection teams from the German government, funds for interdiction and investigation of illicit drug smuggling from the UK's Justice Sector Development Program, and training from the UK Serious Organised Crime Agency, the US Embassy, the German Development Cooperation, and the Italian government.
>
> (Stimson Center 2012: 7)

Many state-based donors contributing to initiatives to address organised crime in Sierra Leone are those affected, either directly or indirectly, by the cocaine trade.

Tensions in the nexus: Sierra Leone 103

With funding coming directly from government donors, either through UNODC or for specific projects, the donor retains some influence over how their funds are spent. As such, funding is driven by the security interests of donors.

The keen interest of international donors, particularly those affected by cocaine trafficking through Sierra Leone, undermines the independence of the WACI and the freedom to engage with issues that are important locally. Some external contributors bring experience in development. For example, UNODC has sought to bring development into their approach to organised crime through alternative development strategies. However, the actors that contributed to the inception and creation of the WACI are primarily state-based actors that maintain direction and control over the initiative. This limits the shift away from a traditional security approach.

Understanding of organised crime

How external actors in Sierra Leone understand organised crime can be established by analysing the language adopted. The language of the WACI is technical, focusing on the tasks to be achieved by the programme rather than the beneficiaries. The project document sets out that

> the vulnerability of states in the West African sub-region to the threats of illicit drug trafficking is due largely to insufficient counter-trafficking measures, poorly trained human resources, insufficient equipment to support effective operations and a limited understanding of the full extent of the illicit drug trafficking problem. Moreover, the permeability of national institutions to corruption, the porosity of borders and structural deficiencies that prevent effective control over their territories and the enforcement of the rule of law, all combine to make West Africa attractive to international organised criminal networks.
>
> (UNODC 2010b: 3)

This passage identifies the threats posed by organised crime and the current deficits in addressing it. The focus is on deficits in law-enforcement capacity rather than human factors such as poverty and unemployment. The result is a clear set of tasks to address organised crime more effectively, focusing on those objectives, rather than the needs of citizens.

The language outlining the focus of the TOCU is also technical. The TOCU is responsible for 'intelligence collection and analysis, surveillance, investigations, tactical operations and international coordination' (UNODC 2010b: 5). By invoking the language of law enforcement, the approach of the TOCU is aligned with security approaches, and responds to incidents of organised crime. Such an approach raises the importance and urgency of organised crime. However, by setting out specific tasks it leaves little space for local law enforcement to determine their own mandate. The language is task oriented and focuses on specific capabilities, prioritising security measures to respond to and address organised

104   *Tensions in the nexus: Sierra Leone*

crime. Language also adopts terms related to security. For example, the WACI seeks to '*combat* drug trafficking and organised crime' (UNODC 2010b: 5, emphasis added).

Despite the security-focused language, the WACI project document highlights avenues to prevent organised crime as it engages with the factors that 'make West Africa attractive to international organised criminal networks' (UNODC 2010b: 3). This preventative focus arises as Sierra Leone is not the most significant case for organised crime within West Africa.[10] However, UNIPSIL argues that it should be a priority because 'once you get crack cocaine coming through here big time, you'll get all the gangster problems that go with that and your police force won't be able to cope'.[11] The focus on prevention shifts away from the reactive focus of security approaches, as it engages with organised crime before it takes root. The preventative approach has created problems in ensuring that the government of Sierra Leone is committed to supporting TOCU in the long term, given more pressing concerns such as poverty and weak governance. This suggests that the urgency applied to security has been removed.

While the preventative approach appears to engage with development approaches, initiatives to address organised crime do not seek to transform structures that allow organised crime to take hold, such as poverty and youth unemployment. Prevention is advanced by building capacity to respond to cases of organised crime to deter criminal networks from using Sierra Leone as a transit point. UNIPSIL notes that 'if it doesn't pay and it constantly gets disrupted, you give up and go somewhere else'.[12] As a result, the approach is more closely aligned with security approaches where organised crime needs to be 'contained through reactive bargaining and coercion' (Cockayne 2011: 5). However, the prevention aspect takes the containment of organised crime to another level, integrating development elements to a certain extent through anti-drug campaigns and demand reduction. While UNIPSIL's understanding of organised crime is primarily security oriented, elements of development are woven in.

The WACI project document also discusses the importance of capacity building. These references become less technical and focus on achieving long-term goals that are locally specific. This aligns with the language of development actors and takes a long-term perspective on addressing organised crime. However, even capacity building is used to refer to capacity in drug interdiction, forensics, intelligence, border management, money laundering and criminal justice (UNODC 2010b). As such, the language of development is mobilised for security purposes. Language related to the anti-drugs programme is more closely aligned with development. The programme identifies 'stakeholders', referring to citizens and civil society, and seeks to engage in 'sensitisations' (UNODC 2011). 'Sensitisation' has become a popular buzzword in Sierra Leone among civil society and NGOs. Although referring to awareness raising, it suggests a one-way flow of information, disregarding the potential for local knowledge to inform approaches to organised crime, or local perspectives on drug use that could be tapped into.

Tensions in the nexus: Sierra Leone 105

While the WACI employs language linked to both security and development, they are not connected. The primary goals and tasks of the WACI are closely aligned with security language, whereas specific aspects of the initiative, such as capacity building and the anti-drugs project, are aligned with development. While security and development elements have been brought in, they refer to separate areas of engagement. However, the use of development language does result in a shift away from a traditional security approach. This aligns with the broader understanding of organised crime within the WACI. External actors have taken a preventative approach. However, this approach still aims to achieve security. The analysis of how organised crime is understood indicates that the institutional underpinnings of external actors addressing organised crime in Sierra Leone are informed by security, with elements of development woven in to the implementation of initiatives.

Approach to organised crime

UNODC and UNIPSIL, the key actors addressing organised crime in Sierra Leone, had a different approach to problems. Cockayne (2011: 6) notes that the WACI 'reflect[s] "local" innovation in response to a pressing problem of peacebuilding' as it is based on regional priorities set out in the ECOWAS Political Declaration and regional action plan. While the objectives of the WACI were based on local innovation and regional priorities, UNODC's approach still resembled a traditional security approach. One of the key goals of the WACI was to institute TOCUs in the four pilot countries. However, the implementation of the TOCU in Sierra Leone ignored existing institutions as UNIPSIL had already set up the Joint Drug Interdiction Task-force (JDITF). The US embassy noted that 'donors have sent assessment teams who appear to want to fit their project model to a Sierra Leone context, rather than understand the context and create the model' (Wikileaks 2009a). Compared to the JDITF, the TOCU has 'the same personnel, just change in name and direction a little bit, more funding and more agencies involved'.[13] While the difference does not appear to be significant, the growth in mandate resulted in tensions between the TOCU and the National Drug Law Enforcement Agency (NDLEA).

'Rivalries between agencies are well known' in West African law enforcement systems (UNODC 2012b). However, in setting up TOCUs in West African countries the WACI has amplified these rivalries rather than alleviated them. In Sierra Leone the NDLEA is constitutionally mandated to address organised crime, while TOCU is not. Yet TOCU receives external funding and support to carry out the work of the NDLEA. The significance of the NDLEA's complaints are debatable. A leaked US embassy cable noted that

> the NDLEA has not been empowered (possibly by design) to carry out its functions. As noted, the Agency's operating budget this year was US$125,000, which has not gone far towards staffing, equipping, and

106 *Tensions in the nexus: Sierra Leone*

> operationalising the Agency. The NDLEA's Executive Director has the right
> to second officers for enforcement purposes, but this has not been exercised.
>
> (Wikileaks 2009a)

Within this context, UNODC's decision to focus on creating the TOCU may have been an attempt to avoid the politics within law-enforcement agencies in Sierra Leone. However, the remaining rivalry between law-enforcement agencies suggests that this could have been managed better by engaging with local law enforcement. By implementing objectives developed at headquarter level, UNODC's practices are more security focused, as they are based on the priorities of donors.

Aside from the establishment of the TOCU, the WACI also seeks to enhance the capacity of law-enforcement agencies to investigate and prosecute complex crimes and reduce illegal activities within Sierra Leone (UNODC 2010b). These objectives move beyond an approach that aims to restore security and withdraw. The WACI aims to build local capacity to address organised crime in the long term. Despite the emphasis on capacity building, there continues to be a focus on technical assistance. For instance, building judicial capacity involves upgrading organised-crime-related legislation (UNODC 2010b: 5). This implies that some elements of the programme need to be done by internationals to pave the way for local action on organised crime.

Capacity building is primarily undertaken on the ground by UNIPSIL. One UNODC officer based within UNIPSIL 'works with the proactive side and sees where the gaps are in training and equipment'.[14] Another UNIPSIL officer 'works on the anti-drugs programme with citizens', raising awareness of the dangers of drug use.[15] UNIPSIL passes intelligence on to TOCU members and provides assistance and advice where needed to ensure that local law enforcement can effectively pursue cases. The UNIPSIL team also refrains from directly guiding the TOCU, preferring them to identify where they need to focus their energy independently. For example, UNIPSIL notes that 'the element that needs to come into TOCU, and they're only just waking up to it, is financial investigation'.[16] Rather than external actors directly recommending work on financial investigation, TOCU is encouraged to identify gaps in their investigation independently. This approach shifts practices closer to development practices as it encourages local solutions rather than imposing internationally defined objectives.

While the WACI has engaged in capacity building with law enforcement seconded to the TOCU, other levels of government remain unable to address organised crime. Security agencies involved in TOCU have developed effective investigation skills to pursue organised criminals. However, regular police have been causing problems with investigations. An interdiction involving Nigerian nationals resulted in police arresting any Nigerians they encountered in Freetown.[17] The problems also extend upwards. Political actors sideswipe cases to look good politically, putting out calls to arrest all individuals being investigated, which compromises the case.[18] Political actors have also been known to stall actions to disguise their involvement in organised crime.

Tensions in the nexus: Sierra Leone 107

By working with state institutions, the WACI adheres to a traditional security approach. Although the WACI aimed to improve the security environment to benefit individuals, the target groups of the project are law-enforcement agencies and the judiciary, including Sierra Leone police, the National Revenue Authority, the Immigration Department, the National Drug Law Enforcement Agency, the Joint Maritime Committee, the Office of National Security (ONS), the Central Intelligence Security Unit and the Financial Investigations Unit.

Partnerships with law enforcement created problems for direct linkages with civilians. Through DfID's earlier SSR programme, the Sierra Leone police have shifted away from 'traditional policing' towards a 'new landscape in policing' which has much more community engagement through community policing visits to communities and schools, and the creation of Local Police Partnership Boards, provincial and district security committees, which included local leaders.[19] An alliance of NGOs including Conciliation Resources, Talking Drum Studios and Mano River Women's Peace Network delivered programmes to promote trust between the police and local communities. However, it remains a taut relationship, which limits the potential shift away from a traditional security approach.

The police also engage with local communities on organised crime through their media office, telling communities to be aware of organised crime.[20] 'We have radio programmes where they talk about these issues, organised crime, advising the public, but also if it comes into the country to be aware of certain people'.[21] The ONS is setting up a hotline for citizens to report early warning signals of organised crime, such as large shipments coming across the border or planes landing at unmarked airstrips in rural areas.[22] They are also using traditional leaders to transmit messages to local communities.[23] 'The police turns up and talks to them, they see them as part of the problem, but if we have traditional leaders joining us it transmits the message, we will get it through more effectively'.[24] These examples highlight a hierarchical relationship between security agencies and local communities where citizens are not seen as agents that can play a role in addressing organised crime.

The lack of direct engagement with local communities limits the shift away from a traditional security approach. It also creates a lack of understanding of local perspectives of organised crime. Some respondents indicated that there is a common perception that Sierra Leoneans should benefit from the cocaine trade.[25] While illicit activities such as illegal logging and diamond smuggling are viewed negatively as they exploit Sierra Leone's natural resources, the cocaine trade is viewed differently as it just uses Sierra Leone as a transit hub.[26] If this is the case, then citizens would be less likely to report incidents of trafficking that they witness in and around their communities.

The priority given to national security agencies over civil society also neglects the issues important to civilians. A number of civil society organisations are working on issues connected with organised crime. The Centre for the Coordination of Youth Activities (CCYA) runs a project aimed at bike riders[27] to encourage them not to get involved in organised crime.[28] The Foundation for

108 *Tensions in the nexus: Sierra Leone*

Democracy and Development Sierra Leone (FDIDSL) conducts seminars, awareness raising and other activities on organised crime and drug use.[29] There are also several organisations providing services and treatment to drug users (UNODC 2011). While many of these organisations receive support and funding from both national and international actors, their work is not viewed as part of the strategy to address organised crime.

There is also reluctance from civil society when engaging with state bodies. Civil society sees their role as making noise, being an intermediary between citizens and the government.[30] Once they have been heard they do not continue to engage or participate in decision making or implementation. State structures may not be conducive to civil society involvement in these areas. However, there is space for civil society to be more proactive. Instead, roles in civil society are often viewed as a pathway to a secure government job. As such, many individuals are reticent to challenge government too much as it may reduce their employment potential.

With partners primarily located at the state level, the WACI adheres to a traditional security approach with an emphasis on law enforcement. Engagement with civil society and citizens seeks to further the objectives and activities of the WACI, which focus on the investigation and prosecution of organised crime cases and a decrease in cases. This further prioritises a law-enforcement approach to organised crime, limiting the role of development.

The structure of UNODC and UNIPSIL also influences how organised crime is approached. While UNODC had staff working in Sierra Leone, they were based within UNIPSIL as UNODC did not have its own office within the country. As a result, UNODC provided the programme objectives remotely. UNIPSIL acted as a mediator through its presence in the country, coordinating international support to address organised crime to minimise duplication and to ensure resources are tailored to the local context.[31] UNODC's role in the WACI adheres to a traditional security approach, but UNIPSIL brought in development aspects as they were closely connected to local actors and built strong relationships (UNPOL 2012).

The relationship between UNIPSIL and local actors remained hierarchical to a certain extent as UNIPSIL controlled the resources, but there was an attempt to break this down. UNIPSIL provided intelligence and advice on interdictions through a mentoring relationship. For example, in 2011 UNIPSIL received intelligence that a shipment of nappies coming through Sierra Leone contained cocaine. The intelligence was shared with the TOCU and UNIPSIL supported their response.

> They were really good, they sat down and said, 'Okay, we've got this intelligence, do we build on that a bit more, or is it just intelligence? Do we go and hit the ports?' – also recognising the port is another mini-village where everyone knows everyone – 'Can we put someone in there?'[32]

While some agencies could be more effective, UNIPSIL found TOCU's approach to organised crime 'sophisticated'[33] as they know what questions to ask

Tensions in the nexus: Sierra Leone 109

and what to consider when approaching a situation. Problems still arose with the Sierra Leonean government wanting to take control of a case to look good politically. When this happens, UNIPSIL plays a key role in supporting the TOCU.

Local and international actors came together through fortnightly coordination meetings. Representatives from UNIPSIL, the British High Commission and the US embassy attended to provide mentoring and technical support.[34] However, the primary aim was to enhance coordination between local law enforcement agencies. Member agencies reported that the meetings had improved 'camaraderie and organisational usefulness to each other'.[35] The relationship between locals and internationals remained unequal though. As the Sierra Leone government did not fund the TOCU, international actors had a significant influence on the mandate of the unit. 'They are the ones with the money, our government is not really owning things. So really, they are driving the process.'[36] For example, as noted earlier, although cannabis was a major concern for local law enforcement, international actors were primarily concerned with cocaine trafficking.

Despite this imbalance, UNIPSIL worked in partnership with local law enforcement. The emphasis on partnerships between international and national actors indicates a merging of security and development. However, the structure was still primarily designed to achieve security outcomes, particularly those of interest to donors, as it remains difficult for external actors to move away from their traditional activities. Regarding the approach to problems, all of the agencies engaged in the TOCU were from the law-enforcement sector. There is no link to other actors that are addressing social and economic concerns related to organised crime. While UNIPSIL's practices, such as capacity building, were closely aligned with development practices, this was only one element of the WACI. Other elements, such as the creation of the TOCU, remained security focused.

Although the approach to organised crime in Sierra Leone brought together elements of security and development, security was a clear priority. With state-based contributors and donors, the institutional architecture of the WACI was security focused. However, how organised crime was understood engaged with elements of development. External actors acknowledged the need for prevention in their approach. The language employed to address capacity building and the anti-drugs programme was linked more closely to development. However, other language employed by external actors was security focused as it was technical and task oriented. While the language adopted within the WACI aligned with both security and development, this was not a merging of the two as the elements remained separate. The approach to organised crime did move away from security as the emphasis was on capacity building. This brought in development elements by seeking to achieve long-term outcomes. The structure of the WACI also moved beyond security by ensuring a collaborative approach between international actors and local law enforcement

These factors highlight that the adoption of the security–development nexus has been influenced by the institutional underpinnings of external actors. In several areas the institutional division between security and development actors

110 *Tensions in the nexus: Sierra Leone*

has broken down. However, underlying each of these innovations was a continued focus on security. The emphasis on deterrence to prevent organised crime aimed to strengthen law enforcement rather than engaging with the underlying influences that allow organised crime to flourish. Capacity building also focused solely on law enforcement. Despite the collaborative approach, the security interests of external actors were still prioritised. While these factors demonstrate an attempt to integrate security and development, the security-based institutional architecture of the WACI ensures that this is done through a security lens, limiting the contribution of development.

Motivational tension

A final tension emerges from the motivations of external actors addressing organised crime in Sierra Leone. The motivational drivers of external actors influence why security and development are being integrated and which elements are prioritised within the nexus. This problem has already been raised in the analysis of the other tensions. Analysis of the conceptual tension highlighted how understandings of security are often framed by each actor's concern over their own security. Analysis of the institutional tension raised questions over whether the primacy of security in the institutional underpinnings of security actors is driven by international security concerns or a lack of understanding among security actors of how to bring development into their initiatives. This section probes the motivations in more depth, analysing why organised crime is prioritised and by whom; the balance between international and local priorities; and how development is included in initiatives to address organised crime.

Prioritising organised crime

The interest in international security was evident in the approach of external actors addressing organised crime in Sierra Leone. At the regional level in West Africa, ECOWAS expressed concerns over the security threat posed by the presence of organised crime within member states. The Political Declaration on Drug Trafficking and Other Organised Crimes in West Africa notes that 'drug abuse, illicit drug trafficking, diversion of chemical precursors and other organised crimes are serious threats to the regional and national security, political, economic and social development of Member States' (ECOWAS 2008a). Although ECOWAS is a regional actor, the focus here is on the threats that extend beyond the countries directly affected by organised crime. The WACI that emerged from this declaration prioritised Sierra Leone, Liberia, Guinea-Bissau and Cote d'Ivoire, which are considered the most unstable countries in the region. This suggests that organised crime is viewed as a further destabilising force. As a result, organised crime was prioritised to prevent security threats that will spread regionally.

The motivations of external actors addressing organised crime in Sierra Leone were also focused on the threat to international security. The US government committed significant funds to the WACI as 'the proceeds of cocaine trafficked through West Africa flow back to the same organisations that move cocaine to the United States, reinforcing their financial strength' (US Department of State 2011: 50). The UK and other European governments also committed funds to stem cocaine flows in Sierra Leone before it reaches Europe.

Donors concerned about cocaine being trafficked to their home country are eager to have a presence in Sierra Leone. 'When you're dealing with a fragile state with corrupt officials you want to know you have your own person on the ground.'[37] Key personnel within UNIPSIL came from the UK and Spain, two of the primary destinations for cocaine trafficked through West Africa. When the term of the Spanish counter-narcotics officer ended, he was replaced by another Spaniard 'because from the point of view of the proactive policing they do, or joint agencies, we want to keep the intelligence going between the countries that have a vested interest'.[38] The US also has a presence as trafficking through West Africa fuels Latin American cartels that are also active in cocaine trafficking to the US (US Department of State 2011).

The presence of particular international actors in Sierra Leone can also be connected to specific cases. When the UK Serious and Organised Crime Agency (SOCA) withdrew from Sierra Leone, they were eager to maintain a British presence to monitor certain cases. This contributed to the recruitment of a British national as the senior police advisor within UNIPSIL in 2011. SOCA had been tracking Mohib Shamel, a Lebanese–British citizen active in the Sierra Leonean mining sector who allegedly had links to Daniel Kinahan, an Irish businessman involved in narco-trafficking throughout Europe (Wikileaks 2009b). Similarly, the Spanish government had a significant interest in Sierra Leone. Spain is one of the primary destination countries for drugs trafficked through Sierra Leone. The Spanish Drug and Organised Crime Unit had also been tracking a Sierra Leone-flagged vessel involved in human smuggling and narcotics trafficking (Wikileaks 2009b).

A UNIPSIL representative noted that 'donors who are suffering from the drug market will put up a certain amount'.[39] As such, the key donors to the WACI, including Germany, the Netherlands and the US, were driven by concerns of cocaine or cocaine-related revenue entering their own country. The interests of international actors in Sierra Leone is recognised by local law enforcement.

> The current senior police advisor is British. So while she is UN, she also has British interests. The counter-narcotics officer is Spanish; he also has Spanish interests. The representative of the US embassy that comes to meetings makes sure US interests are met. The US Africa Command, AFRICOM, they come sometimes for assessment missions.[40]

The presence of external actors directly affected by cocaine trafficking implies that international security concerns are the primary motivation. External actors seek to address or contain the problem within Sierra Leone before it reaches their shores. However, these concerns can also result in a better response.

112 *Tensions in the nexus: Sierra Leone*

Spanish intelligence is more likely to share information with their Sierra Leonean counterparts if it assists their own counter-narcotics operations. Having a Spanish officer based in the country also enhances trust between the two countries. An approach that engages with local needs will have benefits for international security, as organised crime would be addressed in a sustainable way rather than just responding to incidents of organised crime.

Disjuncture between international and local priorities

A disjuncture between international and local priorities was evident in Sierra Leone. As noted already, although illegal exports of timber and diamonds were viewed negatively by locals because they exploit local resources, drug trafficking was not.[41] Many Sierra Leoneans believe the country should benefit from the revenues of drug trafficking, particularly as the country is primarily a transit country.[42] This may change as increasing amounts of cocaine are consumed locally. However, the lack of government support for the TOCU suggests implicit support for organised crime and drug trafficking. A UNIPSIL officer stated that 'the government says it supports [TOCU], and it hasn't done anything to stop it; but it hasn't done anything at all to ensure its continuity'.[43]

The lack of government engagement to address organised crime may arise because international efforts were adequate. This is implied by the government of Sierra Leone's support for the ECOWAS Political Declaration and the WACI Freetown Commitment, pledging their dedication to addressing organised crime. However, the government directly pursues issues of greatest concern to the electorate to ensure they remain in power. An officer from the ONS met with the President on organised crime:

> I emphatically made it clear that there was a lot more that needs to be tackled. If it's not tackled it will slow down development and impede the successful outcomes of the security agencies. It's only when I mentioned the elections that I got his attention. He wants to win again, so he wants to make sure all the obstacles are clear.[44]

Government preoccupation with elections further supports the argument that organised crime is not a pressing concern locally. If it was, the government would be more engaged in order to gain support.

The disjuncture between local and international priorities also arises as local elites may benefit from organised crime. Corruption supports the presence of organised crime in Sierra Leone. Following the 2008 seizure of cocaine at Lungi airport, government officials and security agents were implicated, as well as then Minister of Transport and Aviation (Gberie 2010). In 2009, Sierra Leone's Foreign Minister noted that 'the cartels have not yet corrupted the governments senior levels, but sooner or later they will, because they have millions of dollars and you need to be a saint to reject them' (cited in Kavanagh 2011). When government officials are involved in organised crime, they have an interest in keeping it hidden. As a result, citizens may not be aware of the magnitude of criminal activity.

While it appears as though external actors were investing resources to address problems that are not a concern locally, not engaging with organised crime could have disastrous effects for the host country. UNIPSIL acknowledged that Sierra Leone was not the most pressing case of organised crime in West Africa. However, they also recognised that, if it is not addressed, local law enforcement won't be able to cope if cocaine starts passing through the country at a greater pace.[45] Although significant advances have been made since the war ended, organised crime has the potential to undercut them. With revenues higher than the government, organised crime networks have the potential to undermine state control over the economy, security forces and rule of law. This would limit further progress, as well as affect the wellbeing of citizens. As such, what appears to be an international agenda may be focused on local needs.

Factors such as corruption and the discrete nature of organised crime may explain the disjuncture between local and international priorities. However, externally driven initiatives to address organised crime do not address all elements of organised crime. External actors are addressing the elements that have the greatest impact internationally. The primary focus of Sierra Leone security agencies is on intelligence and operations to target the transport of drugs via air or sea. This means that local priorities related to cannabis production and trafficking within West Africa are given less priority.

Cannabis production and trafficking is becoming a serious concern for law enforcement and government officials within Sierra Leone. A local law enforcement officer noted that cannabis had overtaken food production. 'Food security, which is a national goal, national interest, is under serious threat because of this widespread cultivation.'[46] Many farmers are switching from food production to cannabis production as it is easier and faster to grow and generates a higher income.

> It's easy to go across the border to sell in Guinea and Liberia. A bag of rice is 200,000 Leones, a bag of cannabis, the same weight, 50 kilos, can give you a motorbike and a motorbike is around 5 million Leones. Compare 200,000 to 5 million Leones, and the cannabis grows much faster and is far easier to harvest.[47]

While external actors recognise that cannabis is currently more of a problem than cocaine,[48] it is still not a priority. This primarily stems from the assumption that cannabis is 'relatively harmless since it was intended for the domestic market' (Wikileaks 2009c).

While development actors such as Irish Aid and the Food and Agriculture Organisation (FAO) addressed cannabis cultivation as part of their food security programming, local law enforcement find it hard to maintain a focus on it. Although the work plan of the TOCU is decided jointly by local law enforcement and external actors, international security concerns tend to dominate.

114 *Tensions in the nexus: Sierra Leone*

> There is mutual suspicion, you see, in terms of they want us to do things according to how they want, to benefit their own countries.... They're trying to increase security here by pumping money into our agencies. It's basically to make sure their country is also secure. In the process, we make our country secure, because we have our national interest. So cannabis, cannabis doesn't impact on them, but it does affect us.... If we can do it mutually, we develop it so it suits both sides. But at the same time they are the ones with the money.[49]

While addressing organised crime has local benefits, the emphasis on international priorities suggests that external actors will address organised crime to the extent that it is no longer a threat to their own countries. This suggests a minimal approach that seeks to contain organised crime in Sierra Leone, limiting the spread internationally. Such an approach does not necessarily engage with the underlying factors that make Sierra Leone conducive to organised crime. In the long term, this approach will ensure that organised crime continues to threaten international security even if the threat is minimised in the short term.

The inclusion of development

While it is clear that international initiatives to address organised crime in Sierra Leone are driven by self-interest, it is this self-interest that resulted in the adoption of the security–development nexus to frame international initiatives. As noted earlier in this book, it has become increasingly apparent that a pure security approach is inadequate in addressing organised crime.

To bring development elements into their approach to organised crime, external actors in Sierra Leone had a significant emphasis on capacity building. External actors identified gaps in equipment and training, and provided assistance and advice to ensure local law enforcement were able to effectively pursue cases.[50] The aim was to enhance the investigation and prosecution of crimes and reduce criminal activity by building capacity in drug interdiction, forensics, intelligence, border management, money laundering and criminal justice (UNODC 2010b).

Working with law enforcement to build their capacity in all forms of policing has beneficial consequences beyond addressing organised crime. Enhanced capacity of the police improves the legitimacy of the state and avoids the potential of renewed conflict, particularly in post-conflict countries such as Sierra Leone, where police were involved in the war as combatants. As Brinkerhoff (2007: 5) states, 'unaccountable, corrupt and/or subversive security forces are major barriers to state legitimacy, impede the restoration of basic services and often contribute to reigniting conflict'. As such, capacity building of law enforcement agencies contributes to broader post-conflict reconstruction.

While initiatives to address organised crime in Sierra Leone had a significant focus on capacity building, this does not necessarily equate to the inclusion of development. In this context, capacity building refers to the creation of technical capabilities in law enforcement. There is no linkage to poverty reduction,

Tensions in the nexus: Sierra Leone 115

governance or other elements of development. As such, capacity building is about restoring the status quo rather than engaging in transformative development.

The inclusion of capacity building in this context does, however, point to the integration of security and development. In the long term, capacity building provides local law enforcement with the skills and knowledge to pursue their own objectives, as well as those of internationals. Equipped with the necessary skills, law-enforcement agencies in Sierra Leone would then be able to address the rise in cannabis production as well as cocaine trafficking. However, international priorities will continue to be used to measure success. It is likely that international support will dry up once their objectives have been achieved, even if capacity hasn't been significantly improved. For example, while the US is supporting the WACI, they are not too concerned with organised crime in Sierra Leone, but will devote more resources if it becomes more serious.[51] Unless local priorities are aligned with international security concerns, it may be more difficult to obtain necessary funding.

The focus on capacity building also ensures that international security concerns are addressed in the long term. UNODC's 2009 Transnational Organised Crime Threat Assessment of West Africa noted a decline in trafficking through the region that was partly attributed to external engagement. However, it also noted that

> despite progress, it appears that at least one billion dollars' worth of cocaine continues to be trafficked through the region, and the West African distribution network in Europe remains intact. Should international attention waver, this region retains all of the attractions that drew traffickers here in the first place.
>
> (UNODC 2009: 3)

Building the capacity of local law enforcement to address organised crime maintains pressure on the flow of cocaine, reducing the likelihood that it will increase. However, this statement from UNODC also acknowledges that the other factors that are conducive to organised crime have not been addressed, as the 'region retains all of the attractions that drew traffickers' to West Africa, including weak governance, high unemployment, and a lack of effective border patrols (UNODC 2009: 3).

As capacity building is solely focused on law enforcement, it only addresses the symptoms of organised crime rather than working with local actors to address the causes. The emphasis on building the capacity of local law enforcement enhances their ability to respond to cases of organised crime through investigation, interdiction and prosecution. However, this occurs after the incident. Some internationals understand this strategy to be a deterrent for organised crime: 'I take the view that if it doesn't pay and constantly gets disrupted, you give up and go somewhere else.'[52] However, this underestimates the flexibility and ingenuity of organised crime networks.

116 *Tensions in the nexus: Sierra Leone*

As noted earlier, UNODC engages in community-centred prevention, assistance to victims, juvenile justice, treatment and rehabilitation, and HIV/AIDS prevention and care. Similarly, UNIPSIL focused on drug demand-reduction, treatment, prevention and rehabilitation. While these initiatives were located at the community level through engagement with NGOs and civil society, they were designed to limit the threat posed by organised crime to the state and international security. As such, these strategies were also driven by the motivations of external actors. As with capacity building, this means that drug demand-reduction and treatment may be discontinued once external actors decide that Sierra Leone is no longer a threat. However, once initiated these programmes can continue with support from other sources.

Although capacity building is a key strategy of development actors, development elements have not been a considerable focus of initiatives to address organised crime in Sierra Leone. If development or underdevelopment were a significant concern of external actors, initiatives would move beyond law enforcement to address the underlying factors that provide a conducive environment for organised crime. As discussed in relation to the other tensions, underdevelopment can contribute to organised crime through youth unemployment, poverty and weak governance. Development is not brought in to address these issues in connection with organised crime; rather, development is 'tacked on' to security approaches when it is useful for achieving security. As such, security remains the overarching priority within the security–development nexus, which consequently affects the role of development. While this undermines a comprehensive approach, it does indicate a shift away from traditional security approaches.

Notes

1 This will be explored in more detail in the examination of the institutional tension.
2 Interview, Freetown, January 2012.
3 Interview, Freetown, January 2012.
4 Interview, Freetown, January 2012.
5 The senior police advisor between 2011 and 2013 had previously been contingent commander and head of the War Crimes Unit for the European Union Police Mission in Bosnia & Herzegovina (2003–2004) and as a senior investigator in the UN International Independent Investigation Commission in Lebanon (UNPOL 2012).
6 Interview, Freetown, January 2012.
7 Interview, Freetown, January 2012.
8 This point will be explored in more depth in in the next section, which examines the motivations of donors.
9 Interview, Freetown, January 2012.
10 UNODC considers Guinea-Bissau, Guinea and Nigeria to be urgent cases for organised crime in West Africa. While Sierra Leone remains important, it is not considered on the same scale as these countries (UNODC 2010a).
11 Interview, Freetown, January 2012.
12 Interview, Freetown, January 2012.
13 Interview, Freetown, January 2012.
14 Interview, Freetown, January 2012.
15 Interview, Freetown, January 2012.

16 Interview, Freetown, January 2012.
17 Interview, Freetown, January 2012.
18 Interview, Freetown, January 2012.
19 Interview, Freetown, January 2012.
20 Interview, Freetown, January 2012.
21 Interview, Freetown, January 2012.
22 Interview, Freetown, January 2012.
23 Interview, Freetown, January 2012.
24 Interview, Freetown, January 2012.
25 Interviews, Freetown, January 2012.
26 Interviews, Freetown, January 2012.
27 Bike riders are usually young men who use motorbikes as couriers or transport.
28 Interview, Freetown, January 2012.
29 Interview, Freetown, January 2012.
30 Interview, Freetown, January 2012.
31 Interview, Freetown, January 2012.
32 Interview, Freetown, January 2012.
33 Interview, Freetown, January 2012.
34 Interview, Freetown, January 2012.
35 Interview, Freetown, January 2012.
36 Interview, Freetown, January 2012.
37 Interview, Freetown, January 2012.
38 Interview, Freetown, January 2012.
39 Interview, Freetown, January 2012.
40 Interview, Freetown, January 2012.
41 Interview, Freetown, January 2012.
42 Interviews, Freetown, January 2012.
43 Interview, Freetown, January 2012.
44 Interview, Freetown, January 2012.
45 Interview, Freetown, January 2012.
46 Interview, Freetown, January 2012.
47 Interview, Freetown, January 2012.
48 Interview, Freetown, January 2012.
49 Interview, Freetown, January 2012.
50 Interview, Freetown, January 2012.
51 Interview, Freetown, January 2012.
52 Interview, Freetown, January 2012.

References

Aning, Emmanuel Kwesi (2004). 'Investing in Peace and Security in Africa: The Case of ECOWAS', *Conflict, Security & Development* 4(3): 533–42.

Ayangafac, Chrysantus and Jakkie Cilliers (2011). 'African Solutions to African Problems: Assessing the Capacity of African Peace and Security Architecture', in Chester Crocker, Fen Osler Hampson and Pamela Aall (eds), *Rewiring Regional Security in A Fragmented World.* Washington DC, United States Institute of Peace.

Biondo, Karen Del, Stefan Oltsch and Jan Orbie (2013). 'Security and Development in EU Relations: Converging, But in Which Direction?' in Sven Biscop and Richard G. Whitman, *The Routledge Handbook of European Security.* Abingdon; New York, Routledge.

Boutellis, Arthur (2008). 'Rudolfo Landeros, Interview', *Innovation for Successful Societies.* Princeton, Bobst Center for Peace and Justice, Princeton University.

118 *Tensions in the nexus: Sierra Leone*

Brinkerhoff, Derick W. (2007). 'Introduction – Governance Challenges in Fragile States: Re-establishing Security, Rebuilding Effectiveness, and Reconstituting Legitimacy', in Derick W. Brinkerhoff (ed.), *Governance in Post-Conflict Socieities: Rebuilding Fragile States.* London; New York, Routledge.

Carrier, Neil and Gernot Klantschnig (2012). *Africa and the War on Drugs.* London; New York, Zed Books.

Cockayne, James (2011). *State Fragility, Organised Crime and Peacebuilding: Towards a More Strategic Approach.* Oslo, NOREF.

Cornwall, Andrea (2007). 'Buzzwords and Fuzzwords: Deconstructing Development Discourse', *Development in Practice* 17(4–5): 474–84.

ECOWAS (Economic Community of West African States) (2000). *Protocol Relating to the Mechanism for Conflict Prevention, Management, Resolution, Peacekeeping and Security.* Abuja, ECOWAS.

ECOWAS (Economic Community of West African States) (2008a). *Political Declaration on Drug Trafficking and Other Organised Crimes in West Africa.* Abuja, ECOWAS.

ECOWAS (Economic Community of West African States) (2008b). *Regional Action Plan to Address the Growing Problem of Illicit Drug Trafficking, Organised Crimes and Drug Abuse in West Africa.* Abuja, ECOWAS.

ECOWAS (Economic Community of West African States) (2008c). *The ECOWAS Conflict Prevention Framework.* Ouagadougou, UNODC.

ECOWAS (Economic Community of West African States) (2010). *West Africa Coast Initiative 'WACI' Freetown Commitment on Combating Illicit Trafficking of Drugs and Transnational Organized Crime in West Africa.* Freetown, ECOWAS.

ECOWAS (Economic Community of West African States) (2012). *ECOWAS Vision 2020: Towards a Democratic and Prosperous Community.* Abuja, ECOWAS.

ECOWAS Commission (2008). *Final Communiqué: Thirty-Fifth Ordinary Session of the Authority of Heads of State and Government.* Abuja, ECOWAS Commission.

Gbeho, Victor (2011). *Driving a People-centred Regional Integration: Press Conference to Mark the 36th Anniversary of the Founding of ECOWAS.* Abuja, ECOWAS Commission.

Gberie, Lansana (2010). 'Sierra Leone: Business More Than Usual', *Situation Report.* Pretoria, Institute for Security Studies.

IPA (International Peace Academy) (2006). *Security and Development Nexus: Research Findings and Policy Implications.* New York, IPA.

Kavanagh, Camino (2011). *Background Paper: State Capture and Organised Crime or Capture of Organised Crime by the State.* New York, NYU Centre on International Cooperation.

Newman, Edward (2010). 'Critical Human Security Studies', *Review of International Studies* 36(1): 77–94.

Sen, Amartya (1999). *Development as Freedom.* Oxford, Oxford University Press.

Stiglitz, Joseph (1998). 'Towards a New Paradigm for Development', *9th Raul Prebisch Lecture.* UNCTAD. Palais des Nations, Geneva.

Stimson Center (2012). *UN Police, Justice and Corrections Programming in Sierra Leone: A Compact Case Study.* Washington DC, Stimson Center.

UK Government (2004). *Security Sector Reform Strategy: GCPP SSR Strategy 2004–2005.* London, MoD, FCO, DfID.

UN (2009). *Joint Vision for Sierra Leone of the United Nations Family.* Freetown, UNIPSIL.

Tensions in the nexus: Sierra Leone 119

UNIPSIL (UN Peacebuilding Mission in Sierra Leone) (2012a). 'National Security', http://unipsil.unmissions.org/Default.aspx?tabid=9623&language=en-US accessed 19 December 2012.

UNIPSIL (UN Peacebuilding Mission in Sierra Leone) (2012b). 'UNIPSIL Mandate and Approach', http://unipsil.unmissions.org/Default.aspx?tabid=9613&language=en-US accessed 19 December 2012.

UNODC (UN Office on Drugs and Crime) (1998). *Alternative Development – Drug Control through Rural Development.* Vienna, UNODC.

UNODC (UN Office on Drugs and Crime) (2005). *Alternative Development: A Global Thematic Evaluation: Final Synthesis Report.* New York, United Nations.

UNODC (UN Office on Drugs and Crime) (2007a). *Cocaine Trafficking in West Africa: The Threat to Stability and Development.* Vienna, UNODC.

UNODC (UN Office on Drugs and Crime) (2007b). *Making the World Safer from Crime, Drugs and Terrorism.* Vienna, UNODC.

UNODC (UN Office on Drugs and Crime) (2008a). *An Integrated Response to Organised Crime and Illicit Drug Trafficking: West Africa Coast Initiative.* Dakar, UNODC.

UNODC (UN Office on Drugs and Crime) (2008b). *UNODC Strategy 2008–2011: Towards Security and Justice for All: Making the World Safer from Crime, Drugs and Terrorism.* Vienna, UNODC.

UNODC (UN Office on Drugs and Crime) (2008c). *Drug Trafficking as a Security Threat in West Africa.* Vienna, UNODC.

UNDOC (UN Office on Drugs and Crime) (2009). *Transnational Trafficking and the Rule of Law in West Africa: A Threat Assessment.* Vienna, UNODC.

UNODC (UN Office on Drugs and Crime) (2010a). *Regional Programme for West Africa 2010–2014.* New York, UNODC.

UNODC (UN Office on Drugs and Crime) (2010b). *Project Document: Building Institutional Capacity to Respond to the Threat Posed by Illicit Drug Trafficking and Organised Crime in Sierra Leone.* Dakar, UNODC Regional Office for West and Central Africa.

UNODC (UN Office on Drugs and Crime) (2011). *UNODC Programme in Sierra Leone, Monthly Progress Report, December 2011.* Freetown, UNODC.

UNODC (UN Office on Drugs and Crime) (2012a). *Regional Programme for West Africa 2010–2014.* Vienna, UNODC.

UNODC (UN Office on Drugs and Crime) (2012b). 'West Africa Coast Initiative: Background', www.unodc.org/westandcentralafrica/en/west-africa-coast-initiative.html accessed 10 October 2012.

UNPOL (UN Police) (2012). 'Interview: Janice Mclean', *UN Police Magazine* 9: 39–43.

US Department of State (2011). *Bureau of International Narcotics and Law Enforcement Affairs Fiscal Year 2011 Program and Budget Guide.* Washington DC, US Department of State.

Wikileaks (2009a). 'Coke, Tokes and Inept Folks: Can SL Stay Tough on Drugs? US Embassy Sierra Leone Cable', www.cablegatesearch.net/cable.php?id=09FREETOWN 270 accessed 1 March 2012.

Wikileaks (2009b). 'Sierra Leone Narcotics Wrap-Up, 2009', https://dazzlepod.com/cable/09FREETOWN462/ accessed 20 March 2013.

Wikileaks (2009c). 'Marijuana Cultivation Seen as National Security Threat', http://wikileaks.org/cable/2009/04/09FREETOWN135.html accessed 3 October 2012.

5 Tensions in the security–development nexus: Bosnia

As in Sierra Leone, external actors addressing organised crime in Bosnia readily adopted the security–development nexus. The EU Police Mission (EUPM) was a cross-pillar instrument, deployed as a European Security and Defence Policy (ESDP) mission, which brought together a focus on long-term development, short-term security and justice and home affairs (Juncos 2007). The main goal of EUPM was 'to establish sustainable policing arrangements under Bosnia and Herzegovina ownership in accordance with best European and international practice, thereby raising current Bosnia and Herzegovina police standards' (UN Security Council 2004). In contrast to Sierra Leone, organised crime is more varied in Bosnia. As well as drug trafficking, the country also experiences trafficking in many illicit commodities, from people to high-excise goods, as well as economic crimes.

In the final two phases, EUPM's mandate narrowed to support 'law enforcement agencies in the fight against organised crime and corruption, notably focusing on state level law enforcement agencies, on the interaction between police and prosecutor and on regional and international cooperation' (EUPM 2012c). Although the security–development nexus framed the mission, many of the practices during these phases remained security focused. This chapter examines how the four hypothesised tensions influenced the integration of security and development into a nexus through its implementation in Bosnia.

Conceptual tension

As previously discussed, the way external actors understand security and development can be quite different. These different understandings are rarely directly articulated but they have a significant influence on how the security–development nexus is implemented in practice. In contrast to the multi-agency approach in Sierra Leone, organised crime in Bosnia was primarily addressed through EUPM. However, the potential for divergent understandings of security and development remains, with an influence on the type of nexus that emerges.

Tensions in the nexus: Bosnia 121

Security

The locus of EUPM's initiatives was at the state level as the overarching objective was to enhance internal security. The aim was to build the capacity of Bosnian security institutions – from regular police to specialised agencies such as the State Investigation and Protection Agency (SIPA) and the Border Police – to provide a secure environment. As a result, the understanding of security fits within Quadrant A or B, depending on the referent object.

The emphasis on law-enforcement bodies suggests a state-level referent object as the aim was to strengthen national security. However, strengthening law enforcement may also be a strategy to enhance people's security by ensuring there are mechanisms in place that reduce the impact of organised crime. The rationale behind the focus on organised crime also points to the international level as the referent object of security. 'Bosnia and Herzegovina, geographically located on the infamous Balkan Route, is the last bastion in the fight against all forms of organised crime, from drug trafficking to car thefts to human smuggling, before this evil reaches the European Union' (Osmanović-Vukelić 2012). This statement identifies the containment of organised crime within Bosnia and the Western Balkan region to ensure European security as a key focus of EUPM. With the international level as the referent object and a locus at the state level, this places EUPM's understanding of security in Quadrant B: Hard security.

Scholars have argued that the disjuncture between Bosnian and European security resulted in 'strategic vagueness', incoherent policies and less-effective solutions (Schroeder 2009: 500). The division has implications for whether approaches to organised crime adhere to a hard security approach or become more focused on human security. Focusing on EU security suggests a desire to address organised crime effectively and efficiently. However, focusing on Bosnian security suggests a long-term focus that addresses the concerns of citizens. As Schroeder (2009: 500) argues, in Bosnia 'the EU is torn between its external policy of fostering democratic reforms and human security and between pursuing its quest for domestic security through fighting crime and stabilising its neighbouring "ring of fire"'. Ioannides and Collantes-Celador (2011: 422) argue that the priority often becomes hard security as 'police effectiveness and crime fighting can become more important than longer-term democratic policing and good governance reforms'. This suggests that the international level remains the primary referent object as containing organised crime is prioritised over individual needs.

In contrast to how security was understood within EUPM policy, mission personnel emphasised individual security. An EUPM official noted

> you want to increase the security of the citizens and you want citizens to perceive that they're more secure and safer.... In order to do that you need to make sure that they believe in it, and to do that it needs to be more than a military presence. It needs to be that they have confidence that the police are working for them not the government.[1]

122 *Tensions in the nexus: Bosnia*

These perspectives influenced the development of the Mission Implementation Plan. The result was a focus on developing standards of democratic policing in accordance with human rights principles (EUPM 2012b). While the locus of initiatives remained at the state level, such an approach shifts understandings of security away from hard security measures to focus on individual people as the referent object. Alongside policing, EUPM also engaged in thematic areas such as gender balance, gender mainstreaming, media support and rule of law (EUPM 2012b). These programmes also shift initiatives to address organised crime away from a hard security approach. As such, the understanding of security among EUPM personnel fit within Quadrant A: Top-down benevolence.

As EUPM was designed to contribute to EU policy and peace implementation through policing, the understandings expressed at the strategic or headquarter level also influenced the mandate, objectives and approach of EUPM. For instance, as a European Security and Defence Policy (ESDP) mission, under-standings of security within the ESDP also influenced EUPM's approach. The ESDP sought to 'strengthen security and resolutely combat dangers such as … organised crime' (European Council 1999: 10). Organised crime is considered 'a major obstacle for the consolidation of law and order in former crisis areas' (European Council 2004: 2). This suggests that the post-conflict state is the referent object of EU involvement. However, the ESDP also noted that

> Europe is a prime target for organised crime (cross-border trafficking in drugs, human beings, and weapons accounts for a large part of the activities of criminal gangs) and external action, inter alia through international police missions, can help improve our internal security.
>
> (European Council 2004: 2)

This suggests that ESDP missions such as EUPM seek to strengthen capacity to address security threats to limit their impact on the EU. This points to the inter-national level as referent object, with activities to combat organised crime focused at the state level. The ESDP understanding of security extends across Quadrant B to include both internal and external security. However, it remains focused on hard security approaches.

The European Security Strategy (ESS), drafted in 2003, also influenced the mandate and objectives of EUPM as 'the European Council decided that one of the initial priorities for implementation of the EU Security Strategy should be the elaboration of a comprehensive policy for Bosnia and Herzegovina' (Council of the European Union 2004: 2). Security threats and challenges set out in the ESS include terrorism, weapons of mass destruction, regional conflicts, state failure and organised crime. While these threats do impact on individuals, in this context they are considered as transnational threats that affect security within the EU. By priori-tising European security, the referent object is the international level. The EU seeks to identify and contain these threats before they affect member states.

In practice, the method of addressing these threats moves beyond a hard security approach. The ESS recognises that 'none of these threats are purely military and cannot be tackled by purely military means' (EU 2003: 8). The ESS states that

> [the] best protection for our security is a world of well-governed democratic states. Spreading good governance, supporting social and political reform, dealing with corruption and abuse of power, establishing the rule of law and protecting human rights are the best means of strengthening the international order.
>
> (EU 2003: 11)

This suggests that organised crime should be addressed by ensuring good governance and rule of law in Bosnia. 'Restoring good government to the Balkans, fostering democracy and enabling authorities there to tackle organised crime is one of the most effective ways of dealing with organised crime within the EU' (EU 2003: 7). As the ESS is primarily focused on European security, its understanding of security fits in Quadrant B. The shift away from hard security measures brings security closer to the centre, between Quadrants A and B, as the ESS perceives good governance and rule of law reforms as the most effective strategy to maintain and protect EU security.

While there is some interest in Bosnian security, which suggests a long-term focus that engages with the needs of citizens, there is also a significant emphasis on containing organised crime before it affects the EU. Among EU personnel, citizen security was prioritised. This may suggest that security was not clearly defined within EUPM or that they rejected the mandate and focused more on the needs of citizens. Either way, the locus of initiatives was at the state level as the emphasis was on building the capacity of state institutions. This limits the understandings of security to Quadrants A and B. However, the understanding stretches across both quadrants. As a result, EUPM's understanding of security began to shift away from a traditional security approach.

Development

The reference to good governance and rule of law within the ESS brought elements of development into initiatives to address organised crime in Bosnia. Good governance and rule of law programmes seek to refocus police activities on the needs of citizens, ensuring democratic processes and justice mechanisms are in place. This implies that the understanding of development fits within Quadrant A: Top-down benevolence. It acknowledges the need for programmes to benefit citizens, but initiatives were still implemented at the state level.

Alongside good governance and rule of law programmes, EUPM also focused on economic development. EUPM recognised that 'organised crime is holding back Bosnia by preventing foreign investment, economic growth, and slowing down European integration' (Osmanović-Vukelić 2012: 44). This reiterates the focus on the state level, as the primary concern is investment and growth. While economic growth also has benefits for citizens, the primary concern here is state

124 *Tensions in the nexus: Bosnia*

stability. However, concerns over state stability also point to the international level as referent object, as economic growth contributes to European security. The focus on economic development places development within Quadrant B as it is believed that growth will enhance the stability of Bosnia, ensuring it is less of a threat to European security.

For many EUPM officials the primary aim of the mission was security focused as they worked with law-enforcement agencies across the country. Development was understood to be included within European integration and enlargement policies.[2] As a potential candidate for accession to the EU, Bosnia has been engaged in the Stabilisation and Association Process as part of the EU's enlargement policy. Although there have been a number of setbacks arising from difficulties in meeting their obligations, Bosnia signed a Stabilisation and Association Agreement, which sets out the conditions required for EU membership, in 2008. Membership of the EU requires that the candidate country has achieved stability of institutions guaranteeing democracy, the rule of law, human rights, respect for and protection of minorities, the existence of a functioning market economy, as well as the capacity to cope with competitive pressure and market forces within the Union as set out in the Acquis Communautaire and the Copenhagen Criteria (European Council 1993). As such, development was viewed in the context of broader rule of law reforms and economic development. As with good governance and rule of law, the inclusion of development suggests that initiatives to address organised crime would focus on the needs of citizens, which would place understandings of development in Quadrant A.

Viewing development as connected to the enlargement process has been criticised by development NGOs as it makes the security–development nexus 'essentially about diverting poverty relief into support for Western strategic objectives' (Youngs 2007: 13). While integration and enlargement policies include a focus on development, these policies are designed to maintain the stability and integrity of the EU. From this perspective, development is not focused on individuals' needs but seeks to address the international level as referent object. This would place EUPM's understanding of development into Quadrant B.

There is also a lack of clarity on what the enlargement strategy means for approaches to organised crime. The 2005 Enlargement Strategy considered organised crime to be 'a major threat for Bosnia and Herzegovina's stability and overall socio-economic development' (Commission of the European Communities 2005: 20). Similarly, the 2011 Enlargement Progress Report recognised that organised crime has 'a negative impact on political structures and the economy' (European Commission 2011: 57). Addressing organised crime was viewed as the role of EUPM through security and law-enforcement tasks. This suggests a limited understanding on what development strategies can bring to initiatives to address organised crime even though EUPM was a cross-pillar instrument. During the final two phases of EUPM, progress towards accession was the key focus of the EU Delegation. As such, development was often viewed as the remit of the EU Delegation while EUPM focused on security concerns.

Tensions in the nexus: Bosnia 125

This suggests that understanding development in relation to enlargement creates a separation between security and development.[3]

Although organised crime in Bosnia was primarily addressed through EUPM, rather than through a coalition of actors as in Sierra Leone, conceptual tension remains prevalent. Despite being a cross-pillar instrument that combines security and development, there was no clear understanding of development among actors addressing organised crime. The focus on good governance and rule of law suggests both state-level and individual referent objects. However, EUPM officials considered development to be part of the broader EU enlargement strategy, reiterating the international level as referent object. While enlargement addresses many areas connected to development, organised crime is considered as a security problem. As such, there was no consistency on how development was understood in relation to EU initiatives to address organised crime.

There was also a lack of consistency in how security was understood. At the strategic level the referent object was international security, as EU security was the primary concern. This was translated into EUPM policy which sought to achieve EU security by working at the state level. However, EUPM officials also identified individuals as the referent object. This suggests that, while understandings of security were influenced by EU policy, on the ground they became more human centred. Rather than integrating security and development, initiatives focused primarily on security elements such as law enforcement. References to development through the enlargement strategy suggested a conviction that other actors, such as the EU Delegation, would address development aspects. However, as enlargement does not directly address organised crime, development was neglected in initiatives to address organised crime.

The lack of consensus is evident in Figure 5.1. This diagram differs from the mapping of different actors in Sierra Leone as it maps different elements of the EU approach. In relation to understandings of security, within EUPM there were different perspectives from personnel that focus on individual needs, the emphasis on internal (Bosnian) security and the emphasis on external (EU) security. EUPM was also influenced by two European policies, ESDP and ESS. Although these fall into the same quadrant, they are not aligned with the understandings within EUPM. There were also varied understandings of development. There was a focus on good governance, which primarily falls in Quadrant A, although some policies suggest that this is to bolster European interests rather than just individual needs. The focus on enlargement and economic development remains in Quadrant B, relying on economic understandings of development.

These understandings influence the type of nexus that emerges. The different understandings mean there cannot be a clear security–development nexus across the mission. While some parts of the mission, such as EUPM personnel, began to engage with individual needs, traditional security approaches remain dominant. With understandings of development primarily falling within Quadrant B, it is difficult for development to have a 'humanising' effect on security and contribute to a shift towards an emancipatory approach. Despite this, there

126 *Tensions in the nexus: Bosnia*

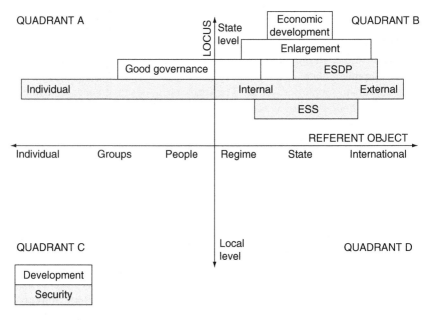

Figure 5.1 Understandings of security and development in Bosnia.

has still been a shift away from a traditional security approach, as some understandings moved into Quadrant A.

Causal tension

The recognition of the relationship between security and development, and the urgency to develop new, comprehensive approaches to complex challenges, suggests that the causal relationship between security and development is uncontested and viewed in the same way by all actors engaging with the nexus. However, there are many different perspectives on the causal relationship. This section examines how security and development are applied in Bosnia and how the linkage between security and development is viewed, which reveals the form of integration between security and development.

Application

As in Sierra Leone, EUPM's perspective on how security is applied adhered to the traditional view: security is an end state where the referent object is secure. EUPM's mandate was to ensure the security of society, as well as maintain EU security through initiatives to address organised crime. This implies that security is an end state to be achieved through EUPM's engagement, whether it is Bosnian security or European security. EUPM supported Bosnian law-enforcement institutions to provide 'the necessary security to the society it serves' (Osmanović-Vukelić 2012: 31). Part of EUPM's approach was to 'contribute to internal security' and extend the area of security to potential member states.[4] These references focus on security as an end state that EUPM is working towards. This approach included 'increasing the security of citizens'.[5] While this is a less tangible understanding of security as it invokes individual perceptions, it still refers to an end state to be achieved. EUPM also focused on threats to security and 'security concerns'.[6] This reinforces the view that security is an end state as it indicates that security is a condition that can be undermined by organised crime. Understanding security as an end state implies that the goal may be predetermined by external actors. However, local needs were brought in to a certain extent, as the mission aimed to increase the security of citizens.

While security is often understood as an end state, development has been more variable. Bosnia differs from Sierra Leone in that it is not a developing country. As such, development has played a less prominent role. Despite this, EUPM lamented that law enforcement did not meet 'hopes for the development of [Bosnia]' in 2009 (Osmanović-Vukelić 2012). Similarly, organised crime was viewed by EUPM as the biggest obstacle in Bosnia's development (Osmanović-Vukelić 2012). Helly (2013: 75) noted that 'fighting organised crime and curbing corruption are key to lasting stability and peaceful development'. These references to development suggest that it was viewed as a desired end state that is undermined by organised crime.

Among the contributing organisations to EUPM there were different perspectives on development, which made its application more ambiguous. For the European Commission, development played a more significant role than it did for the Council. The Commission's approach focuses on institution building and the reform agenda put forward by EUPM (Juncos 2007). While the focus on institution building furthers the perspective that development is a process, it seeks to achieve specific, predefined goals. Such an approach is aligned with arguments that development would be enhanced by the accession agenda, which sets out concrete benchmarks that Bosnia must achieve before it becomes an EU member state.

Within EUPM, security was applied as an end state: the goal to be achieved through external involvement. This adheres to the traditional perspective of security, which suggests that the application of security has not been modified through the security–development nexus. While there is some ambiguity with development, it appeared to be primarily viewed as an end state. With security and development both applied as an end state, these understandings do not raise questions of how the two concepts are integrated – external engagement seeks to achieve both security *and* development as the end goal. However, given the predetermined objectives such as the benchmarks necessary for accession, viewing security and development as end goals undermines the shift away from a traditional security approach towards emancipation, as local communities are excluded from decision making on what the end state of security and development is.

128   *Tensions in the nexus: Bosnia*

Linkages

Within EUPM there were also different perspectives on the linkages between security and development. EU policy acknowledges that 'there cannot be sustainable development without peace and security, and that without development and poverty eradication there will be no sustainable peace' (EU 2007: 1). Yet there remains a lack of consensus on the linkages between security and development. In 2007, the Council of the EU stated that 'the nexus between development and security should inform EU strategies and policies in order to contribute to the coherence of EU external action' (EU 2007: 1). As EU policy on external engagement has developed a strong recognition of the links between security and development, there was an expectation that this would transfer into practice through EUPM. EUPM was a cross-pillar instrument bringing together development, short-term security, and justice and home affairs (Juncos 2007). This implies that EUPM combined security and development in its approach to organised crime in Bosnia. However, as a police mission, EUPM's approach to organised crime prioritised policing and law-enforcement institutions. This suggests that the linkage was not integrated.

Many EUPM officials saw the mission's objectives as security focused. There are 'papers that say that [security and development are linked], but how we actually do this, we are very focused on the security sector. So we have horizontal activities, say gender, human rights activities, outreach, public information, but that's rather horizontal and marginal to what the activity is.'[7] While both security and development elements were brought in to EUPM's approach, they were not connected. However, development institutions fund relevant projects within EUPM that have a focus on security.[8] This suggests a sequential linkage between security and development as the aim was to restore security through policing and law enforcement to create space for development.

EUPM's prioritisation of security to create space for development was further evidenced by the transition of organised crime programmes from EUPM to the EU Delegation. Following the withdrawal of EUPM in June 2012, much of the work on organised crime moved over to the EU Delegation. This shift was viewed as a transition from a crisis management or post-conflict agenda to institution building or enlargement with a focus on the conditions for accession.[9] These separate phases have parallels with a sequential perspective of the security–development nexus. The crisis management/post-conflict phase focused on security issues, whereas the accession logic can be considered part of a development approach as it entailed rule of law reform and institution building to ensure social and economic cohesion with Europe.

The sequential understanding continued with the accession agenda. The EU enlargement strategy sees organised crime as a threat to both security and development. 'Organised crime is considered a major threat for Bosnia and Herzegovina's stability and overall socio-economic development' (Commission of the European Communities 2005: 20). However, the Stabilisation and Association Process progress reports address political criteria, economic criteria and

European standards separately from strategies to address organised crime (European Commission 2010, 2011, 2012). Organised crime is evaluated under 'Justice, Freedom and Security', with a focus solely on law-enforcement strategies (Commission of the European Communities 2009). While organised crime impacts on both security and development, it is addressed solely through security approaches within the enlargement strategy.

Despite the prioritisation of security on the ground, development has increasingly taken a stronger role in EU policy. The Maastricht Treaty noted that in its external relations the EU seeks to 'contribute to peace, security, the sustainable development of the Earth, solidarity and mutual respect among people, free and fair trade, eradication of poverty and the protection of human rights' (EU 1992). The treaty also calls for greater cooperation in addressing organised crime (EU 1992). While security and development are both viewed as important, Article 3 states that 'the Union shall in particular ensure the consistency of its external activities as a whole in the context of its external relations, security, economic and development policies' (EU 1992). This implies a stronger linkage, where security and development policies are consistent with each other. However, it didn't extend to integration in Bosnia.

These linkages were consolidated in the Lisbon Treaty in 2009 which rearranged external engagement to consolidate the different areas of engagement. While the Lisbon Treaty removed the pillar structure that kept security and development policy separate, they continued to be governed by different actors (House of Lords 2008). 'The developmental, long-term institution building remit of the Commission is supposed to complement the security-focused, short-term crisis management remit of the Council' (Ryan 2011: 95). Article 208 of the Consolidated Treaty on the Functioning of Europe, which was amended by the Lisbon Treaty, stipulates that development objectives have to be taken into account by all EU policies (EU 2010). This implies a much closer integration of security and development policies. Sjolinder (2010) argues that increased harmonisation will improve approaches to organised crime. These policy changes indicate a shift towards a more integrated relationship between security and development in EU missions such as EUPM. However, this was not evident in the implementation of initiatives to address organised crime in Bosnia.

The European Security Strategy (ESS), a key driver in EUPM's approach, maintained the separation of security and development. The ESS states that 'security is a precondition for development' (EU 2003: 3). This implies that security is viewed with urgency while development comes later. However, the ESS also considers development as a strategy to achieve security for the EU. Poverty and disease, problems of underdevelopment, are seen to 'give rise to pressing security concerns' (EU 2003: 3). These two arguments see security and development as interconnected in that security is necessary for development and development can be useful to achieve European security. However, they continue to be separate areas of focus. The ESS understanding of the security–development nexus is one of interdependence rather than integration. This may be changing. The ESS also acknowledged that 'we are stronger when we act

130 *Tensions in the nexus: Bosnia*

together ... the challenge now is to bring together the different capabilities, European assistance programmes and the European Development Fund, military and civilian capabilities from Member states and other instruments' (EU 2003: 14).

While this remains in the context of different institutions working together, rather than an integrated approach, the 2008 report on the ESS goes further.

> [By] drawing on a unique range of instruments, the EU already contributes to a more secure world. We have worked to build human security, by reducing poverty and inequality, promoting good governance and human rights, assisting development, and addressing the root causes of conflict and insecurity.
>
> (EU 2008: 2)

While this brings the two concepts closer together, they remain interdependent rather than integrated. This was the case in Bosnia. EUPM sought to combine a range of EU instruments to address organised crime. However, in practice the result was a 'security first' approach. As the aim is to create space for development and development actors, the linkage between security and development was viewed as sequential.

While the EU appears to have entrenched the security–development nexus in their policymaking in external affairs, a divide remained between security and development in the practices of EUPM. Security policies such as the ESS assert that security is a precondition for development. However, the result is not an integrated relationship between security and development. While the two elements are connected, they remain separate and sequential. Bosnia's ranking as an upper middle-income country may explain the low priority given to development and poverty reduction (World Bank 2004). However, the EU Consensus on Development recognises that 'a large number of the world's poor live in [middle income] countries and many are confronted with striking inequalities and weak governance, which threaten the sustainability of their own development process' (EU 2005: 10). Unemployment remains a major concern for Bosnians (Prism Research 2012). Other issues that tend to fall to development rather than security bodies, such as corruption, also remain a significant factor for organised crime. While EUPM did address corruption, the focus was primarily on the law enforcement and criminal justice sectors, rather than the higher levels that facilitate organised crime. While weak governance and poverty provide a conducive environment for organised crime, they are not addressed in this one-sided approach to the security–development nexus.

Within EUPM there is no direct causal relationship between security and development. However, the aim to create space for development creates a shift in the approach of external actors. Although this does not equate to the integration of security and development, it does indicate the beginnings of shift away from a traditional security approach.

Institutional tension

With different institutional architecture, a different understanding of problems and different approaches, the actors and institutions that inform the implementation of initiatives to address organised crime create an institutional tension that influences how security and development are integrated into a nexus.

Institutional architecture

As an EU mission, the institutional architecture of EUPM was influenced by EU policies. While EU crisis-management missions were at the time generally under Pillar II (foreign and security policy), EUPM was a cross-pillar instrument also bringing in Pillar I, with a focus on long-term development, and Pillar III, addressing justice and home affairs (Hansen 2004; Emerson and Gross 2007). However, the Council Conclusions on Security and Development recognised that 'the responsibilities of development and security actors are complementary but remain specific' (EU 2007: 1). Gourlay (2004) and Osland (2004) argue that the pillar structure is a major barrier to civilian crisis management as mandates, goals and financial priorities fall to different pillars. As a result, EUPM was influenced by contributors from both security and development perspectives. However, rather than merging, the two areas remained separate. As Schroeder (2007: 28) notes, 'first and second pillar actors have followed diverging strategies of organisational innovation'.

The division between development cooperation and security policy is entrenched in EU treaties. Article 209 of the Treaty on the Functioning of the EU places development cooperation within the ordinary legislative procedure, whereby the European Commission proposes programmes to be approved by the European Parliament and the Council of the EU (EU 2010). In contrast, Article 24 of the Treaty on European Union provides for unanimous decision making on Common Foreign and Security Policy – which includes the European Security and Defence Policy (ESDP) and now the Common Security and Defence Policy (CSDP) – by the European Council and the Council of the European Union (EU 1992). Merket (2012: 628) argues that 'this treaty-based distinction between development cooperation and security and defence policy tends to jeopardise the intuitive complementarity of both policy fields'.

Under the Lisbon Treaty, the European Council identifies the strategic (security) interests and objectives of the Union in terms of external action, supplying the political direction and priorities that shape the Common Foreign and Security Policy (Mix 2011). Overall direction for EUPM is provided by the Political and Security Council (PSC), the Committee for Civilian Aspects of Crisis Management (CIVCOM) and the Civilian Planning and Conduct Capability (CPCC). The PSC, composed of ambassadors from member states, monitors and assesses international affairs relevant to foreign and security policy, feeds into decision making in these areas, and monitors implementation (Mix 2011). Within the PSC, CIVCOM provides advice on civilian aspects of

132 *Tensions in the nexus: Bosnia*

crisis management while the CPCC provides guidance on the planning, conduct and implementation of Common Security and Defence Policy missions (Youngs and Faria 2010). EUPM reported on the implementation of their objectives to the PSC, CIVCOM and the CPCC.[10] The focus on civilian involvement shifts beyond a military approach. However, the focus is still on the security sector, specifically policing, rule of law, civil administration and civil protection. With its focus on crisis management, the European Council is closely aligned with security approaches. This ensures that the institutional architecture of EUPM was influenced by the security perspective of the European Council.

As well as the European Council, the European Commission played a role in the management and oversight of civilian missions such as EUPM. As the European Commission housed European development policy, it was well placed to ensure that security and development approaches were connected in initiatives to address organised crime. With its focus on the judiciary and human rights, many Commissioners saw EUPM's mandate within their rule of law programme (Matthiessen 2013). Yet while the Maastricht Treaty states that the Commission is 'fully associated' with decisions on CFSP, in practice this is primarily consultative (Derks and More 2009). As a result, security interests remain the overriding priority. Although EU Civilian Crisis Management can draw on a wide range of mechanisms, Gourlay (2004: 404) argues that the 'institutional structure and limited approach to developing crisis management capabilities within the intergovernmental decision-making context of the ESDP means that its response to crises is neither integrated nor coherent'.

The security focus is amplified by the contributions of personnel by member states. While EU crisis-management systems have shifted to incorporate civilian elements, procedures within member states haven't adapted accordingly.

> [T]hese crisis management centres in countries, most of them were set up by foreign ministries to second staff from the interior ministries because they wanted police officers.... If you look at Finland, their crisis management centre, they have agreements with all of their ministries; most of the good experts that were not from policing came from Finland. They sent us prison experts, ex-prison directors; all of our customs and duties experts.... Whereas if you look at other countries, they've never moved on from, 'Well, we can send you police officers', so they don't have arrangements with their ministries of justice to find you prosecutors.[11]

When EU member states do send police, it's often military police.

> They're already armed. So they've already got gun training, but they're not really police officers ... [T]heir role in their own country is different, and they don't have the experience of dealing with organised crime and corruption like you would get in England, London say. There are different skill sets that you need in these missions.[12]

As such, EUPM personnel were primarily drawn from a security background, many without civilian training.

While the Commission sought to influence the mandate of EUPM by bringing in elements of development, the primary contributor was the European Council, with a strong security mandate, and EU member states, which were keen to address organised crime before it reached their borders. As a result, the contributors to EUPM were security focused. However, funding for EUPM was more diverse, resulting in a shift away from a traditional security approach.

Funding for EUPM primarily came from the European Commission through the Directorate of External Relations (DG RELEX). Although the Commission didn't have significant input into the implementation of EUPM, its contribution in terms of funding shifted the mission away from a pure security focus. One EUPM official noted that 'development wasn't second fiddle because it played a huge role in European funding of relevant projects'.[13] As a result, 'some Commission officials argued that the mission in fact had "two chains of command": one budgetary to the Commission and one political to the High Representative ... and the Council' (Matthiessen 2013: 17).

Although DG RELEX was integrated into the European External Action Service (EEAS) in December 2010, the 'European Commission still plays an important role ... as it is responsible for drafting the proposal for the EU budget, including allocations for Common Foreign and Security Policy' (EPLO 2012: 8). As well as funding EUPM directly, Commission funds also contributed to other initiatives to address organised crime in Bosnia. Community Assistance for Reconstruction, Development and Stabilisation (CARDS) was used for a project on integrated border management (Flessenkemper 2013). CARDS also funded communication systems using voice over internet protocol (VoIP) and terrestrial trunked radio (tetra), and the automated fingerprint identification system.[14] The Instrument for Pre-accession Assistance (IPA) funded an anti-corruption project and the law-enforcement project that succeeded EUPM (Flessenkemper 2013).

Some of these projects overlapped with the work of EUPM. As the European Commission had limited decision-making power over EUPM, these projects can be viewed as attempts by the European Commission to ensure that initiatives to address organised crime fit within their rule of law agenda, and furthered European Commission goals and objectives in Bosnia. While the projects included both security and development elements as they approached organised crime from the Commission's perspective, their separation from EUPM, and their overlap with EUPM projects, revealed a deeper disconnect and competition between security and development institutions within the EU. Flessenkemper (2013: 60) noted that 'towards the last phase of the mission (2010–2012), EUPM competed almost directly for qualified personnel with Community projects'. Similarly, Schroeder (2007: 35–6) noted that 'the convergence of Council and Commission activities in the field of civilian crisis management and peacebuilding has led to a deterioration of their relationship rather than to better coordination of their work'.

134 *Tensions in the nexus: Bosnia*

Other donors also contributed to EUPM, adding other interests to the mandate and approach. Member states provided funding directly to certain projects. For example, Norway and the UK jointly funded a project on police–prosecutor cooperation that was implemented by EUPM.[15] As a result, member states also influenced EUPM's approach to organised crime by pushing particular objectives. This means there were a number of influences on EUPM's approach to organised crime.

While the key contributor to EUPM was the European Council, the European Commission also played a key role as the primary donor of the mission. This ensures that development elements are brought in to a certain extent. However, the efforts of the European Commission to implement its own projects that overlapped with EUPM initiatives suggests that security influences dominate.

Understanding of organised crime

Organised crime was given greater priority by EUPM than by the local population (Juncos 2007). This implies that organised crime was understood as a security threat to the European Union, resulting in more attention than the local-level criminality that concerned citizens. However, some EUPM officials considered the problem greater than it appeared.

> You'll find some evidence of organised crime and corruption in the Balkan route in assessments of Bosnia, but because everyone in the country does not have the same intelligence sharing, nobody can give you an overall picture. If you want a true picture of it, you won't be able to find one. Any threat assessment of the Balkans will show Bosnia as a bit of 'not too bad', but that only represents a lack of information.[16]

While this can still indicate that organised crime is a threat to the EU, it also highlights that it should be a priority for local actors.

Although EUPM sought to address organised crime before it became visible to citizens, it was still understood as a problem that could be addressed through a responsive approach, where police come in once a crime has been committed.[17] Police became more proactive, developing relationships with communities to avoid and prevent problems.[18] However, police sought to prevent organised crime by making it more difficult, rather than addressing the underlying factors that make organised crime possible and allow it to flourish in Bosnia. The aim of EUPM was to enhance the capacity of law-enforcement bodies to ensure they were better able to respond to incidents of organised crime. This approach maintained a focus on coercive strategies. As a result, the understanding of organised crime adhered to a traditional security approach.

The language adopted by EUPM also indicates that organised crime is understood in security terms. The mission location was referred to as the 'theatre'.[19] This has become common in military operations and peacekeeping missions; it is linked to Clausewitz (1832), who used 'theatre' to 'denote properly such a

Tensions in the nexus: Bosnia   135

portion of the space over which war prevails'. Staffing was referred to as 'force generation' (Flessenkemper 2013). Even the term 'mission' is usually reserved for security programmes, being employed by NATO and the UN to refer to security operations to end and manage violence and maintain peace.

The language employed by EUPM was technical and task oriented. The focus was primarily on the pursuit of organised crime networks, addressing 'investigative capacity' (EUPM 2010a: 1). As with Sierra Leone, EUPM also included a focus on capacity building. However, language related to capacity building was also task oriented, focusing on specific objectives. The aim was 'to assist in building an increased ability to plan and implement measures that are designed to fight organised crime and corruption within corruption resistant organisational structures', and increase 'capability to identify, investigate and dismantle organised crime networks' (EUPM 2010b: 1). The language employed by EUPM suggests that security threats need to be addressed in the most efficient way.

Although EUPM sought to engage with local priorities and employed capacity building to achieve their objectives, organised crime was understood in security terms. EUPM responded to incidents of organised crime rather than seeking to transform the structures that allow organised crime to flourish. This understanding is supported by the technical, security-focused language employed by EUPM.

Approach to organised crime

The EU's objective in Bosnia was 'to upgrade national capacities and intra-regional cooperation and to support the "hot pursuit" and arrest of criminals who cross country borders' (Montanaro-Jankovski 2005: 22). However, EUPM did not seek to achieve these objectives and withdraw. Because of the Europeanisation agenda, EU engagement was more long term than other missions that are 'based on an in-and-out model' (Emerson and Gross 2007: 6), resembling a traditional security approach. Initially the focus was very technical. The emphasis was on 'technical assistance and professionalising the police. It was institution building mostly, with a lot of training on different technical aspects of police, surveillance, so setting up systems.'[20] The focus on institution building 'provided expert advice and monitored the creation and strengthening of various institutions (the Ministry of Security, SIPA, SBS and Interpol) to increase the local capacity' (Juncos 2007: 59).

EUPM gradually shifted from a policing mission to a rule of law mission and the practices became more strategic.[21] The mission aimed to promote effectiveness and accountability and build the capacity of local law enforcement. This was often done through a needs analysis.

> We would work on these particular cases that we select as the most difficult and we work with them to overcome the problems, but we use that process as a needs analysis and gap analysis to identify in that process what doesn't work and how we can help and we can then work on the technical side with training.[22]

136 *Tensions in the nexus: Bosnia*

Some EUPM officials perceived the emphasis on organised crime as a broader attempt to improve the capacity of the police force overall. 'Looking at it from a technical point of view, if you are able to conduct an investigation into organised crime, which is one of the most complex, then you are capable of any kind of investigation.'[23]

Despite debates over the rationale for the focus on organised crime, EUPM aimed to work in partnership with local law enforcement. Penska (2008: 29) notes that 'on the basis of its mandate [EUPM] utilised a bottom-up, functional approach', identifying areas of focus in collaboration with local counterparts. An EUPM official stated that this was put in practice by respecting 'that these are police officers, they know their job, so go in at a level where you are there to support them as opposed to telling them how it should be done'.[24] This wasn't always the case. The same official added: 'I'm not saying internationals didn't try and come over to individually impose things, but it wasn't an EUPM position to impose things.'[25] EUPM was not an executive mission, so it was unable to impose decisions: 'we've got no policing powers and if they don't do it properly we can't do it for them. We don't have the power to – we've just got powers of persuasion.'[26] This means it was in the best interests of EUPM to develop strong collaborative relationships with local counterparts. Such an approach shifts away from a traditional security approach, which aims to directly implement programmes.

Problems with high-level corruption often made it difficult for local authorities to directly pursue some cases. One respondent noted that Bosnian police and prosecutors fear dealing with corruption more than death; 'they are not willing to deal with organised crime where people get killed over links with corruption.'[27] In these cases, international involvement can be useful. Some members of local law enforcement state that they 'need support from the international community to strengthen their approach'.[28]

> There's relatively little interest in the Bosnian government in fighting corruption and organised crime. That said, when pressure comes from the outside, especially in the form of task forces, or other countries, neighbouring countries that are particularly interested in arresting someone, they sometimes will act, so there is activity, but the systemic organised crime that exists in the country, that's not an outside force, they tend not to do a whole lot.[29]

While international assistance is useful, without an executive mandate EUPM did not always achieve successful outcomes. An EUPM official noted that corruption extends from organised crime to the highest level. 'For us, when we are trying to implement something without imposition, you have to make sure it's strong enough to make an impact but weak enough to not get opposition.'[30] With powerful interests blocking initiatives, it was difficult to achieve reform. 'The things we wanted to achieve that we haven't achieved is because the politicians don't want it – money laundering laws, intelligence sharing between police agencies, coordination and cooperation.'[31]

In some instances, these challenges resulted in a stronger partnership between EUPM and their local allies. During needs analysis, when problems were discovered, EUPM and local law enforcement identified the most effective way to achieve their goals.

> If we discovered a problem with SIPA on how they worked when we were working on a case, we ask, 'Why don't you speak to your chief of investigation?' and they say, 'Pfft', we would speak with them. We would say.... 'We have this suggestion.' We're always mediating trying to get improvements.[32]

However, there is a risk that this approach generates reliance on internationals to do the difficult tasks.

Despite being a police mission, EUPM's practices did not strictly adhere to a traditional security approach. This becomes apparent when comparing EUPM to the EU's military force – EUFOR Bosnia. 'Several operations were launched by the EUFOR to support local law enforcement to combat illegal activities such as weapons and drug smuggling, human trafficking and illegal logging ... by participating actively in operations against organised crime' (Juncos 2007: 59). Rather than supporting local law enforcement, EUFOR engaged directly in pursuing organised crime. EUFOR had an executive mandate to provide a safe and secure environment, whereas EUPM aimed to build the capacity of local law enforcement to address organised crime themselves. Although EUPM still sought to achieve security outcomes, the practices moved beyond a traditional security approach. In this regard, EUPM's approach to problems demonstrates a merging of security and development.

Although EUPM aimed to achieve a joint approach with local law enforcement, the structure of the partnership remained hierarchical.

> EUPM has stepped in with training and seminars and conferences and taken members from the police force away to see how it could be done differently, more for a joint approach than changing it, to see what has worked in other places.[33]

The focus on training and exchanges implies that internationals brought expertise that was lacking locally. This perspective was amplified by the mentoring relationship between EUPM and local law enforcement. EUPM aimed to achieve their objectives by co-locating European police with local law enforcement as mentors. At its peak, co-location was widespread.

> We had a relationship with every police agent at every level; we had field officers that worked not only in different locations but different offices and different agencies in those locations. So if there's a field office of the border police in Bijeljina, we had a team working in the field office in Bijeljina. We were everywhere, even the cantonal police station.[34]

138 *Tensions in the nexus: Bosnia*

Referring to the mentoring relationship, one EUPM official noted: 'I think the stipulation is that you have 15 years' service to mentor, but the mentee may have 25, and it's not to say you're lacking, because you could have technically been doing that job for 15 years, but it's the level of respect.'[35] An Italian officer serving in Banja Luka noted: 'if someone had come to me in Italy and said you had to do it like this, and if I didn't agree, or I didn't respect them, or they didn't come in at my level, I'd have my back up'.[36] The hierarchical relationship was compounded by the lack of domestic capacity to drive changes. 'Institutions are immature, internal plans are still evolving. They are not at the stage where they can tell donors what's needed.'[37] As a result, local law enforcement was influenced by the aims of EUPM.

The focus on partnerships with local law enforcement did result in a shift away from a traditional security approach, however, particularly as co-location and mentoring aimed to support local actors to find solutions. Despite this shift, a number of problems arose from working with government bodies. Many advances in addressing organised crime were blocked because of corruption or a lack of political will. Several EUPM officials expressed frustration over political blockages that prevented them from fulfilling their mandate. In particular, politicians blocked money laundering laws, international sharing between the police agencies, and initiatives to enhance cooperation and coordination.[38] Political blockages also prevented different police bodies from working together effectively. 'It's the political and ... state-level corruption that is not facilitating that wheel to turn properly.'[39] As these influences are not always apparent, it can create false hypotheses of what needs to be addressed within the police bodies. 'When international agencies target the police, they don't get the results that they envisaged because there were other factors that they weren't aware of, or didn't acknowledge they were so strong.'[40]

As EUPM was not an executive mission, personnel relied solely on the powers of persuasion to improve policing in Bosnia. One EUPM official noted that

> the mandate of missions ... need to be far more detailed and agreed – we're working towards this, this is the overall end vision and this is what needs to be done to achieve that and we'll come and do that if you sign up to the fact that you want us to do it, but you're responsible for getting all your local counterparts to sign up to that too and not to block us so we're not fighting them all the time.[41]

However, the international community did not necessarily take their lead from local institutions. The Republika Srpska Ministry of Security requested support to develop new databases and train police on how to use them. Their request was turned down, so they raised funds to do it themselves.[42] It took several years before an adequate number of police were trained to use the new databases but, once they were, it was an effective policing tool.[43] In response, the international

Tensions in the nexus: Bosnia 139

community supported the same project in police departments in the Federation of Bosnia and Herzegovina.[44]

EUPM aimed to shift the approach of the police from protecting the state to protecting citizens. However, when it comes to law enforcement and ministries engaging with civil society, problems arise. Government bodies now have a responsibility to hold public hearings on new legislation to get feedback from civil society. However, civil society is rarely involved in preparing legislation; this is left to ministry staff and experts.[45] This suggests that the knowledge and expertise of civil society is not valued. When juvenile delinquency became an issue of concern in Bosnia in recent years, a local academic who had worked on two major studies of juvenile delinquency in Bosnia contacted the Ministry of Security offering to make the data available.[46] The Ministry did not respond but instead contacted an American academic for advice on doing their own research; the American academic then informed the Ministry this research had already been done by local academics.[47]

Some bodies have improved their relationship with civil society. The Ministry of Security has been particularly effective in this area. When developing its anti-corruption strategy

> the Ministry of Security was inviting NGOs to participate in the working group that was working on the anti-corruption strategy and action plan and the law that would set up the anti-corruption agency.... There was some hesitation in the beginning, sometimes their relationship is a conflictual one by nature, between the NGOs wanting to see some progress and the authorities that are moving slow, so in this regard they had to overcome some even mutual prejudices ... [T]he NGOs also saw how difficult it is to get consensus among the different institutions really to agree on something, so it was a learning process and the authorities saw that the NGOs are not unreasonable, just criticising, that they want to have a constructive part in the whole process.[48]

However, as corruption is a key element of EU accession, the EU Delegation heavily supervised the process. When it is an accession issue, the EU insists on civil society participation.[49]

The Ministry of Security remains hesitant on civil society engagement in relation to organised crime. There was uncertainty over what information was classified and how much could be shared with civil society.[50] The relationship with civil society and the Ministry of Security remains difficult. Civil society worked to create a relationship with the ministry as commentators. They have then fed into policymaking and become part of implementation. However, they are then less likely to criticise implementation. There is also a fluid relationship between the Ministry and civil society, with movement of staff between the two. Civil society wants to keep their funding and requires approval from the Ministry to continue to operate. As such, they require buy-in from the Ministry, which dilutes the capacity of civil society to criticise the Ministry.[51]

140 *Tensions in the nexus: Bosnia*

> Civil society is seen as a stepping-stone to state institutions. You get involved in civil society, you get to know the people, get to know the institutions that you [are] working with and ultimately get a big job in state institutions. Because that is seen as a secure job and something you can rely on, while civil society is something dependent on cyclical funding and short-term projects.[52]

EUPM attempted to encourage activism at the civil society level. For example, the head of EUPM, Stefan Feller, discussed corruption on a TV show filmed in front of a live audience that were mostly students.

> All the young people said, 'What are you going to do about corruption?' and Stefan said, 'Well, what are you going to do about corruption? This is your country, we're doing what we can.' So they formed a group, we invited them back to our building, gave them lunch, had an all-day conference where they all discussed it. 'Okay, what are you going to do about it?' And they came up with some suggestions and they formed the Jolly Ambassadors' Club.[53]

With EUPM's support and encouragement, the group launched a campaign to encourage citizens to take action on corruption through roundtable discussions, presentations and media events (EUPM 2012c).

While these relationships extended beyond law enforcement and a traditional security approach, they still aimed to further the security objectives of EUPM. There was no link with programmes that engage in development activities to address factors that contribute to organised crime. Several development actors have addressed weak governance in Bosnia. USAID engaged in a democracy and governance project that aimed to make government institutions more functional, transparent and accountable and focused on meeting the needs of citizens (USAID 2012). The programme aimed to enhance the effectiveness of judicial, executive and legislative branches of government and increase citizen participation in governance (USAID 2012). UNDP also addressed weak governance. 'The social inclusion and governance cluster assists BiH central, entity and local governments to achieve higher standards of governance effectiveness through better planning, budgeting, provision of public goods to citizens and accountability' (UNDP 2012). While these programmes didn't directly address organised crime, they engaged with some of the key contributing factors. However, there was no link between these strategies and the work of EUPM that directly responded to organised crime. Referring to the work of development actors, one EUPM official noted: 'we are aware of what they are doing when it impacts on what we do.'[54] As a result, these initiatives coexisted but they were not connected, limiting the integration of security and development.

The EU crisis-management structures further limited the shift away from a traditional security approach. The ministries of security and interior of EU member states were reluctant to second their personnel to international missions.

Tensions in the nexus: Bosnia 141

'No chief constable ... wants to send their best people away ... [N]o one wants to lose someone for a year, let alone two or three.'[55] Although officers deployed to an international mission develop many new skills, it is not valued as beneficial experience.[56] As a result, EUPM experienced a high turnover of staff. This affected the ability of the mission to base their initiatives within the local context.

All international engagement brings individuals that seek to model initiatives on programmes that have worked elsewhere, labelled by one respondent as ' "You know what works really well at home" trainers'.[57] However, there is often a concerted effort to engage with the local context. Short secondments make this difficult. 'The issues are so complex that you don't get a handle on them over-night, and you don't build relationships overnight.'[58] The result is reliance on predetermined objectives. For example, some EUPM officers were eager to initiate intelligence-based policing. However, this would be difficult in a country like Bosnia with 16 police bodies and limited coordination and trust between them.[59] The high turnover of staff also affected the mentoring approach of EUPM. 'We failed in the mentoring ... [M]ost of our seconded people stay for one year. In order to do mentoring you need to create interpersonal relationships. In one year you are unable, or if you are then you leave.'[60] While the approach of EUPM moved beyond a security framework, the structure remained linked to a traditional security approach.

Motivational tension

Prioritising organised crime

European security was clearly a driver behind the EU's response to organised crime in Bosnia. The ESS considers Europe a prime target for organised crime and lists it as one of the five key threats to the EU (EU 2003). The prioritisation of organised crime within the ESS suggests that external engagement focused on organised crime is designed to directly contribute to European security. The ESS goes further to state that 'restoring good government to the Balkans, fostering democracy and enabling authorities there to tackle organised crime is one of the most effective ways of dealing with organised crime within the EU' (EU 2003: 6). As a result, ensuring stability in Bosnia by addressing organised crime was driven by concerns over European security.

Self-interest also meant that some member states were more involved than others. Dwan (2003) notes that EUPM had a ready supply of organised crime experts as EU member states were eager to address trafficking and transnational crime that may affect them. Montanaro-Jankovski (2005) points out that Balkan organised-crime groups are particularly active and violent in Austria and the Netherlands, both countries which had police liaison officers in Bosnia that were directly engaged in initiatives to address organised crime. Many internationals referred to self-interest when explaining their presence in Bosnia. One EU member state noted that 'a country that close to our borders we want to be under

142 *Tensions in the nexus: Bosnia*

EU control'.[61] Another EU member state acknowledged that building the capacity of local police is 'partly self-servicing, getting the bad guys arrested before they leave the country'.[62] The presence of internationals seeking to further their own interests is summed up by an EUPM official: 'The UN Charter should say protection of civilians, but it won't because people are only willing to politically commit to things when they have an interest.'[63]

Disjuncture between international and local priorities

A disjuncture between international and local perspectives was evident in Bosnia. EUPM's focus on organised crime as the key issue for policing has been contested. Merlingen and Ostrauskaite (2005: 312) argue that the EU's estimations of organised crime are not accurate as they are 'as much based on speculation as on empirics'. Claims that organised crime is not a significant problem in Bosnia suggest that the EU is addressing issues of concern for European security rather than local security needs. Referring to EU approaches to the Western Balkans more broadly, Ryan (2009: 328) argues that 'the EU appears to be creating the impression of internal security, while merely engaging in technocratic modifications that affect control over the rims of these states'. Government representatives in Bosnia view the focus on organised crime as an international agenda. 'We've signed and ratified the Convention against Organised Crime, so we have certain obligations on this. Practically, though, the initiative came from [internationals].'[64] Some internationals perceive citizens to be more concerned by local-level criminality than organised crime as it affects them more directly.[65] However, a 2010 Gallup survey found that 66 per cent of respondents in the Federation and 46 per cent in Republika Srpska felt affected by organised crime 'in daily life' or 'occasionally' (Gallup 2010).

The difficulty with organised crime is that it is not always visible. An EUPM official noted that

> if you look at threat assessments for organised crime it's like a photographic negative. Where it looks like you have no problem, especially the smaller the area because the smaller places tend to be more corrupt anyway, it tends to be where the biggest problems are.[66]

As such, citizens may not be aware of the extent of the problem, which influences how they view the importance of initiatives to address organised crime. As outlined earlier, EUPM noted that 'any threat assessment of the Balkans will show Bosnia as a bit of not too bad, but that only represents a lack of information'.[67]

Organised crime can also remain hidden when local elites benefit, as they have an interest in keeping it hidden. In Bosnia, EUPM notes that there are 'a number of different high-level criminal organisations working with particular people in high-level political parties for their own good'.[68] The most prominent example is the alleged links between Nasser Kelmendi, a key organised crime

Tensions in the nexus: Bosnia 143

figure in the Western Balkans, and Fahrudin Radončić, owner of *Dveni Avaz* newspaper, head of the Union for a Better Future political party and, since 2012, Bosnia's Minister of Security (Hopkins 2012). As such, politicians and elites with beneficial ties to organised crime are reluctant to acknowledge or address organised crime networks. They are more likely to downplay the presence of organised crime so that it is not addressed.

EUPM's focus on organised crime in Bosnia emphasised the accession agenda. While this focus was based on the argument that organised crime is 'a major threat for Bosnia and Herzegovina's stability and overall socio-economic development' (Commission of the European Communities 2005: 20), its framing as a condition of EU membership points to a strategy to prevent organised crime entering the EU. Some observers perceive this approach as emerging from the rapid inclusion of several central Eastern European countries into the EU.

> I think the EU got a real wake-up call when they let Bulgaria and Romania in. That was pretty much a disaster for them and they're trying to avoid that in the future ... [A] tremendous amount of people took advantage of it.[69]

Once the borders of Eastern Europe opened after 1989, many criminal networks had already flocked to the region, aided by the visa-free regime that was in place throughout much of Eastern Europe (Hignett 2004; Glenny 2008). At the time these countries gained EU membership, many criminal networks were already well established despite attempts to address organised crime in the region.

As a result, there was a reluctance to allow a repeat with aspiring members from the Western Balkans. More stringent conditions regarding organised crime were implemented and the EU was more actively involved to ensure these conditions were fulfilled. As Ioannides and Collantes-Celador (2011: 416) argue, 'EU reforms in the area of freedom, security and justice aim at gradually transforming post-conflict societies into democratic and rule of law abiding states, but also enable the EU to achieve its own internal security objectives.' By framing responses to organised crime as a condition of accession, the EU also had the ability to turn EU priorities into local priorities. An EU official noted that 'the requirement from an accession perspective for us should be the same as the interests of the local actors if they have an accession agenda'.[70] While this approach seeks to impart local ownership for reforms related to organised crime, it wasn't based on local needs.

The inclusion of development

Bosnia has had much less development engagement than Sierra Leone. It is not a developing country and the political system prior to conflict was not open to external assistance. However, development tools were still brought in to EUPM's approach to organised crime. As in Sierra Leone, capacity building was a key aspect of EUPM's programming. Working in partnership with local law enforcement on specific cases, EUPM conducted a needs analysis to identify

144 *Tensions in the nexus: Bosnia*

gaps in capabilities.[71] The aim was 'to assist in building an increased ability to plan and implement measures that are designed to fight organised crime' (EUPM 2010b: 2).

As well as ensuring the long-term capability to address organised crime, building capacity in relation to organised crime also increased the capacity of law enforcement more broadly.

> Looking at it from a technical point of view, if you are able to conduct an investigation into organised crime, which is one of the most complex, then you are capable any other kind of investigation. So from that point of view we were working on organised crime. Organised crime also has particular rules, you also have to do some financial investigations on members and so on, so it's a huge range and if you can do that you're capable of many things.[72]

By using investigations into organised crime to build the capacity of law enforcement, agencies were becoming equipped to address most challenges they are likely to face.

While capacity building draws on the experiences and practices of development, in this context the limited focus on law enforcement suggests that it is mobilised for security purposes. EUPM defines capacity as the 'increased ability to plan and implement measures that are designed to fight organised crime and corruption within corruption resistant organisational structures' (EUPM 2010c: 1). Building capacity also has specific success indicators, such as implementing national strategies on organised crime and corruption, developing action plans, and developing mechanisms to identify, address and prevent corruption (EUPM 2010b). Capacity building in this context is significantly different from its use in development programming.

Glenny (2008) notes that organised crime networks are usually several steps ahead of law enforcement. When law enforcement strategies are effective, it merely pushes organised crime groups in other directions. For example, in 2008 Bosnian smuggling networks had built private roads across the border near Foča and Trebinje to facilitate smuggling (OCCRP 2008). Similarly, Cockayne (2011) argues that cocaine trafficking in West Africa increased as production and trafficking in Central America and the Caribbean came under scrutiny. As such, measures that address the symptoms of organised crime by enhancing the capacity of law enforcement are unlikely to deter individuals from engaging in organised crime.

While development elements were brought into initiatives to address organised crime, development was 'second fiddle'.[73] This supports the assumption that international security concerns are the primary motivational driver of external actors addressing organised crime in Bosnia. As a result, development was employed as an extension of security practices. Other areas of development that would contribute to initiatives to address organised crime – such as attempts to address weak governance but also strategies aimed to increase employment and create sustainable livelihoods – were not included. These strategies would make criminal activity less viable and provide citizens with other options.

Notes

1 Interview, Sarajevo, March 2012.
2 Interview, Sarajevo, October 2011.
3 This issue will be examined in more detail in the following section on causal tension, which analyses the linkages between security and development.
4 Interview, Sarajevo, October 2011.
5 Interview, Sarajevo, March 2012.
6 Interview, Sarajevo, October 2011.
7 Interview, Sarajevo, October 2011.
8 Interview, Sarajevo, October 2011.
9 Interview, Sarajevo, March 2012.
10 Interview, Sarajevo, March 2012.
11 Interview, Sarajevo, March 2012.
12 Interview, Sarajevo, March 2012.
13 Interview, Sarajevo, October 2011.
14 Interview, Sarajevo, March 2012.
15 Interview, Sarajevo, March 2012.
16 Interview, Sarajevo, March 2012.
17 Interview, Sarajevo, March 2012.
18 Interview, Sarajevo, March 2012.
19 Interview, Sarajevo, March 2012. See also Flessenkemper (2013).
20 Interview, Sarajevo, March 2012.
21 Interview, Sarajevo, March 2012.
22 Interview, Sarajevo, March 2012.
23 Interview, Sarajevo, March 2012.
24 Interview, Sarajevo, March 2012.
25 Interview, Sarajevo, March 2012.
26 Interview, Sarajevo, March 2012.
27 Interview, Sarajevo, March 2012.
28 Interview, Sarajevo, March 2012.
29 Interview, Sarajevo, March 2012.
30 Interview, Sarajevo, March 2012.
31 Interview, Sarajevo, March 2012.
32 Interview, Sarajevo, March 2012.
33 Interview, Sarajevo, March 2012.
34 Interview, Sarajevo, March 2012.
35 Interview, Sarajevo, March 2012.
36 Interview, Sarajevo, March 2012.
37 Interview, Sarajevo, March 2012.
38 Interview, Sarajevo, March 2012.
39 Interview, Sarajevo, March 2012.
40 Interview, Sarajevo, March 2012.
41 Interview, Sarajevo, March 2012.
42 Interview, Sarajevo, March 2012.
43 Interview, Sarajevo, March 2012.
44 Interview, Sarajevo, March 2012.
45 Interview, Sarajevo, March 2012.
46 Interview, Sarajevo, March 2012.
47 Interview, Sarajevo, March 2012.
48 Interview, Sarajevo, March 2012.
49 Interview, Sarajevo, March 2012.
50 Interview, Sarajevo, March 2012.
51 Interview, Sarajevo, March 2012.

146 *Tensions in the nexus: Bosnia*

52 Interview, Sarajevo, October 2011.
53 Interview, Sarajevo, March 2012.
54 Interview, Sarajevo, March 2012.
55 Interview, Sarajevo, March 2012.
56 Interview, Sarajevo, March 2012.
57 Interview, Sarajevo, March 2012.
58 Interview, Sarajevo, March 2012.
59 Interview, Sarajevo, March 2012.
60 Interview, Sarajevo, March 2012.
61 Interview, Sarajevo, March 2012.
62 Interview, Sarajevo, March 2012.
63 Interview, Sarajevo, March 2012.
64 Interview, Sarajevo, March 2012.
65 Interview, Sarajevo, March 2012.
66 Interview, Sarajevo, March 2012.
67 Interview, Sarajevo, March 2012.
68 Interview, Sarajevo, March 2012.
69 Interview, Sarajevo, March 2012.
70 Interview, Sarajevo, March 2012.
71 Interview, Sarajevo, March 2012.
72 Interview, Sarajevo, March 2012.
73 Interview, Sarajevo, October 2011.

References

Clausewitz, Carl von (1832). *On War.* Princeton, NJ, Princeton University Press.

Cockayne, James (2011). *State Fragility, Organised Crime and Peacebuilding: Towards a More Strategic Approach.* Oslo, NOREF.

Commission of the European Communities (2005). *2005 Enlargement Strategy Paper.* Brussels, Commission of the European Communities.

Commission of the European Communities (2009). *Bosnia and Herzegovina 2009 Progress Report.* Brussels, Commission of the European Communities.

Council of the European Union (2004). *European Security Strategy: Bosnia and Herzegovina/Comprehensive Policy.* Brussels, Council of the European Union.

Derks, Maria and Sylvia More (2009). *The European Union and Internal Challenges for Effectively Supporting Security Sector Reform: An Overview of the EU's Set-Up for SSR Support anno Spring 2009.* The Hague, Clingendael Institute.

Dwan, Renata (2003). 'Capabilties in the Civilian Field', *European Union Security Strategy: Coherence and Capabilities Seminar.* Swedish Institute for International Affairs.

Emerson, Michael and Eva Gross (eds) (2007). *Evaluating the EU's Crisis Missions in the Balkans.* Brussels, Centre for European Policy Studies.

EPLO (European Peacebuilding Liaison Office) (2012). *Common Foreign and Security Policy Structures and Instruments after the Entry into Force of the Lisbon Treaty.* Brussels, EPLO.

EU (1992). *Treaty of Maastricht on European Union.* Maastricht, EU.

EU (2003). *A Secure Europe in a Better World: European Security Strategy.* Brussels, EU.

EU (2005). *The European Consensus on Development.* Brussels, EU.

EU (2007). *Council Conclusions on Security and Development: 2831st External Relations Council Meeting 19–20 November 2007.* Brussels, EU.

EU (2008). *Report on the Implementation of the European Security Strategy: Providing Security in a Changing World.* Brussels, EU.

EU (2010). *Treaty on the Functioning of the European Union.* Brussels, EU.

EUPM (European Union Police Mission) (2010a). *EUPM Joint Vision 2010/11.* Sarajevo, EUPM.

EUPM (European Union Police Mission) (2010b). *EUPM Mission Implementation Plan 2010.* Sarajevo, EUPM.

EUPM (European Union Police Mission) (2010c). *EUPM Strategic Objectives 2010/11.* Sarajevo, EUPM.

EUPM (European Union Police Mission) (2012a). 'Mandate', www.eupm.org/Our Mandate.aspx accessed 19 December 2012.

EUPM (European Union Police Mission) (2012b). ' "Genuine Partnership is the Key to Success": Reflections on a Decade of EUPM with Head of Mission Stefan Feller', *Mission Magazine* 95: 3–5.

EUPM (European Union Police Mission) (2012c). 'Fighting Corruption Begins with Me! Veseli Ambasadori', www.eupm.org/Detail.aspx?ID=46&TabID=8 accessed 15 February 2013.

European Commission (2010). *Bosnia and Herzegovina 2010 Progress Report.* Brussels, European Commission.

European Commission (2011). *Bosnia and Herzegovina 2011 Progress Report.* Brussels, European Commission.

European Commission (2012). *Bosnia and Herzegovina 2012 Progress Report.* Brussels, European Commission.

European Council (1993). *Presidency Conclusions: Copenhagen European Council 21–22 June 1993, Relations with the Countries of Central and Eastern Europe.* Copenhagen, European Council.

European Council (1999). *Presidency Conclusions, Cologne European Council, 3 and 4 June 1999.* Cologne, European Council.

European Council (2004). *Declaration of EU Chiefs of Police following the Meeting on Police Aspects in the ESDP Framework.* Warnsveld, Netherlands, European Council.

Flessenkemper, Tobias (2013). 'Lessons from Staffing and Equipping EUPM. Learning by Doing?' in Tobias Flessenkemper and Damien Helly (eds), *Ten Years After: Lessons from the EUPM in Bosnia and Herzegovina 2002–2012.* Paris, EU Institute for Security Studies.

Gallup (2010). *Balkan Monitor: Summary of Findings: Insights and Perceptions: Voices of the Balkans.* Brussels, Gallup.

Glenny, Misha (2008). *McMafia: A Journey through the Global Criminal Underworld.* New York, Alfred A. Knopf.

Gourlay, Catriona (2004). 'European Union Procedures and Resources for Crisis Management', *International Peacekeeping* 11(3): 404–21.

Hansen, Annika S. (2004). 'Security and Defence: The EU Police Mission in Bosnia-Herzegovina', in Walter Carlsnaes, Helene Sjursen and Brian White (eds), *Contemporary European Foreign Policy.* London, Sage.

Helly, Damien (2013). 'EUPM@10: Lessons for the EU's External Action, CSDP and CFSP', in Tobias Flessenkemper and Damien Helly (eds), *Ten Years After: Lessons from the EUPM in Bosnia and Herzegovina 2002–2012.* Paris, EU Institute for Security Studies.

Hignett, Kelly (2004). 'Organised Crime in East Central Europe: The Czech Republic, Hungary and Poland', *Global Crime* 6(1): 70–83.

148 *Tensions in the nexus: Bosnia*

Hopkins, Valerie (2012). 'US Blacklists Balkan Businessman Naser Kelmendi', www.reportingproject.net/occrp/index.php/en/ccwatch/cc-watch-indepth/1539-us-blacklists-balkan-businessman-naser-kelmendi accessed 12 August 2012.

House of Lords (2008). *The Treaty of Lisbon: An Impact Assessment.* London, The Stationery Office.

Ioannides, Isabelle and Gemma Collantes-Celador (2011). 'The Internal–External Security Nexus and EU Police/Rule of Law Missions in the Western Balkans', *Conflict, Security & Development* 11(4): 415–45.

Juncos, Ana E. (2007). 'Police Mission in Bosnia and Herzegovina', in Michael Emerson and Eva Gross (eds), *Evaluating the EU's Crisis Missions in the Balkans.* Brussels, Centre for European Policy Studies.

Matthiessen, Michael (2013). 'The Institutional Genesis of the EUPM', in Tobias Flessenkemper and Damien Helly (eds), *Ten Years After: Lessons from the EUPM in Bosnia and Herzegovina 2002–2012.* Paris, EU Institute for Security Studies.

Merket, Hans (2012). 'The European External Action Service and the Nexus between CFSP/CSDP and Development Cooperation', *European Foreign Affairs Review* 17(4): 625–52.

Merlingen, Michael and Rasa Ostrauskaite (2005). 'Power/Knowledge in International Peacebuilding: The Case of the EU Police Mission in Bosnia', *Alternatives: Global, Local, Political* 30(3): 297–323.

Mix, Derek E. (2011). *The European Union: Foreign and Security Policy.* Washington DC, Congressional Research Service.

Montanaro-Jankovski, Lucia (2005). *Good Cops, Bad Mobs? EU Policies to Fight Transnational Organised Crime in the Western Balkans.* Brussels, European Policy Centre.

OCCRP (Organised Crime and Corruption Reporting Project) (2008). 'Smuggling in Bosnia', www.reportingproject.net/occrp/index.php/en/projects/tobacco-project/32-bosnia-and-herzegovina/60-smuggling-in-bosnia accessed 20 August 2013.

Osland, Kari M (2004). 'The EU Police Mission in Bosnia and Herzegovina', *International Peacekeeping* 11(3): 544–60.

Osmanović-Vukelić, Sanela (2012). *10 Years of EU Police Mission in Bosnia and Herzegovina: The Story of the EU Police Mission in Bosnia and Herzegovina.* Sarajevo, EUPM.

Penska, Susan (2008). 'Lessons Identified from BiH: Strategies for Developing Domestic Reform Agendas', Andreja Dolnicar Jeraj, Ivana Bostjancic Pulko and Tobias Flessenkemper (eds), *Seminar on Police Reform in Bosnia and Herzegovina: Security Sector Reform and the Stabilisation and Association Process.* Sarajevo, Centre for a European Perspective.

Prism Research (2012). *EUPM Public Opinion Research 2011.* Sarajevo, Prism Research.

Ryan, B. J. (2009). 'The EU's Emergent Security-first Agenda: Securing Albania and Montenegro', *Security Dialogue* 40(3): 311–31.

Ryan, Barry (2011). *Statebuilding and Police Reform: The Freedom of Security.* Abingdon; New York, Routledge.

Schroeder, Ursula (2007). 'Governance of EU Crisis Management', in Michael Emerson and Eva Gross (eds), *Evaluating the EU's Crisis Missions in the Balkans.* Brussels, Centre for European Policy Studies.

Schroeder, Ursula (2009). 'Strategy by Stealth? The Development of EU Internal and External Security Strategies', *Perspectives on European Politics and Society* 10(4): 486–505.

Sjolinder, Henrik (2010). *Fighting Organised Crime in the EU: A New Era with the Lisbon Treaty and the Stockholm Programme.* Stockholm, Institute for Security and Development Policy.

UN Security Council (2004). *Report of the Secretary-General and High Representative for the Common Foreign and Security Policy of the European Union on the Activities of the European Union Police Mission in Bosnia and Herzegovina Covering the Period from 1 January to 30 June 2004.* S/2004/709. New York, UN Security Council.

UNDP (UN Development Programme) (2012). 'Bosnia and Herzegovina: Democratic Governance', www.undp.ba/index.aspx?PID=25&RID=27 accessed 3 March 2013.

USAID (US Agency for International Development) (2012). *Country Development Cooperation Strategy for Bosnia and Herzegovina 2012–2016.* Washington DC, USAID.

World Bank (2004). *Bosnia and Herzegovina: Post-Conflict Reconstruction and the Transition to a Market Economy.* Washington DC, World Bank.

Youngs, Richard (2007). *Fusing Security and Development: Just Another Euro-Platitude.* Centre for European Policy Studies. Brussels.

Youngs, Richard and Fernanda Faria (2010). *European Conflict Resolution Policies: Truncated Peace-Building.* Fride. Madrid.

6 Inhibiting integration?

External actors addressing organised crime in Sierra Leone and Bosnia have recognised that a comprehensive approach that integrates security and development is necessary. In Sierra Leone it was recognised that organised crime was a threat to security and development, but also that poverty, weak institutions and youth unemployment were key contributing factors to the presence of organised crime. In Bosnia, organised crime was viewed as an impediment to development, and corruption and weak governance were understood as barriers in addressing organised crime.

The recognition of the benefits of an integrated approach is part of a broader trend in post-conflict reconstruction. Building on the lessons and challenges of the post-Cold War interventionist phase, external actors engaged in post-conflict reconstruction have acknowledged the need for comprehensive approaches that engage with the diverse challenges that arise in the post-conflict period. In particular, the connections between security and development have been recognised. In response, external actors have drawn on traditionally separate epistemological approaches, and created new tools and policies to inform their engagement with post-conflict reconstruction. The integration of security and development is expected to result in a comprehensive approach. Such an approach is understood by external actors to be more sustainable as it engages with the full range of challenges in a balanced way but also seeks to achieve local 'buy in' as it shifts away from a focus on the state to engage with the needs of individuals and communities.

While security and development have been enthusiastically merged in policy, integrating the two areas into a nexus in practice raises a number of challenges. The adoption of the security–development nexus to frame initiatives to address organised crime in Sierra Leone and Bosnia has resulted in a shift in approach. However, it does not equate to an emancipatory approach as defined by human security. The gap between policy and practice in relation to the security–development nexus has been the focus of critical scholars who argue that the nexus is one sided, resulting in the securitisation of development. While this may reflect the outcome of the security–development nexus, it does little to elucidate what inhibits the integration of security and development into a nexus.

By investigating the tensions in the two different case studies, the analysis aimed to identify contextual factors that may influence the integration of security and development.

Tensions in the security–development nexus

Conceptual tension

The first tension arises from the varied understandings of security and development. The integration of security and development into a nexus that results in emancipation relies on understandings of the two concepts that fit within Quadrant C of Figure 2.1 – human security/human development. Yet it is evident that there is no clear understanding of the security–development nexus among actors adopting the concept, as external actors have different understandings of security and development. Although security and development have become closely related through parallel shifts towards human security and human development, the concepts remain highly ambiguous. How external actors understand security and development is rarely articulated directly.

The two cases represent different approaches to organised crime: Sierra Leone was a multi-agency initiative, whereas EUPM was the primary actor addressing organised crime in Bosnia. The Sierra Leone case highlights the difficulties of collaborating under the security–development nexus framework. ECOWAS created the documents that served as the foundation for the WACI. Despite inconsistency between the ECOWAS Commission and member states, there was a shift towards Quadrant A: Top-down benevolence in the ECOWAS understanding of both security and development. However, ECOWAS's understanding of security and development differed from that of UNODC and UNIPSIL. Although security and development had different loci, they were both focused on the state/international level as the referent object. As UNODC and UNIPSIL sought to operationalise the regional action plan on drug trafficking and organised crime, the different understandings of security and development suggest that implementation of the WACI is significantly different from the aims of the ECOWAS Commission in drafting the regional action plan. While ECOWAS aims to move towards people-centred understandings of security and development, UNODC and UNIPSIL's understandings of security and development moved implementation in the other direction, adhering closely to a traditional security approach.

Bosnia provides a different insight. As initiatives to address organised crime were driven by a single actor, the EU, there is an expectation that understandings of security and development will be more consistent. Despite a strong EU policy on the security–development nexus, this was not the case in practice. There were varying understandings of security, both on the ground and in EU policy. There was a lack of clarity on how development contributes to initiatives to address organised crime. As a result, there were different perspectives on the referent object of development. Although EUPM is a cross-pillar instrument of the EU,

152 *Inhibiting integration?*

tension remains in how security and development are understood. With diverse understandings of security and development in two significantly different contexts, it can be implied that consistent understandings of security and development among actors addressing organised crime is rare. The number of actors – whether one or several – does not appear to affect the consistency of how security and development understood.

These different understandings ensure that there is no clear understanding of what the security–development nexus is, with implications for the type of nexus that emerges. Different understandings of security and development ensure that the nexus cannot be defined as adhering to a traditional security approach, nor as shifting towards emancipation, as there are is no consistency across the external actors addressing organised crime. The ECOWAS Commission seeks a shift towards people's security and EUPM personnel acknowledged the need for individual security. However, understandings of security overwhelmingly fit within Quadrant B: Hard security. With its focus on hard security measures implemented at the state level, and a referent object focused on international and state security, Quadrant B adheres to a traditional security approach rather than a new approach that engages with emancipation as defined by human security.

The integration of security and development into a comprehensive approach requires collaboration across the two areas. However, the approach is not balanced, as development is understood in relation to security. In Sierra Leone, external actors implemented a range of development strategies at the community level, including drug demand-reduction, treatment, prevention and rehabilitation. These initiatives address the impact that organised crime has on individuals and communities. Similarly, the focus on good governance, rule of law and human rights strategies in Bosnia adds a new dimension to initiatives to address organised crime. Rather than seeking to address the immediate threat of organised crime, the focus is on strategies to achieve long-term sustainable change by drawing on the tools and strategies of development. However, these elements were secondary to security concerns.

In Sierra Leone, UNODC and UNIPSIL's understanding of development fits within Quadrant D: Containment. Although strategies were implemented at the local level, they do not seek to address individual and community insecurity. Drug demand-reduction, treatment, prevention and rehabilitation seek to neutralise the threat drug use poses to the state as it can have a destabilising effect that has implications for international security. Working to contain the impact of organised crime at the local level seeks to limit the spill over of organised crime both regionally and internationally. From this perspective, development is understood to be secondary to security concerns rather than an equally important element. This does indicate a degree of comprehensiveness, as development is recognised as an important factor. However, development is brought in to enhance security outcomes.

A similar form of integration occurred in Bosnia. Although the focus on good governance, social and political reform, corruption, rule of law and human rights in Bosnia sought to address the effect of organised crime on individuals, these strategies were also designed to bolster the state to limit threats to international security. The European Security Strategy understands these strategies as 'the best means of strengthening international order' (EU 2003: 10). As such, security took precedence over development.

Rather than following the trajectory towards emancipation, understandings of security in the two case studies are aligned with traditional security approaches as the focus is on state and international security. This affects the integration of security and development as the urgency of security concerns ensures that understandings of development are shaped by security needs. In both case studies, the use of development tools and strategies broadens the approach of external actors addressing organised crime, as they engage in long-term strategies rather than seeking to immediately neutralise threats. However, rather than being understood as an essential element of a comprehensive approach because of their contribution to the wellbeing of individuals and communities, development tools are deployed to achieve security outcomes.

The prioritisation of security influences the type of nexus that emerges. The use of the tools and strategies of development to achieve security outcomes will still have benefits for individuals and communities. However, when development is focused on international security, these benefits are a positive side effect or end result of external engagement. The inclusion of development is primarily designed to achieve state and international security. This points to the dominance of security within the security–development nexus. As a result, the conceptual tension contributes to an explanation of why the security–development nexus achieves the outcomes outlined by critics. With understandings of security centred on the state/international level as referent object, and with initiatives implemented at the state level, security is not people centred and the inclusion of development initiatives is further sidelined. As a result, the nexus adheres to a traditional security approach rather than shifting towards emancipation.

The way the security–development nexus is invoked in theory suggests that it is a fixed concept that easily merges security and development. However, there are divergent understandings of security and development that are not always compatible. These divergent understandings inhibit the integration of security and development into a nexus. As understandings of security continue to align with traditional security approaches, security is deemed to be the most important priority, with development goals – improving lives – given less priority. The inclusion of development does have benefits for individuals, though. However, this is far from a comprehensive approach that engages with the needs of both individuals and the state. As such, the conceptual tension highlights how external actors can understand security and development in ways that inhibit the integration of security and development. The result of this kind of nexus aligns with the outcome of securitisation which features in critiques of the security–development nexus.

154 *Inhibiting integration?*

Causal tension

The second tension emerges from different perspectives on the causal relationship between security and development. Security and development are purported to be intrinsically linked in that there can be no security without development, and no development without security. However, the cause and effect between security and development is rarely defined.

An integrated security–development nexus that results in emancipation relies on the application of security and development as processes. However, among actors addressing organised crime in Sierra Leone and Bosnia there are different perspectives on how security and development are applied, whether they are processes or a desirable end state. The adoption of the security–development nexus has not changed how the application of security is viewed. As Luckham (2007) notes, security has traditionally referred to an existential goal. In the two case studies, security is universally regarded as a condition to be restored rather than a process. As this perspective maintains the traditional view of how security is applied, it suggests that security approaches are more rigid and less open to change, making it difficult to contribute to a nexus that integrates security and development into a comprehensive approach. It also suggests that security is a clearly understood condition, which negates a role for local engagement to determine what is most important and how it should be achieved.

The ambiguity of perceptions of development fits in with the broader lack of consensus on how development is applied within development policies. However, in this context it creates difficulties in defining a specific 'security–development nexus'. As the application of development is not clearly articulated by any of the actors addressing organised crime, it suggests that actors addressing organised crime are not familiar with development and there is no direct input by development actors. While there is variability among development actors in how development is applied, each actor has a clearly articulated approach. Among external actors addressing organised crime in Sierra Leone and Bosnia, the application of development is only vaguely defined in policy texts. This suggests that development is being implemented from a security perspective. Security actors are more likely to approach development in a similar way to security, considering it as a condition to be restored through their engagement rather than a strategy of social transformation.

The variability of how development is applied also raises the question of whether and how different applications can be combined into a nexus. With security understood as a condition and development as a process, this may imply that development processes seek to achieve conditions of security. As a process, development is expected to address organised crime, which will result in the end goal of security. The result would be a one-sided nexus that is preoccupied with security in line with the arguments on the securitisation of development. When both security and development are conceived as a condition or the end state, it implies the goal of the security–development nexus is to achieve both security and development. However, this type of goal does not necessarily require a strong linkage between the two concepts. Particular activities are seen to contribute to security and development conditions, but security and development strategies are not integrated.

Examining how external actors perceive the linkages between security and development adds another analytical layer to the application of development, and the causal relationship between security and development. Figure 6.1 sets out the spectrum of perspectives on the linkages between security and development. While some actors, such as ECOWAS, have recognised an integrated, mutually constitutive relationship between security and development, the majority of actors view the linkage as separate. This is primarily in the form of sequential linkage, where the attainment of security will create space for development. While this approach acknowledges the difficulty of achieving development advances in insecure environments, it neglects the role that development can play in enhancing security and addressing organised crime. Underdevelopment has been identified by all external actors as a conducive factor for organised crime. By not engaging with this aspect of organised crime, security practices continue to dominate the security–development nexus.

As security practices are understood to make space for development, development does not play a significant role in addressing organised crime. Rather than engaging with the factors that allow organised crime to flourish, initiatives

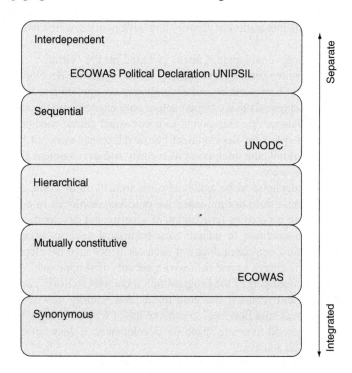

Figure 6.1 How external actors perceive the linkage between security and development.

156 *Inhibiting integration?*

continue to be reactive as they respond to incidents of crime. Similarly, by creating space for development, the end goal of external engagement is not redefined around the needs of individuals and communities, rather it continues to emphasise state and international security outcomes. Such an approach is based on the perspectives of external actors on how to address organised crime, not on local needs and priorities.

Viewing both security and development as the end state of external engagement implies that an integrated security and development approach is not necessary to address organised crime. For example, in the WACI Freetown Commitment, organised crime is understood as a threat to security and development. From this perspective, responding to organised crime does not require a joint response. Rather, it suggests that addressing organised crime will remove the threat to security and development. The end goal of initiatives to address organised crime has changed to respond to the threat to development *and* security. However, the processes implemented to address organised crime do not need to change. Traditionally, responses to organised crime have involved law-enforcement, military and policing strategies. As long as these strategies effectively address organised crime, they create space for development which will be implemented later. As a result, many external actors do not view the security–development nexus as a new approach. As one EUPM official noted '[T]here are these new words for old things,... as it wasn't done before?'[1] However, this perspective undermines the integration of security and development, as the two concepts remain separate.

In theory, the security–development nexus is based on the 'virtuous' cycle, where development ensures security and security creates space for development. However, the analysis of how security and development are applied and how the linkages are understood reveals that external actors only engage with the second part of this dyadic relationship. This points to a one-sided causal relationship, where security creates space for development but development does not play a significant role. This inhibits the integration of security and development as they are understood to be separate.

Development is understood to be achieved once security is in place. As an end product, development does not influence the practices employed to address organised crime as there is no cross-fertilisation of security and development. As a result, the practices continue to adhere to a traditional security approach. However, a 'security first' approach does not necessarily enhance development. The SSR programme in Sierra Leone followed a security-first approach. At the end of the security-focused part of the programme, 'there was security, but there was no development, and whilst it was true to say that security now required development, no one was sure how best to achieve this' (White 2008: 2). While security may be understood to create space for development, it does not ensure that development will be achieved.

The causal tension influences the form of the integration between security and development. Perspectives on how security and development are applied affect what is integrated with what. How external actors understand the linkage between security and development affects the balance between the two concepts and how they come together. In both Sierra Leone and Bosnia, security and development are separate rather than integrated.

Institutional tension

The third tension arises from the institutional drivers of security and development actors. Traditionally security and development have had a different institutional architecture, they have had different understandings of problems and thus have had different approaches. While the adoption of the security–development nexus seeks to bring the two areas together, there is a risk that these institutional underpinnings will continue to influence the practices of external actors, affecting the extent of the integration between security and development.

The adoption of the security–development nexus by external actors addressing organised crime in Sierra Leone and Bosnia has resulted in significant changes in their practices. While some factors continue to adhere to the institutional underpinnings of security, other factors are more flexible, adopting elements of development. The two cases highlight that there is no consistency in which factors integrate security and development. In Sierra Leone, elements of development contributed, to a varying extent, to the language employed by the WACI, how organised crime is understood more broadly, the approach of the WACI, and the structure of UNIPSIL. In contrast, in Bosnia the language and structure of EUPM were closely aligned to a traditional security approach. However, development influenced the broader understanding of organised crime and EUPM's approach to problems.

These differences highlight the multi-layered institutional tension in the security–development nexus. Rather than integrating security and development in a consistent way, the institutional underpinnings result in an ad hoc and haphazard nexus. Traditionally, organised crime has been addressed by security actors. While development is brought into the security–development nexus, it is clear that security actors remain dominant as the contributors and donors of the external actors addressing organised crime in Sierra Leone and Bosnia primarily adhered to a traditional security approach. This ensured that the starting point of external actors in both Sierra Leone and Bosnia was informed by security. As a result, the inclusion of development into initiatives to address organised crime is through a security lens.

Development is implemented as it is understood by security actors. Such an approach does not take on the best practice of development as it does not understand the evolution behind current practices. For example, EUPM is dominated by security actors. From their perspective, development is viewed within the context of the accession agenda as it focused on economic development, market reforms and rule of law reform.[2] However, Youngs (2007: 13) points out that this approach has been heavily criticised by development organisations as it 'provides evidence that the security–development link is essentially about diverting poverty relief into support for Western strategic objectives in middle income states'.

158 *Inhibiting integration?*

Although the institutional tension arises from the dominance of security, development practice has still had an influence on security. In Sierra Leone, UNIPSIL regards local law-enforcement bodies as agents of change, empowering them to address organised crime and providing training to address any shortfalls in skills and experience. However, UNODC takes a different approach. Without a presence in the country, the inception of the WACI was not based on local knowledge and context. In Bosnia, EUPM worked in partnership with local law enforcement. As in Sierra Leone, this approach regarded local law enforcement as agents of change and empowered them to identify gaps in addressing organised crime. However, the hierarchical relationship between international and local actors valued international knowledge over local knowledge and experience.

In both cases, external actors have recognised a need for prevention. While the focus remains on coercive strategies, it is still a shift away from responding to the symptoms of organised crime. Rather than directly addressing organised crime and withdrawing, there is also an emphasis on capacity building to ensure the long-term capability of local law enforcement. This is a key area where the modalities of development are brought into initiatives to address organised crime in both Sierra Leone and Bosnia. UNIPSIL and EUPM aimed to build the capacity of local law enforcement as part of a long-term strategy. Eade (2007: 630) argues that capacity building 'is surely about enabling those on the margins to represent and defend their interests more effectively'. However, in Sierra Leone and Bosnia capacity building is being employed to ensure the ability to address and deter organised crime in the long term, an objective that adheres more to international objectives than local interests, particularly as organised crime is not viewed as the most pressing concern locally in either case. Development actors can also use capacity building in a way that is not emancipatory. However, in this context, the use of capacity building adheres to a traditional security approach as it seeks to ensure security at the state and international level.

The dominance of security in the institutional underpinnings of external actors suggests that a hierarchy exists within the three factors examined. This hierarchy is displayed in Figure 6.2. External actors have chosen to adopt the security–development nexus to frame their initiatives and they have taken steps to merge the two in their approach to organised crime. As such, in both case studies it is evident that development is influencing how external actors approach the problem of organised crime, including their structure. However, the next layer is more difficult. While development has been brought into the understanding of organised crime, in both cases the understanding remains underpinned by security thinking through a focus on coercive strategies. As such, this level is less malleable. Further up the hierarchy, the institutional architecture of external actors remains even more difficult. The European Commission influenced EUPM to a certain extent. However, the European Council and its security interests remained the dominant contributor. This hierarchy supports the argument that development is brought in through a security lens, as the higher levels remain security focused with development playing more of a role lower down the hierarchy, as long as it meets security needs.

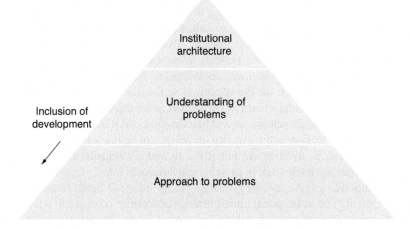

Figure 6.2 The influence of development on the institutional underpinnings.

The institutional underpinnings of security and development actors are difficult to overcome. Even in 'joined up' approaches, such as the links between DfID, MoD and FCO in the UK's Conflict Prevention Pools, each institution still maintained its own personality and mandate and delivered programmes in line with their traditional way of working (Kent 2007). Security and development actors remain two different institutional cultures trying to imitate each other. They can adopt the modalities of the other but. without the institutional memory and background, the meaning behind certain elements is lost and implementation becomes very different. While security and development actors may employ the tools of the other, the tools are implemented within their own frame of reference, limiting the extent of integration between the two concepts.

The ad hoc nature of the integration between security and development revealed by the institutional tension also has an unintended effect on external engagement more broadly. The lack of a clear and cohesive nexus has generated uncertainty among partners in both countries. Despite participating in the larger project to address organised crime implemented by EUPM and UNIPSIL, other actors instituted their own initiatives that overlapped. In some instances these initiatives employ another mix of security and development elements. For example, in Sierra Leone the FCO supported civil society through their small bilateral fund for initiatives to address security threats, notably drug trafficking and political violence, and to tackle corruption, promote democracy, human rights and consolidate the rule of law.[3] The US Bureau for International Narcotics and Law Enforcement Affairs (INL) has developed the West African Cooperative Security Initiative (WACSI) that involves many of the same elements of the WACI and is implemented across the region.

160 *Inhibiting integration?*

In Bosnia, many EU member states are addressing organised crime through their own police liaison officers.[4] One police liaison officer noted that there are 'a lot of countries pumping money in creating negative competition'.[5] In relation to EU engagement, an NGO noted a lack of cohesion as there are 'different police forces who are interested in different things'.[6] Even the European Community engaged in separate but overlapping projects. Flessenkemper (2013) highlights a number of overlapping programmes, including a European-funded project financed under the Instrument for Pre-accession Assistance (IPA) on corruption; and several projects on border management funded under the Community Assistance for Reconstruction, Development and Stabilisation (CARDS). This suggests that the institutional tension in the security–development nexus inspires a lack of confidence, resulting in overlapping initiatives to address organised crime that further undermines the integration of security and development.

The institutional tension creates problems in the interface between security and development. The institutional underpinnings of security continue to wield a strong influence over initiatives to address organised crime. As organised crime has traditionally been addressed by security actors, the institutional architecture of external actors addressing organised crime in Sierra Leone and Bosnia remains security focused, which limits the inclusion of development. Although development has influenced practices in some areas, security and development elements continue to 'speak past each other' (Spear and Williams 2012: 10). Development modalities are brought into initiatives to address organised crime through a security lens, to achieve security outcomes, without understanding the rationale behind them. As a result, the institutional tension influences the extent of integration.

Motivational tension

The final tension arises from the motivational drivers of external actors adopting the security–development nexus. The security–development nexus is expected to enhance the effectiveness and sustainability of international initiatives. This may be to enhance outcomes for individuals and communities or it may be driven by concerns over international security. The different motivations influence why security and development are being integrated and the prioritisation of each concept within the nexus.

Arguments on the securitisation of development argue that the adoption of the security–development nexus is driven by self-interest. The emphasis on self-interest is particularly relevant to initiatives to address organised crime, as organised crime is transnational by nature. This is evident in both Sierra Leone and Bosnia. Sierra Leone has attracted international attention as it is a transit point for cocaine being trafficked from Latin America to Europe. Bosnia has also become a concern for the EU and its member states due to its proximity to Europe's borders and aspirations for accession. While self-interest is one of the key motivational drivers of external engagement in both Sierra Leone and Bosnia, it is not necessarily a negative feature. By drawing on security and

Inhibiting integration? 161

development elements, the security–development nexus holds the promise to enhance security by improving lives.

Despite the potential for a mutually beneficial approach, in Sierra Leone and Bosnia the self-interest of external actors ensured that security is prioritised over development. In both cases the disjuncture between international and local priorities signified that international security concerns were the key priority. In Sierra Leone, this limited the focus on cannabis production, despite concerns over food security. In Bosnia, initiatives to address organised crime adhered to the accession agenda with little room for movement. In both cases, there was limited space for local input into what should be a priority. As a result, the approach is disconnected from local concerns, which tend to be focused more on development needs. The approach of external actors has shifted away from achieving a specific goal and withdrawing. However, with goals centred on international security, external actors may withdraw before issues such as unemployment and weak governance that contribute to organised crime are effectively addressed, as long as organised crime no longer poses a threat to international security.

Rather than resulting in a shift towards an emancipatory approach in Sierra Leone and Bosnia, the inclusion of development modalities such as capacity building and anti-drugs programmes seek to contain organised crime. As noted in the analysis of the conceptual tension, containment is associated with building capacity to address challenges locally, 'the capacity to positively or successfully adapt to external problems or threats' (Chandler 2012: 217). Containment suggests a people-centred approach, as it emphasises locally developed strategies to respond to problems and empowering individuals to take responsibility for security challenges. Such an approach links to Sen's (1999: xiii) arguments in *Development as Freedom*, which posit individuals as 'active agents of change, rather than passive recipients of dispensed benefits'. However, the focus is not on addressing problems in collaboration with local actors to minimise their impact. The aim is building local capacity to respond to ensure that organised crime does not spill over with consequences for regional and international security. As such, development is brought into initiatives to address organised crime to the extent that it contributes to international security outcomes. This approach is far removed from the core mandate of development actors.

The emphasis on international security outcomes does not prevent the integration of security and development. In actuality, such an approach would ensure security problems were addressed more sustainably with benefits for international security. However, international security concerns have maintained their grasp on international approaches to address organised crime. While external actors frame their engagement as 'enlightened self-interest', it is not enlightened at all. As noted in previous chapters, elements of development are utilised to enhance security outcomes. However, they are only employed superficially. As a result, in both cases, the motivational drivers of external actors influence why security and development are integrated. As international involvement is driven by concerns over international security, this ensures that security is prioritised, with development brought in only when it enhances security outcomes.

162 *Inhibiting integration?*

Factors limiting integration

While the security–development nexus may appear to equate to a comprehensive approach, security and development are not mutually complementary, as the nexus does not focus on development outcomes – improving lives. Analysis of the institutional tension highlighted that initiatives to address organised crime have a security perspective as their starting point. As such, development elements that are deemed important for security outcomes are brought into their approaches. However, the focus remains on security and continues to respond to the problem rather than taking a comprehensive and balanced approach to organised crime. The security focus is reinforced by the motivational tension which ensures that the drivers behind international engagement remain focused on international security needs. This arises from what Roe (2012: 254) refers to as 'panic politics: we must do something now, as our very survival is at stake.' The result is an attempt to contain organised crime in Sierra Leone and Bosnia before it affects donors, rather than directly resolving the problem. Such an approach neglects the contribution that development can make to achieve international security.

The investigation of the four hypothesised tensions revealed two overarching trends that inhibit the integration of security and development into a nexus. First, although the nexus is posited as a new and comprehensive approach, it continues to prioritise international concerns rather than the concerns of individuals and communities in post-conflict countries. Second, despite the enthusiasm of policymakers regarding an integrated approach, the security–development nexus is dominated by security actors. These factors point to a one-sided security–development nexus where security dominates.

Prioritising international concerns

The continued prioritisation of international concerns was highlighted most prominently by the motivational tension. By its nature organised crime is transnational, which creates a desire to address it at its source or in transit countries before it reaches donor countries. However, organised crime also has a negative effect on transit countries – from encouraging corruption to undermining legitimate business activities and, in the case of drug trafficking, increasing local consumption. As a result, addressing organised crime has benefits for both recipient and donor countries.

The interest of countries affected by organised crime at the end of the supply chain ensures that resources are devoted to addressing organised crime in source and transit countries. This explains the presence in Sierra Leone and Bosnia of external actors that are directly affected by organised crime flows. However, in both countries there is a disjuncture between international and local priorities. Organised crime is not viewed as the most pressing security concern in either Sierra Leone or Bosnia, and initiatives to address organised crime emphasise the elements that are most likely to affect donors. In Sierra Leone the cocaine trade was the key priority, despite the effect cannabis production and trade has on food security. In Bosnia, initiatives were closely tied to the accession agenda to ensure that the EU was not exposing its borders to traffickers. In neither case did initiatives address the conditions that make Sierra Leone and Bosnia conducive to organised crime, which would reduce the impact of organised crime on the two countries. Instead, initiatives responded to instances of crime, building capacity for interdictions, arrests and prosecutions. This approach attempts to contain the problem in Sierra Leone and Bosnia before it affects donors rather than addressing the impact of organised crime on post-conflict countries.

Analysis of the conceptual tensions also highlights this trend. ECOWAS's involvement in addressing organised crime in Sierra Leone represents an outlier as there is an attempt to adopt a people-centred approach to security. However, member states retained a focus on state security. For the two international actors – UNODC and UNIPSIL – concerns extended to international security. UNODC was concerned about Sierra Leone's capacity to maintain rule of law and sovereignty in the face of organised crime, which would threaten state stability with regional and international implications. UNIPSIL sought to build the capacity of Sierra Leone's security forces to prevent spill over to the regional and international level. This highlights the aim of external actors to contain organised crime before it poses a risk to international security. Similarly, in Bosnia, while EUPM officials aimed to enhance individual security, the policy of the mission was to strengthen state-level institutions to prevent organised crime crossing into the EU and negatively effecting EU security. As such, initiatives to address organised crime in Sierra Leone and Bosnia were driven by concerns over international security.

The continued prioritisation of international security concerns is also evident in the analysis of the causal tension. Through the security–development nexus, the application of security has remained unchanged. It is still understood as an end goal to be achieved through international involvement. While this end goal could focus on what security means locally, analysis of the conceptual tension revealed that security is primarily understood in terms of state and international security. As such, it can be implied that the end goal is the containment of organised crime to limit the threat it poses to international security.

Within this context, the expectation of a comprehensive approach seeks to link international security with local development. The linkages between security and development were often understood as sequential, where the attainment of security will create space for development. With security focused on the state and international level, this suggests that the security–development nexus is used to justify international self-interest, as addressing international security concerns will create space for local development. However, international security concerns remain the overarching priority.

Another common understanding of the relationship between security and development viewed organised crime as a threat to both security and development. From this perspective, if organised crime is addressed then security and development will improve. This perspective leaves limited space to engage with

164   *Inhibiting integration?*

local security and development concerns, and assumes that these issues will be easily achieved once organised crime is addressed. However, organised crime is rarely 'addressed'. Even European countries with effective law enforcement and rule of law continue to be affected by organised crime. In 2013, EUROPOL identified an estimated 3600 organised crime groups active in the EU (EUROPOL 2013). This suggests that local security and development are less important than preventing the spread of organised crime to donor countries.

The institutional tension also points to the prioritisation of international security concerns. In both cases, the contributors and donors to initiatives to address organised crime adhere to a traditional security approach. Although the European Commission provided funding for EUPM, there was limited contribution to decision making. The involvement of security actors suggests that international priorities will remain dominant. As Carrier and Klantschnig (2012) point out, UNODC's mandate is informed by the law enforcement priorities of its key donors. As such, initiatives to address organised crime in Sierra Leone and Bosnia were heavily influenced by the security concerns of contributors and donors.

Within policy, the security–development nexus is adopted on the basis that it will contribute to a new and comprehensive approach to post-conflict reconstruction. By adopting the security–development nexus as a framework to guide their initiatives, it can be expected that external actors will combine the security interests of donors with the needs of individuals and communities. However, investigation of the four tensions reveals that the interests of individuals and communities in post-conflict countries are relegated in favour of international security concerns.

The prominence of security actors

Although initiatives to address organised crime in Sierra Leone and Bosnia are implemented within the framework of the security–development nexus, they are primarily implemented by security actors. This was elucidated most clearly in the discussion on the institutional tension. In Sierra Leone, the contributors were the member states of ECOWAS as well as UNODC and UNIPSIL. All of these bodies are state-based actors that sought to address organised crime in response to the threat it posed to security. The personnel deployed to UNIPSIL to implement the WACI were primarily drawn from a law-enforcement background. As such, they sought to reinstitute security in Sierra Leone. In line with this, funding for the WACI came from donors concerned about the impact of organised crime on their own countries, either because it was a destination for organised crime or because the revenue from trafficking in Sierra Leone supported cartels that operated in their own territory.

While EUPM was a cross-pillar instrument, it was driven by the security priorities of the European Council as part of the EU's Common Foreign and Security Policy (CFSP). EUPM's operations were overseen by a number of security bodies, including the Political and Security Council (PSC), the Committee for

Inhibiting integration? 165

Civilian Aspects of Crisis Management (CIVCOM) and the Civilian Planning and Conduct Capability (CPCC). As in Sierra Leone, the majority of EUPM personnel were seconded from their national police force, and many were from military police forces which adhere more to militaristic strategies than their civilian counterparts. Although funding was derived from the European Commission, which is linked to EU development policy, the Commission did not have a significant influence on implementation. This highlights the security background of the external actors addressing organised crime in Sierra Leone and Bosnia. As a result, development is brought into the security–development nexus through a security lens.

The other tensions also point to the primacy of security actors. The divergent understandings of security and development arising from the conceptual tension suggest that development is understood through a security lens. In both cases, understandings of security adhered to 'hard security', with a focus on the state/ international level as referent object. While understandings of development shifted away from Quadrant B: Economic development, with its focus on the state/international level as referent object and programmes implemented at the state level, development was not understood in terms of human development. Security perspectives influenced how development was understood. In Sierra Leone, the focus on demand reduction, treatment and rehabilitation seeks to contain problems connected to drug trafficking to ensure state security. In Bosnia, while some elements of development focused on individual needs, it remained a top-down process and these initiatives were seen to contribute to enhanced security. With development focused on improving security rather than improving lives, it suggests that development has been skewed by the prominence of security actors.

The causal tension displays a similar trend. The ambiguity on how development is applied – whether an end goal or a process – suggests a lack of clarity on what development can bring. Considering development as an end goal places it in the same category as security. This arises as security actors understand development through their own frame of reference, rather than understanding development as a transformative process. However, it also means that the activities implemented to address organised crime do not need to change. As White (2008) noted in relation to SSR in Sierra Leone, though, this does not mean external actors know how to achieve development once security is in place. This issue is also raised by the understandings of the linkages between security and development. The majority of actors addressing organised crime in Sierra Leone and Bosnia acknowledge a sequential linkage, where the attainment of security will achieve development. As such, the benefits that development can bring are not recognised, suggesting a lack of familiarity with development.

The prominence of security actors is also evident in the analysis of the motivational tension. Development actors such as Denmark and Canada's development agencies, DANIDA and CIDA, have begun to recognise the role of development in addressing international security concerns. For example, the 2005 annual report of DANIDA states that 'development assistance is useful, if

166 *Inhibiting integration?*

necessary for our own security' (DANIDA 2005: 15). Similarly, CIDA acknowledged that 'the weakness of failed states makes them obvious breeding grounds for terrorist networks and organised crime, which can directly threaten the security of Canadians' (CIDA 2005: 13). However, in these examples addressing international security concerns is a benefit of existing development practices, rather than pointing to a need to adopt development strategies specifically to achieve security outcomes. In Sierra Leone and Bosnia, development is used to achieve security, with security the primary concern. This points to security actors as the driver behind initiatives to address organised crime.

The implementation of the security–development nexus by security actors further strengthens the prioritisation of international security concerns. However, it also ensures that development is implemented from a security perspective. This undermines the core focus of development on improving lives.

The securitisation of development?

While the prioritisation of international security actors and the prominence of security actors within the security–development nexus appears to support the arguments of critical peacebuilding scholars on the securitisation of development, the inclusion of development has still resulted in a shift in approach. In Sierra Leone, external actors have been encouraging a preventative focus on organised crime as enhancing law enforcement is believed to be a deterrent. This shifts away from a traditional, responsive security approach. However, it does not extend to addressing the factors that encourage organised crime, such as youth unemployment and weak governance.

In other areas of external engagement, the contribution of development has been embraced to a greater extent. There has been an emphasis on community engagement to gain a better understanding of organised crime, but also to raise awareness of the risks. UNIPSIL has implemented a drug-users programme. Rather than seeking to neutralise the threat directly, external actors have been building the capacity of local law enforcement. External actors in Bosnia have taken a similar approach, focusing on capacity building rather than direct engagement and seeking to prevent organised crime through law enforcement. EUPM has also included a focus on good governance and corruption, areas that begin to engage with the factors that allow organised crime to flourish.

These factors point to a shift away from a traditional security approach. There is a focus on long-term, sustainable outcomes; external actors have engaged with the local community; and there is an acknowledgement of the factors that encourage organised crime. However, because development is implemented through a security lens, it is always going to be skewed in favour of security needs. This was particularly evident in the analysis of the institutional tension, which highlighted the difficulty in moving away from the institutional underpinnings of security actors.

The implementation of the security–development nexus through a security lens appears to support the arguments on the securitisation of development, as

Inhibiting integration? 167

development is implemented to enhance security outcomes. However, proponents of the securitisation of development argument contend that development is being co-opted by security actors to further their own agenda. For example, Goodhand (2001a) noted fears that development would be driven by the political and strategic interests of the North. Similarly, Waddell (2006: 253) highlights how 'many in the development sector are concerned about a subordination of development to the West's domestically inspired security priorities'. These arguments derive from earlier attempts at integrating security and development, such as counter-insurgency strategies to 'win hearts and minds', where development tools were employed to directly support military objectives. This suggests that the use of development to enhance security is an explicit strategy.

In contrast, the adoption of the security–development nexus derives from the acknowledgement that a broader strategy is required to address the multifaceted challenges present in the post-conflict context. It also draws on the lessons of earlier attempts at post-conflict reconstruction, recognising the role of non-state actors in conflict and post-conflict agreements, the impact of violence on civilians, the role of inadequate state structures, and the neglect of human and social capital. In relation to organised crime, the focus shifts away from the security threat to its impact on public health, governance and the rule of law. This suggests a more sophisticated approach than the one-sided relationship outlined by critical peacebuilding scholars in the securitisation of development literature.

Tacit knowledge

While the focus of this research was on the epistemic knowledge of external actors addressing organised crime, their tacit knowledge was a key factor. Analysis of the four tensions reveals that, rather than the dominance of security being an explicit strategy, it derives from the tacit knowledge of external actors addressing organised crime. As Pouliot (2010: 12) argues, 'an essential dimension of practice is the result of inarticulate, practical knowledge that makes what is to be done appear self-evident or commonsensical'. However, there is disagreement on what constitutes tacit knowledge. Within critical security studies, the practice turn draws heavily from Bourdieu, who was interested in how practices emerge. For Bourdieu (1977), practices are derived from *habitus* – the internalised and informal subjective dispositions of actors – and *doxa* – the unquestioned beliefs of these actors. This implies that tacit knowledge exists and can be understood. However, other approaches to practice theory have criticised Bourdieu's approach. For example, De Certeau has focused on *metis*, which is learned action: 'a wide array of practical skills and acquired intelligence in responding to a constantly changing natural and human environment' (Scott 1998: 313). This highlights the changing nature of tacit knowledge: it is learned and evolving rather than just existing. This debate focuses on how tacit knowledge is formed and exists. However, both perspectives agree that tacit knowledge and presuppositions underpin activities. In the context of the security–development nexus, tacit knowledge informs the integration of security and development.

168 *Inhibiting integration?*

The prominence of security actors addressing organised crime suggests that their tacit knowledge informs the implementation of the security–development nexus. The four tensions support this notion. The conceptual tension revealed that understandings of security primarily adhere to a 'hard security' approach, through a focus on the state/international level as referent object. This understanding of security has a significant bearing on how development is understood and how it relates to security, as the urgency of security ensures that development is shaped by security needs. In both case studies, development tools and strategies broadened the approach of external actors addressing organised crime. Rather than immediately addressing threats, strategies became more long term. However, rather than being an essential element of an integrated approach, development tools are deployed to achieve security outcomes. In Sierra Leone, development was focused on the state/international level as referent object. In Bosnia, development was focused on individual and community needs. However, initiatives were implemented at the state level. This suggests that the understanding of development is influenced by the tacit knowledge of security actors as development is positioned in relation to security rather than aligning with human security.

The causal tension also revealed that the security–development nexus was influenced by the tacit knowledge of security actors. The application of security remained unchanged in both case studies: it is a condition to be restored. However, the application of development is ambiguous. In many cases it is understood in the same way as security, which suggests that security actors are applying their own frame of reference. However, in some instances development is understood as a process. With security as an end goal, this implies development is understood as a strategy to achieve security. In terms of linkages, the security–development nexus is primarily understood to create space for development. This also implies that the security–development nexus is driven by the tacit knowledge of security actors as the potential contribution development can make to organised crime is not realised.

Rather than integrating security and development in a consistent way, the institutional tension results in an ad hoc and haphazard nexus. Traditionally, organised crime has been addressed by security actors. While development is brought into the security–development nexus, it is clear that security actors remain dominant as the starting point of external actors addressing organised crime in Sierra Leone and Bosnia primarily adhered to a traditional security approach. As a result, the integration of development into initiatives to address organised crime is through a security lens. This means that development elements are brought in to initiatives to address organised crime as they are understood by security actors.

The motivational tension highlighted the self-interest of external actors addressing organised crime in Sierra Leone and Bosnia. This has the potential to ensure an integrated approach as it would contribute to better outcomes for international and local actors. However, the disjuncture of international and local priorities ensures that development is brought into initiatives to address organised

Inhibiting integration? 169

crime in order to achieve security outcomes. While this isn't exactly an example of tacit knowledge, as external actors do acknowledge their motivations, it still ensures that development is implemented superficially despite acknowledgement of its importance for effectively addressing organised crime.

As Salter (2013: 85) argues, 'fields have particular logics, specific rules of the game, that structure the competition over the form of economic, cultural, social or symbolic capital at stake'. The tacit knowledge that frames the practice of external actors ensures that development is brought into the security–development nexus through a security lens. This has implications for the integration of security and development. However, it is not a deliberate attempt to co-opt development to achieve security outcomes as suggested by the securitisation of development argument. Rather, development is removed from its evolution and best practices as development is implemented the way it is understood by security actors.

Use of tacit knowledge: capacity building

The tacit knowledge of security actors has a significant impact on how security and development come together. This was particularly evident in the use of capacity building as a development tool to address organised crime. Although adopted as a tool in both countries, the use of capacity building to address organised crime differed significantly from its use by development actors.

While it is often referred to as jargon or a fad in development practice, capacity building is an essential part of people-centred development. For Oxfam, 'strengthening people's capacity to determine their own values and priorities, and to act on these is the basis of development' (Eade 1997: 3). Oxfam takes the time to identify existing capacities and situates capacity building in the social, economic and political environment: 'understanding this environment is critical in order to understand who lacks what capacities, in any given context, why and why this matters' (Eade 1997: 3). In this setting, capacity building gives individuals the skills and knowledge to participate in decision making on how resources can be used to improve their lives in a way that is meaningful to them. As a result, capacity building contributes to emancipation – it is embedded in the local context, it relies on local knowledge, seeks to empower individuals, treats them as agents in the change process, and it is holistic, engaging with social, economic and political factors.

Within development practice, capacity building is interpreted and applied differently. Rather than being a people-centred approach, Eade (2007) notes that capacity building has also been employed as a top-down process, where development actors are focused on retaining power and view capacity building as a one-way transfer of knowledge. For instance, it is 'today commonly used to further a neo-liberal "pull-yourself-up-by-your-bootstraps" kind of economic and political agenda' (Eade 2007: 632). A top-down approach to capacity building depoliticises it and it then becomes technocratic, emphasising the techniques rather than the meaning behind them (Leal 2007: 544). This type of capacity

170 *Inhibiting integration?*

building undermines emancipation as 'genuine empowerment is about poor people seizing and constructing *popular power* through their own praxis. It is not handed down from the powerful to the powerless' (Leal 2007: 545).

The tacit knowledge of security actors has a similar effect. In both Sierra Leone and Bosnia, capacity building was employed by external actors addressing organised crime to enhance the capabilities of local law enforcement. The impetus was to ensure that both countries were equipped to respond and address organised crime to limit the spill over into donor countries. This concern over international security resulted in a top-down, instrumental approach to capacity building. The focus of the programmes was confined to the priorities of internationals. In neither country was organised crime viewed as the most pressing security concern by local actors. Although some internationals argue that this is based on a lack of knowledge, the continued belief that resources would be better used elsewhere means that there was no attempt to address this knowledge deficit. This further reinforces the focus on international priorities regardless of local concerns.

Accordingly, capacity building was limited to the bodies seen as relevant to achieve international priorities. In both cases capacity building focused on local law-enforcement agencies. Programmes have expanded to the criminal justice system in order to improve law-enforcement approaches. However, other bodies that may have a role to play in addressing organised crime, particularly bodies that are locally specific, with a contribution not immediately obvious to internationals, are excluded. While one EUPM official argued that improving capabilities to address organised crime ensures that law enforcement is better equipped to address other areas, the focus of local law enforcement was limited to the areas of concern to internationals. As highlighted in the analysis of the motivational tension, Sierra Leonean law enforcement had difficulty getting cannabis production on the agenda as internationals were primarily interested in addressing the cocaine trade.

This approach to capacity building highlights its instrumental nature. It is employed as a technical tool to achieve the goals of international actors. As a result, it has been stripped of the qualities that underpin it when employed as part of a people-centred approach to development. This undermines the emancipatory potential of capacity building. Local context and knowledge is subdued in favour of international priorities. Local actors are not empowered to contribute to the process. It is top-down, with external actors driving the agenda. Local law enforcement has had to fight for their concerns to be included. The approach is not holistic as it focuses narrowly on international concerns. This version of capacity building appears to support the argument on the securitisation of development, as the tools of development have been employed to further security objectives.

Rather than being a concerted attempt to co-opt the tools of development, this approach to capacity building and other development tools has arisen as security actors do not understand how the tool has emerged and evolved. Since its first emergence, people-centred development – of which capacity building is a core component – has changed significantly.

Inhibiting integration? 171

After two early attempts in the 1950s and 1980s, people-centred approaches became a key element of development in the mid-1990s.

> Critics of the top-down approach began to complain that many large-scale, centralised, government-initiated development programmes – from schooling to health to credit to irrigation systems – were performing poorly, while rapidly degrading common-pool resources and having significant negative environmental and poverty impacts.
>
> (Mansuri and Rao 2004: 28)

During this period, development actors were drawing on the work of radical thinkers that explored the potential of participation. In *Pedagogy of the Oppressed*, Friere (1970) called for 'dialogic' education that embraced diverse forms of knowledge. Chambers (1983) called for local involvement in decision making on how resources were used, with development actors playing a supporting role. Successful grassroots, locally driven projects were also coming to light, including the Self-Employed Women's Association in India, the Orangi Slum Improvement Project in Pakistan, and the Iringa Irrigation Project in Tanzania, displaying the potential of bottom-up programming (Krishna *et al.* 1997).

Coupled with the increased role of NGOs in development in the 1980s, these factors contributed to a third wave of people-centred development. Since then participatory approaches have become a key element of development. Mohan (2008: 46) argues that there is 'a growing acceptance regarding the importance of local involvement'. Similarly, Cornwall (2000) points out that participatory development has become a new orthodoxy. However, there have been numerous criticisms. For example, without empowerment participation is meaningless; participation creates cheap labour; communities are treated as homogenous; and it does not address the larger, global problems that contribute to underdevelopment (Cornwall 2000). While this is a very condensed summary of the evolution of people-centred approaches, it highlights that these approaches have been influenced by earlier failures, critical writing on the subject and grassroots projects. Despite flaws in each wave, there is a concerted attempt to continue to improve the approach based on the lessons learned.

Not all development actors engage with a people-centred approach, and those that do can still be flawed. However, the adoption of tools and modalities derived from people-centred approaches is more difficult for security actors. Security actors are not aware of the evolution of the people-centred approach or the lessons that inform current practice. As Spear and Williams (2012) note, 'specialists in each area sometimes see each other as possessing new and improved tools to adapt to tackle the problems they face without necessarily understanding the difficulties that need to be overcome or understanding the mixed records of each approach'. The dominance of security actors and the role of tacit knowledge in implementing the security–development nexus ensures that the lessons that have gradually improved the people-centred approach to development do not inform initiatives to address organised crime. This affects how the modalities

172 *Inhibiting integration?*

of development are put into practice. As a result, development is stripped of its emancipatory qualities and becomes focused on enhancing security objectives.

Engagement with development

The comparison of the implementation of the security–development nexus in Sierra Leone and Bosnia highlighted many similarities despite the different contexts of the two peacebuilding missions. Despite subtle differences among the four tensions, in both case studies all four had an influence on the integration of security and development. However, one key difference was the level of engagement with development among external actors addressing organised crime. In this sense, the external actors that participated in the WACI had a stronger focus on development than EUPM. Alongside the emphasis on law enforcement, the WACI included a drug-users programme, the institutional underpinnings of the WACI were further away from a traditional security approach, and there was an emphasis on community engagement within law enforcement.

In part, this arises from the actors involved in the programme. As highlighted in the analysis of the institutional tension, EUPM was staffed by police and in many cases military police, ensuring a strong emphasis on law enforcement. The WACI also had a strong police presence. However, the mandate of UNIPSIL extended to many areas with a development focus, whereas EUPM focused solely on SSR. UNODC also has a history of engaging in alternative development strategies, which indicates a shift away from a traditional security approach. The multi-agency engagement in the WACI also requires negotiations between the various actors on how to address organised crime. This suggests that factors that influence the implementation of security and development are specifically articulated. As such, UNODC and UNIPSIL have similar understandings of security and development. In contrast, within EUPM, because it is expected to be more consistent, the understanding of specific concepts is not directly articulated, resulting in significantly different interpretations.

The depth of engagement with development can also be attributed to how development is understood in each country. As Sierra Leone is a 'less developed country', there is a strong presence of development actors. There is also a long history of development engagement within the country, which means local communities have participated in development processes. Even law-enforcement agencies have worked closely with development actors as DfID managed the SSR process. As external actors in Sierra Leone have worked closely with local law enforcement, it is likely that these influences were filtered into initiatives to address organised crime. In contrast, Bosnia has little history with development engagement due to the political context. While some development actors have been active in the country since the war ended, development is often seen in a negative light as many local actors do not consider the country to be in need of development assistance.

These differences reveal that the level of engagement with development depends on the extent to which external actors are security focused and what

Inhibiting integration? 173

interaction exists with development actors and practices. However, even in Sierra Leone, where there has been much more interaction with development practice, security actors still dominate the security–development nexus and international security concerns remain the priority. As such, it is likely that the adoption of the security–development nexus to address organised crime in other cases will have the same result as long as security actors are driving the process, as engagement will be influenced by their tacit knowledge. While this appears to point to a failure in integrating security and development into a nexus, it actually points to the latent potential of the security–development nexus.

The latent potential of the security–development nexus

A key idea within the Welsh School of Critical Security Studies is the concept of unfulfilled potential, which is contained within immanent critique. Immanent critique was employed to analyse the four tensions as it compares the outcomes with the stated objectives – a comprehensive approach that integrates security and development. The analysis uncovered the factors that inhibit the integration of security and development, resulting in a rich and detailed explanation of why the security–development nexus results in the outcomes outlined by critics. However, the analysis also points to the latent potential of the security–development nexus as it is currently constituted.

Despite the barriers created by the prioritisation of international security concerns and the prominence of security actors, the adoption of the security–development nexus results in the beginnings of a shift away from a traditional security approach towards emancipation. In both cases, external actors have engaged in a range of activities that extend beyond a traditional security approach, from the drug-users programme to capacity building. However, as noted above, development is brought into initiatives to address organised crime through a security lens. The tacit knowledge of security actors ensures that development tools and modalities are removed from their people-centred, emancipatory nature.

For the security–development nexus to become less one sided, development actors need to play a more active role in addressing organised crime. Direct engagement of development actors would ensure that development concerns that create a conducive environment for organised crime, such as youth unemployment and corruption, receive more attention. It would also ensure that the needs of individuals and communities were addressed, rather than just international security concerns. The use of development practices would also remain consistent with their underlying principles such as local ownership, participation and empowerment.

When development actors have engaged with security issues it results in a significantly different approach that moves beyond traditional security approaches. DfID's approach to SSR in Sierra Leone was implemented in a 'security first' framework based on the understanding that an improved security sector would create space for development. Rather than just reforming the security sector, the programme included the creation of civil oversight bodies to

174 *Inhibiting integration?*

monitor the practices of the security sector, and the mandate of security forces was refocused on citizen security rather than state security (UK Government 2004). This represents a significant shift in how security issues are addressed. DfID's approach created space for local involvement and refocused the security sector on the needs of individuals and communities.

In Bosnia, UNDP engaged in security issues by creating community safety forums. Through their work at the local level, communities conveyed a desire for their security concerns to be integrated into municipal development plans and strategies.

> However, they didn't have means and they didn't have knowledge. What we gave them, we helped them to think strategically about risks and threats posed at the local level, and to give them an opportunity to discuss and decide what are the most appropriate actions to be taken and who is responsible. So what we have now at the level of the municipality, we have community safety forums, which are literally chaired by the mayor, but it also includes the police, the protection agency, it includes representatives of IDPs [internally displaced persons], women NGOs and centres for social welfare. So they sit around the table, they discuss issues and problems and so on and they discuss what would be the immediate, mid-term and long-term measures they need to undertake in terms of minimising.[7]

This adheres to an emancipatory approach as it engages with the local context and knowledge, and it empowers local actors and treats them as agents in the change process. It is also holistic, as

> what comes up as a risk and threat by the population is for instance the misuse of the local stadiums, and you have issues like floods, disaster prevention, interventions, and we have issues in quite a few municipalities of stray dogs. So there are a number of issues that they identify that do not necessarily fall under security; they require more integrated approaches.[8]

Despite the increased involvement of development actors on security issues, in particular SSR, there remains a reticence to engage with organised crime. As Cockayne (2011: 7) noted:

> a review of key development actors' guidance and assessment tools for peacebuilders ... reveals that not one of them includes indicators or assessment methodologies for mapping or analysing organised crime.... The new Rule of Law indicators developed by the UN Department of Peacekeeping Operations seek to take a comprehensive approach, but also exclude organised crime. The OECD [Organisation for Economic Co-operation and Development] DAC [Development Assistance Committee] has recognised that organised crime is a factor in peacebuilding, but has offered no comprehensive guidance on what to do about it.

Some progress has been made. USAID has produced a programming guide on drug trafficking in Africa (USAID 2013). DfID has commissioned research on what development can offer initiatives to address organised crime, resulting in the report *Getting Smart and Scaling Up: Responding to the Impact of Organised Crime on Governance in Developing Countries* (Kavanagh 2013). Yet there has been limited engagement in practice. One development professional noted that it has taken a long time to acknowledge the relationship between security and development and development actors are still not there. Organised crime is another step beyond: 'we're where we were 10 years ago with human security.'[9]

Development engagement with organised crime

The current reticence to engage with organised crime, but increasing recognition of the links between organised crime and development, has parallels to the growing involvement of development in conflict in the 1990s. As development actors began linking their initiatives to conflict, many scholars grappled with the emerging connections. Goodhand created a framework to map the contribution that development actors could make to conflict resolution and post-conflict reconstruction. 'Working *around* war' pointed to early development engagement with war, as development actors sought to avoid direct involvement but continued their activities where possible (Goodhand 2001b). Development actors 'working *in* war' acknowledged the relationship between development and conflict and sought to minimise their impact, but didn't seek to address war directly (Goodhand 2006a). The final category, 'working *on* war', was the most proactive approach and saw development actors directly engage in peacebuilding activities (Goodhand 2006b).

The current approach of development actors to organised crime has parallels to 'working around war', where conflict is an 'impediment or negative externality that is to be avoided' (Goodhand 2001b: 61). From this perspective, development was understood to automatically contribute to peace, which means nothing additional is required (Uvin 2002). Existing development programmes engage with the factors that encourage organised crime, such as corruption, poverty and unemployment. This suggests that development practice does not need to change to address organised crime, as it already is. However, this type of engagement neglects the power of organised crime to undercut advances achieved by development actors, particularly in relation to governance. While the impact of organised crime on development has been increasingly recognised, most notably by the World Bank's 2011 *World Development Report*, there has been little effort by development actors to directly engage with organised crime.

The dangers of this were highlighted by the crisis in Mali during 2012 and 2013. Mali has often been praised as a development success. During a visit to the country in 2010, UNDP director Helen Clark commended the country on its progress towards the Millennium Development Goals (MDGs) and democratic governance (UNDP 2010). While the transition from fragile state to democracy was considered a success in Mali, external actors

176 *Inhibiting integration?*

neglected to acknowledge that an independent source of resources in the sub region over the last decade has been the proceeds of drug trafficking. The continued failure to address the problem makes those behind the trafficking bolder and more aggressive in seizing new opportunities across a broader geographic area.

(Shaw 2012: 2)

As Lacher (2012: 1) noted:

up until Mali's military coup of March 2012, state complicity in organised crime was the main factor involved in AQIM's [Al-Qaeda in the Mahgreb's] growth and driver of conflict in the north of the country. Actors involved in organised crime currently wield decisive political and military influence in Northern Mali.

Even when discussions turned to rebuilding Mali's institutions and democratic elections, the involvement of organised crime remained a blind spot for all actors (Reitano and Shaw 2013). By not acknowledging the criminal factors in Mali, development actors perceived the country to be a development success with democratic governance in place. However, this ignored the penetration of organised crime, which undermined state institutions and the governance that development actors were so proud of.

Development actors can become more engaged with organised crime by becoming crime-sensitive. This has parallels with 'working in war', where development actors are conscious of the relationship between conflict and development and the potential impact their activities can have on conflict. 'Agencies working in areas of active violence have attempted to mitigate war-related risks and also to minimise the potential for programmes to fuel or prolong violence' (Goodhand 2006a: 264).

In relation to drug trafficking, USAID recognises that

development efforts could unintentionally foster drug trafficking by: (1) bolstering the power of those complicit in drug trafficking, (2) deincentivising opposition to drug trafficking, (3) facilitating the movement of drugs, and (4) facilitating money laundering.

(USAID 2013: 33)

Building the capacity of government structures inadvertently supports officials connected to crime; transparency measures discourage open opposition to crime; enhancements in trade and the transportation of development supplies provides new shipment opportunities for trafficking; new banking infrastructure and innovative small-scale banking mechanisms such as mobile banking provides money-laundering opportunities (USAID 2013).

Crime sensitivity also requires attention on the impact crime can have on development. For instance, criminal groups can siphon development resources

Inhibiting integration? 177

for their own purposes. Similarly, individuals are more open to the opportunities and services provided by organised crime when faced with few other options. 'While knowledge on the overarching impact of organised crime is still limited … under dire socio-economic conditions, people are more receptive to supporting, engaging in, or turning a blind eye to illicit activity' (Kavanagh 2013: 26). This can undermine development programmes. However, implicit support for organised crime can also have negative public health consequences and affect food security through the production of illegal crops. Natural resources exploitation has negative environmental consequences, the services providing by organised crime groups can undermine legitimate service provision by governments, and there are also cases where governments have supported organised crime to enhance their legitimacy on the basis of the services provided by criminal groups. While crime sensitivity minimises the unintended consequences of development that may foster organised crime, it does little to contribute to an integrated approach.

Goodhand's final category, 'working on war', outlines a role for development actors to become directly involved in preventing and resolving conflict. A parallel would be programmes that were directly focused on addressing organised crime. A study by the Centre of International Cooperation at New York University highlighted five core areas where development can engage with organised crime: protecting the political process; modernising and strengthening law enforcement and the judiciary; supporting crime-sensitive economic and social development; engaging civil society and the media; and deepening the knowledge base (Kavanagh 2013).

Combating corruption is a key area where development actors can address organised crime as it is an area where many development agencies are already active. In many countries, 'political and public sector corruption has allowed organised crime to develop or flourish, undermining the legitimacy of state institutions, and providing limited incentives for citizens not to engage in, or benefit from, organised crime' (Kavanagh 2013: 14). Particularly in post-conflict countries where state revenue is low, government representatives may find it difficult to resist funds offered by organised crime groups. Corruption also makes it difficult to address organised crime as state institutions are implicated. In Jamaica, DfID engaged in a police reform project improving equipment and conducting training. However, 'corruption within the system blocked reform as police were de facto accountable to criminal "dons"' (USAID 2013: 29). Even when law-enforcement agencies aren't directly implicated in organised crime, there is still reticence in pursuing senior figures that are. In Bosnia many prosecutors are fearful of addressing corruption.[10] As such, development initiatives focused on corruption make a significant contribution to addressing organised crime.

Development actors have already begun participating in, or even leading, security sector reform and judicial reform. However, in some instances enhancing the skills of law enforcement and the judiciary can have negative consequences, such as increased violence or corruption.

178 *Inhibiting integration?*

> Unless the mechanisms are in place, strengthened security can also lead to increases in violence, while a strengthened judiciary or empowered economic or financial crimes unit can actually lead to enhanced corruptibility and the use of organised crime-related intelligence tools for political or financial gain.
>
> (Kavanagh 2013: 24)

Effective civil-oversight bodies can monitor security and judicial bodies to ensure their power is restricted. This is often beyond the remit of security actors who focus on transmitting technical expertise, which creates a key role for development agencies in addressing organised crime.

As already noted, organised crime can provide lucrative income-generating opportunities. This is particularly prevalent in the post-conflict period when there may be few other opportunities and the state is unable to provide basic services. Referring to West Africa, Alemika (2013: 28) has recognised as a key factor in promoting organised crime the role of dysfunctional and unproductive economic systems that are unable to ensure social welfare, employment, goods and services, or good governance, rule of law and democracy. Kavanagh (2013: 26) reports how organised crime has taken advantage of the state's inability to deliver social services and promote socio-economic development, becoming providers of services and employment themselves, and in turn generating social capital and legitimacy. As such, there is a key role for development actors in providing alternative opportunities and basic services to undermine the lure of criminal entrepreneurs and undercut their legitimacy before criminal groups become an integral part of economic and governance structures. Shaw and Reitano (2013: 21) add that 'development initiatives need to be targeted at the groups that are vulnerable to being co-opted along the supply chain, with a focus on the root causes of gang membership and illicit activity'.

As development actors often have a close relationship with civil-society actors, they can also enhance community engagement with organised crime. This is not always forthcoming as there are fears of reprisals. In 2011, several bloggers were killed by drug cartels in Mexico for criticising the drug situation (Kavanagh 2013). However, with support, civil society and media reporting on organised crime can be an effective tool to address organised crime. Ralchev (2004: 329) identifies key areas where civil society can play a key role in the fight against organised crime, including: 'raising public awareness, informing the general public and influencing public attitudes; conducting research and analysis on issues inter-related with organised crime; and cooperating with state institutions in charge of combating organised crime'. Shaw and Reitano (2013) also recommend the creation of local democratic structures where people can express grievances to strengthen community responses to organised crime.

A final area where development actors can contribute is expanding the knowledge base. Official data on organised crime is often derived from statistics on arrests and seizures. However, this only provides a snapshot of organised crime. Through contact with civil society, development actors can gain a deeper

Inhibiting integration? 179

understanding of how organised crime operates, as well as local reactions to it, which can contribute to a stronger understanding of the nuances of organised crime in each context.

These elements highlight the programmatic contributions that development can make to initiatives to address organised crime. The involvement of development actors in this way points to a significantly different approach to organised crime that engages with the factors that make a country conducive to organised crime, the impact organised crime has on individuals and communities, and also factors that create insecurity, both locally and internationally. Alongside security elements that emphasise law-enforcement strategies, the engagement of development actors in programmes that directly respond to and address organised crime would contribute to a comprehensive approach that integrates security and development elements. However, many development practitioners consider this to be too significant a leap away from their core mandate.

The reluctance to address organised crime despite the recognition of the connection between security and development is similar to the reluctance to address conflict in 1990s. Development engagement with conflict was seen 'as part of a worrying trend in which development assistance is driven by political and strategic interests; in effect it becomes another policy tool through which the North projects its power and influence on the South' (Goodhand 2001a: 32). This is connected to the fear of the securitisation of development. Attempts to link development and organised crime raise the same concerns. As noted above, while the implementation of the security–development nexus appears to support the arguments on the securitisation of development, this is not a concerted attempt by security actors to co-opt development strategies to achieve their goals. Rather, because development tools and modalities are implemented through a security lens, they are influenced by the tacit knowledge of security actors. As a result, the 'humanising' effect of development is often removed, as highlighted by the use of capacity building.

As it stands, the adoption of the security–development nexus reveals a glimpse of emancipation as practices shift away from a traditional security approach. In Sierra Leone and Bosnia, external actors engage in a number of activities set out as potential development interventions in relation to organised crime. In Sierra Leone this includes raising awareness through the drug use programme, as well as the establishment of a hotline for citizens to report incidents of organised crime. In Bosnia, external actors strengthened the criminal justice system and aimed to address corruption. However, because these activities are implemented through a security lens, they were designed to contribute to international security objectives. As with capacity building, they are removed from the context of people-centred development. For example, the hotline established in Sierra Leone to receive individual complaints on organised crime was instituted by law enforcement to enhance their interdiction capacity, rather than being part of a strategy to empower and promote local activism to bolster political will to address organised crime. Similarly, strengthening the Bosnian criminal justice system was an addition to the law enforcement approach to facilitate

180 *Inhibiting integration?*

prosecutions after arrests were made. When development actors engage directly in programmes to prevent and address organised crime, they maintain control over their practices. This would ensure that development tools are applied as they were intended: to improve conditions for individuals and communities.

Of course, such an approach relies on a specific type of development engagement: a people-centred approach. As highlighted by the conceptual tension, there are multiple understandings of development. This means the inclusion of development does not immediately address the tensions in the security–development nexus. The inclusion of development does not automatically imply a shift towards an emancipatory approach, either. Duffield (2001) points out that development can be an imperial force to contain problems, but at its heart 'development embodies an urge to protect and better others less fortunate that ourselves. As such, it indicates a noble and emancipatory aspiration' (Duffield 2007: 227). Despite emancipatory objectives, development is not a magic wand to address organised crime.

Other difficulties also arise from the inclusion of development. For example, addressing organised crime through development is much harder to measure. If initiatives were successful in addressing the factors that make Sierra Leone and Bosnia conducive to organised crime, the result would be a reduced presence of organised crime. As organised crime groups seek to be discrete in their activities, this is not always obvious. It is also impossible to know exactly what causes a reduction. As UNDP noted in relation to their community safety forums in Bosnia:

> one of the key challenges we have is how do you measure things. It's very difficult when you have zero baseline and you start from zero, how to measure your impact, and most of our projects are of a long-term impact rather than short-term.[11]

Despite these challenges, the direct involvement of development actors in initiatives to address organised crime would also have a positive effect on international security. However, this is not the primary goal. Felbab-Brown (2010) argues that standard law-enforcement programmes can have unintended consequences: 'the weakest criminal groups can be eliminated through such as approach, with law enforcement inadvertently increasing the efficiency, lethality and coercive and corruptive power of the remaining criminal groups'. As a result, the softer, people-centred elements of development engagement can garner more effective results. As USAID (2013: 30–1) argues, 'the longer term democracy, rights and governance programming implemented by development agencies has a crucial role to play in establishing the systems, policies and practices necessary to effectively deter drug trafficking' and other forms of organised crime.

The use of development to directly address organised crime also aligns with current donor trends to focus on countries and issues that will have a benefit for national security (see for example CIDA 2005; DANIDA 2005; Watt 2010).

Inhibiting integration? 181

However, when implemented by development actors, initiatives to address organised crime will be focused on individual needs and local engagement. Development actors also recognise that all programmes need to be based on an analysis of the political economy. When addressing organised crime, they would assess the potential complicity and opposition of government officials (USAID 2013). Within this framework, development would have a 'humanising' effect on security.

Fears of the securitisation of development ensure that development actors are reluctant to engage with organised crime. Analysis of the two case studies reveals that rather than an explicit strategy to co-opt development, what appears to be securitisation is merely the tacit knowledge of security actors, which informs how development is implemented. This suggests that direct involvement of development actors would prevent securitisation as they would maintain control over development tools and modalities. However, unless development activities are implemented in coordination with security strategies, there is a risk that implementation of the security–development nexus will be reversed. Rather than the securitisation of development, the result will be the developmentalisation of security, as security practices would be implemented through a development lens. Unless the two sides are balanced, initiatives to address organised crime will not achieve an integrated security–development nexus. Analysis of the four tensions revealed that implementation of the security–development nexus is not currently balanced, pointing to a need for more proactive development engagement in partnership with security actors. This raises further challenges regarding coordination and collaboration, as well as the four tensions examined here.

The focus on the latent potential of the security–development nexus appears to align with the critiques of orthodox peacebuilding scholars in that it takes a problem-solving approach to enhance the nexus in practice. While the analysis does indicate strategies to harness the positive potential of the nexus, the focus has not been on what would make the nexus more effective. Rather, analysis has engaged with what would make the nexus achieve its emancipatory potential in line with immanent critique. The latent potential does not rest on quick fixes such as better coordination and sequencing. What is needed is more fundamental: it is a shift away from the dominance of security to expand the role of development. As a result, this research challenges both critical and orthodox approaches to the security–development nexus. It 'raises questions about existing institutions, policy assumptions and the interests they serve' (Newman *et al.* 2009: 23) but also engages with the latent potential of the nexus.

Notes

1 Interview, Sarajevo, October 2011.
2 Interview, Sarajevo, October 2011.
3 Correspondence with UK FCO, Sierra Leone.
4 Interview, Sarajevo, March 2012.
5 Interview, Sarajevo, March 2012.

182 *Inhibiting integration?*

6 Interview, Sarajevo, March 2012.
7 Interview, Sarajevo, October 2011.
8 Interview, Sarajevo, October 2011.
9 Interview, New York, March 2013.
10 Interview, Sarajevo, March 2012.
11 Interview, Sarajevo, October 2011.

References

Alemika, Etannibi (2013). 'Conference Input: Organised Crime in West Africa – Trends, Impacts and Responses', *Being Tough is Not Enough – Curbing Transnational Organised Crime, International Expert Conference.* Berlin, Friedrich-Ebert-Stiftung.

Bourdieu, Pierre (1977). *Outline of a Theory of Practice.* Cambridge, Cambridge University Press.

Carrier, Neil and Gernot Klantschnig (2012). *Africa and the War on Drugs.* London; New York, Zed Books.

Chambers, Robert (1983). *Rural Development: Putting the Last First.* Harlow, Pearson Education.

Chandler, David (2012). 'Resilience and Human Security: The Post-Interventionist Paradigm', *Security Dialogue* 43(3): 213–29.

CIDA (Canadian International Development Agency) (2005). *Canada's International Policy Statement: A Role of Pride and Influence in the World.* Ottawa, Department of Foreign Affairs and Trade.

Cockayne, James (2011). *State Fragility, Organised Crime and Peacebuilding: Towards a More Strategic Approach.* Oslo, NOREF.

Cornwall, Andrea (2000). *Beneficiary, Consumer, Citizen: Perspectives on Participation for Poverty Reduction.* Stockholm, SIDA.

DANIDA (2005). *DANIDA's Annual Report 2005.* Copenhagen, Ministry of Foreign Affairs of Denmark.

Duffield, Mark (2001). *Global Governance and the New Wars: The Merging of Security and Development.* London, Zed Books.

Duffield, Mark (2007). *Development, Security and Unending War: Governing the World of Peoples.* Cambridge, Polity Press.

Eade, Deborah (1997). *Capacity-building: An Approach to People-centred Development.* Oxford, Oxfam.

Eade, Deborah (2007). 'Capacity Building: Who Builds Whose Capacity?' *Development in Practice* 17(4–5): 630–9.

EU (2003). *A Secure Europe in a Better World: European Security Strategy.* Brussels, EU.

EUROPOL (2013). *EU Serious and Organised Crime Threat Assessment 2013.* The Hague, EUROPOL.

Felbab-Brown, Vanda (2010). 'The Design and Resourcing of Supply-Side Counternarcotics Policies', www.brookings.edu/research/testimony/2010/04/14-drug-funding-felbabbrown accessed 19 May 2013.

Flessenkemper, Tobias (2013). 'Lessons from Staffing and Equipping EUPM. Learning by Doing?' in Tobias Flessenkemper and Damien Helly (eds), *Ten Years After: Lessons from the EUPM in Bosnia and Herzegovina 2002–2012.* Paris, EU Institute for Security Studies.

Friere, Paulo (1970). *Pedagogy of the Oppressed.* New York, Herder and Herder.

Goodhand, Jonathan (2001a). 'Violent Conflict, Poverty and Chronic Poverty'. *CPRC Working Paper 6.* Manchester, UK, Chronic Poverty Research Centre.

Goodhand, Jonathan (2001b). *A Synthesis Report: Kyrgyzstan, Moldova, Nepal and Sri Lanka. Conflict Assessments.* London, Conflict, Security and Development Group, Kings College.

Goodhand, Jonathan (2006a). 'Preparing to Intervene', in Helen Yanacopulos and Joseph Hanlon (eds), *Civil War, Civil Peace.* Oxford, James Currey.

Goodhand, Jonathan (2006b). 'Working "In" and "On" War', in Helen Yanacopulos and Joseph Hanlon (eds), *Civil War, Civil Peace.* Oxford, James Currey.

Kavanagh, Camino (2013). *Getting Smart and Scaling Up: Responding to the Impact of Organized Crime on Governance in Developing Countries.* New York, NYU Centre on International Cooperation.

Kent, Randolph (2007). 'The Governance of Global Security and Development: Convergence, Divergence and Coherence', *Conflict, Security & Development* 7(1): 125–65.

Krishna, Anirudh, Norman T. Uphoff and Milton J. Esman (1997). *Reasons for Hope: Instructive Experiences in Rural Development.* West Hartford, CT, Kumarian.

Lacher, Wolfgang (2012). *Organised Crime and Conflict in the Sahel-Sahara Region.* Washington DC, Carnegie Endowment for International Peace.

Leal, Pablo Alejandro (2007). 'Participation: The Ascendancy of a Buzzword in the Neo-Liberal Era', *Development in Practice* 17(4–5): 539–48.

Luckham, Robin (2007). 'The Discordant Voices of "Security"', *Development in Practice* 17(4–5): 682–90.

Mansuri, Ghazala and Vijayendra Rao (2004). 'Community-Based and -Driven Development: A Critical Review', *World Bank Research Observer* 19(1): 1–39.

Mohan, Giles (2008). 'Participatory Development', in Vandana Desai and Robert B. Potter (eds), *The Companion to Development Studies, 2nd edition.* Oxford; New York, Routledge.

Newman, Edward, Roland Paris, and Oliver Richmond (2009). 'Introduction', in Edward Newman, Roland Paris, and Oliver Richmond (eds), *New Perspectives on Liberal Peacebuilding.* Tokyo, United Nations University Press.

Pouliot, Vincent (2010). *International Security in Practice: The Politics of NATO–Russia Diplomacy.* Cambridge; New York, Cambridge University Press.

Ralchev, Plamen (2004). 'The Role of Civil Society in Fighting Corruption and Organised Crime in Southeast Europe', *Southeast European and Black Sea Studies* 4(2): 325–31.

Reitano, Tuesday and Mark Shaw (2013). 'Check Your Blind Spot: Confronting Criminal Spoilers in the Sahel', *Policy Brief No. 39.* Pretoria, Institute of Security Studies.

Roe, Paul (2012). 'Is Securitisation a "Negative" Concept? Revisiting the Normative Debate over Normal Versus Extraordinary Politics', *Security Dialogue* 43(3): 249–66.

Salter, Mark (2013). 'The Practice Turn: Introduction', in Mark Salter and Can E. Mutlu (eds), *Research Methods in Critical Security Studies: An Introduction.* London; New York, Routledge.

Scott, James, C. (1998). *Seeing Like a State: How Certain Schemes to Improve the Human Condition Have Failed.* New Haven, CT, Yale University Press.

Sen, Amartya (1999). *Development as Freedom.* Oxford, Oxford University Press.

Shaw, Mark (2012). *Leadership Required: Drug Trafficking and the Crisis of Statehood in West Africa.* Pretoria, Institute of Security Studies.

Shaw, Mark and Tuesday Reitano (2013). *The Evolution of Organised Crime in Africa.* Pretoria, Institute for Security Studies.

184 *Inhibiting integration?*

Spear, Joanna and Paul D. Williams (2012). 'Conceptualizing the Security–Development Relationship', in Joanna Spear and Paul D. Williams (eds), *Security and Development in Global Politics: A Critical Comparison.* Washington DC, Georgetown University Press.

UK Government (2004). *Security Sector Reform Strategy: GCPP SSR Strategy 2004–2005.* London, MoD, FCO, DfID.

UNDP (UN Development Programme) (2010). 'Helen Clark Concludes Mali Visit', www.undp.org/content/rba/en/home/presscenter/articles/2010/05/04/helen-clark-concludes-mali-visit/ accessed 3 December 2013.

USAID (US Agency for International Development) (2013). *The Development Response to Drug Trafficking in Africa: A Programming Guide.* Washington DC, USAID.

Uvin, Peter (2002). 'The Development/Peacebuilding Nexus: A Typology and History of Changing Paradigms', *Journal of Peacebuilding and Development* 1(1): 1–20.

Waddell, Nicholas (2006). 'Ties that Bind: DfID and the Emerging Security and Development Agenda', *Conflict, Security & Development* 6(4): 531–55.

Watt, Nicholas (2010). 'Protests as UK Security Put at Heart of Government's Aid Policy', *Guardian*, 30 August: 1.

White, Mark (2008). 'The Security and Development Nexus: A Case Study of Sierra Leone 2004–2006', in Peter Albrecht and Paul Jackson (eds), *Security System Transformation in Sierra Leone, 1997–2007.* London, SSR Network.

Youngs, Richard (2007). *Fusing Security and Development: Just Another Euro-Platitude.* Centre for European Policy Studies. Brussels.

Conclusion

External actors engaged in post-conflict reconstruction have enthusiastically adopted the security–development nexus as a framework to inform their approach. The institutionalised linkage between security and development has emerged at a particular historical point as a response to earlier failures in post-conflict reconstruction. With the end of the Cold War, new forms of insecurity were recognised, such as weak or failed states, which require new approaches to address the multifaceted challenges they pose. More recently, additional security challenges, such as organised crime, have gained further attention. With an impact on both security and development, organised crime cannot be adequately addressed through a security approach. It requires a comprehensive approach that engages with both security and development. External actors engaged in post-conflict reconstruction have readily taken this on board and broadened their approach. The desire for a new and comprehensive approach suggests a shift away from a traditional security approach towards emancipation.

Although security and development have been linked in earlier approaches, the contemporary security–development nexus is qualitatively different. Rather than pursuing security and development objectives in tandem, the two concepts are integrated in deeper, more institutionalised ways. In response, there has been an attempt to integrate security and development in practice. Governments have allocated additional resources and transformed institutions to bring security and development together into a comprehensive approach. For organised crime, this has included the pairing of alternative development strategies and programmes focused on rule of law and good governance with law-enforcement approaches, 'making use of the full range of military, development and crime prevention tools available' (UNODC 2008: 55).

Despite the enthusiasm of policymakers and practitioners, the security–development nexus has also received significant criticism. The primary critique emerges from critical peacebuilding scholars who argue that, rather than an integrated approach, the nexus is one sided, with security continuing to dominate. The argument on the securitisation of development contends that development is being employed to further security objectives. Underdevelopment is understood as dangerous and needs to be addressed to curb the impact it has on international security. Rather than an end goal, development strategies such as

186 *Conclusion*

poverty reduction are focused on addressing insecurity rather than individual wellbeing. Such an approach undermines a shift away from a traditional security approach even though new strategies may be employed to achieve security outcomes.

As outlined in Chapter 2, these criticisms appear to be borne out in practice. In Sierra Leone, the policy document that informed the West Africa Coast Initiative (WACI) recognised a two-way relationship between security and development. Poverty, weak institutions and Sierra Leone's weak position on the Human Development Index foster organised crime, while organised crime, drug use and an increasing crime rate undermine development (UNODC 2010: 55). Youth were identified as a particular priority as high rates of youth unemployment creates an entry point for organised crime, but they are also the most susceptible to the increased drug use that accompanies a rise in drug trafficking. However, in practice the approach of external actors remained security focused. The WACI established the Transnational Organised Crime Unit (TOCU) and enhanced the capacity of law enforcement. Other elements have broadened the focus, such as the emphasis on drug demand-reduction and treatment. As highlighted by the analysis of the conceptual tension, these programmes were understood to contribute to national, regional and international security.

Although the EU already had a detailed policy on the security–development nexus, the practices of the EU in Bosnia were even more security focused. The EU Police Mission (EUPM) had a mandate that brought security, development and organised crime together. However, the primary focus was on law enforcement. The key tasks of EUPM included the strengthening of operational capacity and joint capability of the law-enforcement agencies engaged in the fight against organised crime and corruption; assisting and supporting the planning and conduct of investigations in the fight against organised crime and corruption; assisting and promoting the development of criminal investigative capacities; enhancing police–prosecutor cooperation and police–penitentiary cooperation; and ensuring a suitable level of accountability (EUPM 2010).

Arguments about the securitisation of development primarily focus on the outcome of the security–development nexus. The nexus is taken as a fixed concept; there is no analysis of how or why this outcome is reached. In line with the Copenhagen School of Security Studies, the security–development nexus is viewed negatively, resulting in calls for desecuritisation. This research has taken a different approach. Based on the Welsh School of Critical Security Studies, the security–development nexus is understood to be imbued with a positive result. The starting point is the expectation that the nexus will result in a new and comprehensive approach that enhances the effectiveness and sustainability of post-conflict reconstruction, with benefits for individuals and communities rather than just the state. As the securitisation of development literature argues that the nexus is one sided, this research investigated the relationship between security and development. The focus is on the processes of external actors to identify what inhibits the integration of security and development into a nexus. Four hypotheses were developed of tensions that influence the integration of security

Conclusion 187

and development. Investigating these tensions through the case studies of internationally driven initiatives to address organised crime in Sierra Leone and Bosnia revealed a much more complex picture than the securitisation of development literature suggests.

The conceptual tension revealed the ambiguity of how the security–development nexus is understood, as there are diverse understandings of security and development. This has implications for collaboration as the nexus holds a different meaning for different actors. However, more importantly, understandings of security overwhelmingly adhere to a 'hard security' perspective, prioritising state and international referent objects and implementing initiatives at the state level. As a result, understandings of security do not correspond with the shift towards human security. Understandings of development also lack a focus on individual needs. In Bosnia, aspects of development were focused on individuals and communities through an emphasis on good governance. However, the primary referent object remained the state/international level. In Sierra Leone, development initiatives were implemented at the community level. However, as in Bosnia they continued to focus on the state and international level as the referent object. These different understandings affect the integration of security and development as they influence the type of nexus that emerges.

As with the conceptual tension, there is a lack of understanding of how security and development come together. Causal tension emerges from the divergent understandings of how security and development are applied and how they are linked. Although both security and development are valued by external actors addressing organised crime in Sierra Leone and Bosnia, their approach primarily deploys security strategies to create space for development. In part this arises because there is no clear understanding of how development is applied, while security is more tangible. However, it also arises from the belief that organised crime threatens security and development. Such a perspective does not require an integrated response. The tendency is to rely on traditional strategies to address organised crime to achieve security and development as end goals. This understanding fails to benefit from the contribution that development can make to initiatives to address organised crime. It also affects the form of integration between security and development.

The institutional underpinnings of security and development continue to influence the interface between security and development. Rather than overcoming the division between the two, the institutional underpinnings of security continue to dominate. Development does influence some areas of practice through the security–development nexus. In Sierra Leone, elements of development contributed to the language employed by the WACI, how organised crime is understood, the approach of the WACI and the structure of UNIPSIL. In Bosnia, development influenced the understanding of organised crime and EUPM's approach to problems. However, in both countries the primary contributors were security actors. The institutional tension influences the extent of integration between security and development, as development was brought in to address organised crime through a security lens.

188 *Conclusion*

A final tension emerges from the motivational drivers of external actors addressing organised crime. A primary argument behind the securitisation of development is that international responses to security threats are driven by concerns of these threats spreading internationally. However, it is self-interest that has driven the search for more effective approaches to post-conflict reconstruction. A comprehensive approach would be mutually beneficial, improving the lives of individuals and communities with sustainable security outcomes. However, the urgency of international security concerns ensures that development is brought in to initiatives to address organised crime to the extent that it enhances international security outcomes. These concerns have also influenced development actors, with many now considering their activities a response to security threats. The drivers of external actors addressing organised crime influences why security and development are integrated and which element is prioritised.

These tensions reveal two trends in the implementation of the security–development nexus: international security concerns are prioritised and security actors remain the key implementers of initiatives to address organised crime. These trends appear to support the argument on the securitisation of development, as development is employed to achieve security outcomes. However, the analysis of the tensions revealed that this is not an explicit strategy of the security–development nexus but merely a consequence of the tacit knowledge of the key implementers of initiatives to address organised crime – security actors. While it is recognised that security strategies alone are inadequate to address organised crime, development actors remain reluctant to directly engage in initiatives to address organised crime. As a result, security actors are adopting the tools and strategies of development through a security lens. Without understanding the history of particular tools – how they have evolved, their mixed records and the challenges that have had to be overcome to ensure success – they are stripped of their political meaning and emancipatory potential. The use of development tools in this way supports the arguments on the securitisation of development.

Despite the appearance of the securitisation of development, a deeper analysis reveals that development practices have had a significant impact on the processes of the security–development nexus. In Sierra Leone, although ECOWAS's approach still primarily focuses on the state, this is driven by a desire to improve the wellbeing of citizens. UNODC and UNIPSIL engaged in initiatives at the community level that focused on drug demand-reduction and treatment. Although they contributed to international security, they also engaged with the needs of individuals affected by increased drug flows through the country. While there is no direct causal relationship between security and development, the relationship still reveals a shift in the approach of external actors. The sequential relationship reveals that creating space for development is now an objective of external engagement. Although this is not the same as directly engaging in development, it does indicate a shift away from a traditional security approach. The institutional tensions also highlighted areas where external actors have shifted away from a pure security focus. The understanding of organised crime

Conclusion 189

engaged with elements of development. In terms of their approach, external actors have acknowledged the need for prevention and they have engaged in capacity building to achieve long-term objectives. The language related to capacity building and the anti-drugs programmes also shifted away from security.

In Bosnia, the focus on good governance and rule of law focused on both state-level and individual referent objects, expanding beyond just protecting the state. The sequential relationship also indicated a shift in approach as EUPM sought to create space for development. How EUPM understood organised crime has resulted in a shift away from a traditional security approach. As in Sierra Leone, to a certain extent the approach aimed to prevent organised crime and build capacity to ensure a long-term approach. This was bolstered by the shift from a policing mission to a rule of law mission. The approach to organised crime also shifted, working in partnership with local law enforcement through mentoring and co-location. EUPM engaged in a broader range of activities beyond law enforcement, including gender and human rights programmes and outreach and public information campaigns. While these were seen as horizontal and marginal to the primary focus, they still broadened the approach. Accordingly, EUPM encouraged civil society involvement on corruption and organised crime and improved their interaction with key ministries within Bosnia.

These changes challenge the dominant thinking on the security–development nexus. Although proponents of the securitisation of development argument point to a one-sided nexus, the analysis of the two case studies reveals integration of security and development in some areas. While security continues to dominate, the adoption of the security–development nexus in Sierra Leone and Bosnia reveals glimpses of emancipation. In contrast to the focus on the outcomes of the nexus among its critics, this book has explained why and how these outcomes arise, highlighting that the outcomes are more complex than the label of securitisation suggests. The emphasis on securitisation also dismisses the latent potential of the security–development nexus.

Fear of securitisation has deterred development actors from directly engaging in initiatives to address organised crime. This lack of engagement has resulted in the use of development tools by security actors which removes them from their underlying philosophy. The direct involvement of development actors would ensure they maintain control over development tools, preserving the people-centred approach that underpins them. While the examination of the latent potential appears to align with problem-solving critiques, it also challenges this approach. Rather than a quick fix, what is required is a more fundamental shift to engage with development as it was intended. This is the key contribution of the book – analysing the security–development nexus through the lens of human security, it engages with the positive potential of the nexus. From this perspective, the book challenges the arguments of critical scholars and their call for desecuritisation, but also the quick fixes of problem-solving approaches, instead making the argument for deeper integration.

190   *Conclusion*

References

EUPM (European Union Police Mission) (2010). *EUPM Strategic Objectives 2010/11.* Sarajevo, EUPM.

UNODC (UN Office on Drugs and Crime) (2008). *Drug Trafficking as a Security Threat in West Africa.* Vienna, UNODC.

UNODC (UN Office on Drugs and Crime) (2010). *Crime and Instability: Case Studies of Transnational Threats.* Vienna, UNODC.

Index

accession 124, 127, 128, 133, 139, 143, 157, 160, 161, 163
accountability 64, 76, 135, 140
advance fee fraud 66
Æopiæ, Zoran 73
Afghanistan 16, 17, 32, 33, 72, 73
African Union 1
Agamben, Giorgio 35
agency 13, 33, 34, 35, 45, 47, 78, 107
agents of change 158, 161, 169, 174
airport control 69
Albrecht, Peter 75
Ali Gasi, Muhamed 73
alternative development 61, 62, 91, 100, 102, 103, 172, 185
ammunition 72
Aning, Kwesi 87
Annan, Kofi 1, 9, 48
anti-drugs programme 70, 71, 99, 101, 104, 105, 106, 109, 164, 189
Antrobus, Peggy 33
Aradau, Claudia 16
assumptions 4, 19, 53, 69, 99, 113, 144, 181
authoritarianism 49
awareness raising 45, 70, 71, 77, 99, 104, 106, 108, 166, 178, 179
Axworthy, Lloyd 47

Balkan organised crime 141, 143
Balkan route 73, 121, 134
Ball, Nicole 9
balloon effect 79
Bank of Sierra Leone 69
bare life 35
basic needs approach 13
Beall, Jo 15, 16
beneficiaries 20, 33, 45, 47, 50
benevolence 33, 34, 88, 90, 122, 123, 151

Benn, Hilary 49
Berdal, Mats 10
Biafra 9
bike riders 107
Blair, Tony 15
Bolivia 61
Booth, Ken 20, 23
border management 70, 104, 114, 133, 160
borders 8, 31, 47, 48, 51, 72, 89, 103, 133, 135, 141, 143, 160, 163
Bosnia-Herzegovina 2, 4, 9, 22, 23, 37, 38, 40, 43, 53, 63–5, 71–8, 79, 120–44, 150, 151, 152, 153, 154, 157, 158, 160, 161, 162, 163, 165, 166, 168, 170, 172, 174, 177, 179, 180, 186, 187, 189
Bosnian Ministry of Security 135, 138, 139
bottom-up approach 33, 34, 38, 42, 46, 65, 136, 171
BRICS 32
Bulgaria 143
buy in 139, 150
buzzwords 104

cannabis 61, 67, 102, 109, 113, 114, 115, 161, 163, 170
capabilities approach 13, 32, 34
capacity 13, 22, 38, 45, 50, 52, 59, 60, 66, 67, 76, 96, 103, 104, 115, 124, 135, 138, 139, 144, 161, 163, 179, 186
capacity building 35, 69, 70, 76, 89, 98, 100, 104, 105, 106, 109, 110, 114, 115, 116, 121, 122, 123, 134, 135, 136, 137, 142, 143, 144, 158, 161, 163, 166, 169–72, 173, 176, 179, 189
Caribbean 79, 144
cartels 68, 111, 112, 164, 178
causal relationship 35–41, 93, 95, 99, 126, 130, 154, 155, 156, 188

Index

ceasefire 12
Central America 78, 144
chain of command 45, 46
Chandler, David 3, 12, 18, 33, 34, 50, 64, 161
Christie, Ryerson 20
cigarette smuggling 71, 73
citizens 8, 9, 59, 87, 88, 91, 94, 99, 100, 103, 104, 106, 107, 108, 113, 121, 123, 124, 127, 134, 139, 140, 142, 144, 177, 179, 180
civil oversight 173, 178
civil society 14, 23, 46, 91, 104, 107, 108, 116, 139, 140, 159, 177, 178, 189
civilian casualties 12, 63
Civilian Planning and Conduct Capability (CPCC) 131, 132, 165
civilians 8, 9, 44, 47, 61, 63, 72, 107, 142, 167
Clausewitz, Carl von 134
climate change 14, 31
co-location 137, 138, 189
coca plant 61
cocaine 66, 67, 73, 78, 79, 94, 102, 103, 104, 107, 108, 109, 111, 112, 113, 115, 144, 160, 162, 170
cocaine trafficking 66, 102, 103, 109, 111, 115, 144
Cockayne, James 44, 45, 50, 59, 60, 61, 78, 104, 105, 144, 174
coercion 44, 47, 104
coexistence 1, 30
Cold War 7, 8, 9, 11, 12, 31, 48, 50, 150, 185
collaboration 18, 70, 77, 95, 136, 152, 161, 181, 187
Collier, Paul 9, 36
collusion 61
Colombia 66, 100
combatants 8, 10, 72, 114
Committee for Civilian Aspects of Crisis Management (CIVCOM) 131, 132, 165
Common Foreign and Security Policy (CFSP) 132, 164
communism 7, 63, 72
community 7, 33, 39, 46, 70, 71, 87, 91, 92, 93, 107, 116, 152, 166, 168, 172, 174, 178, 180, 187, 188
Community Assistance for Reconstruction, Development and Stabilisation (CARDS) 133, 160
community engagement 107, 166, 172, 178

community safety 174, 180
comparability of cases 4, 58, 63–6
comprehensive approach 1, 3, 4, 6, 8, 10, 11, 15, 17, 20, 22, 23, 30, 31, 42, 46, 48, 49, 53, 60, 69, 75, 79, 92, 93, 97, 116, 126, 150, 152, 153, 154, 162, 163, 164, 173, 174, 179, 185, 186, 188
conceptual framework 4, 6
Conciliation Resources 107
conflict 3, 4, 7, 8, 9, 10, 11, 12, 15, 16, 30, 33, 36, 37, 41, 47, 49, 50, 51, 58, 59, 60, 63, 64, 68, 72, 74, 88, 97, 98, 99, 114, 122, 130, 143, 167, 175
conflict prevention 10, 36
conflict resolution 8, 175
conflict trap 36
conflict-affected states 3, 47, 50, 59
constructivism 19, 21
consultation 46, 47
consumption 31, 67, 68, 162
containment 33, 34, 50, 91, 104, 121, 152, 161, 163
contradiction 4, 17, 30
contributors 43, 96, 100, 102, 103, 109, 131, 133, 157, 164, 187
conventional security 12
cooperation 1, 62, 69, 70, 76, 77, 120, 129, 131, 134, 135, 136, 138, 186
coordination 18, 70, 71, 76, 77, 97, 103, 109, 133, 136, 138, 141, 181
Copenhagen criteria 124, 125
Copenhagen School of Security Studies 2, 16, 186
Cornwall, Andrea 38, 45, 92, 171
corruption 16, 23, 44, 45, 60, 62, 64, 73, 74, 76, 77, 78, 79, 87, 88, 94, 96, 103, 112, 113, 120, 123, 127, 130, 132, 133, 134, 135, 136, 138, 139, 140, 144, 150, 152, 159, 160, 162, 166, 173, 175, 177, 179, 186, 189
Costa Rica 66
Cote d'Ivoire 68, 87, 100
Council Conclusions on Security and Development 74, 131
counter-insurgency 8, 17, 167
counter-narcotics 101, 111, 112
counterfeiting 73, 79
coup d'etat 176
crack cocaine 67, 104
crime prevention 62, 101, 185
crime sensitivity 176, 177
criminal groups 53, 59, 72, 176, 177, 178, 180
criminal intelligence 101

Index 193

criminal justice 70, 96, 101, 104, 114, 130, 170, 179
criminality 37, 70, 134, 142
criminology 59, 101
crisis management 74, 128, 129, 131, 133, 140
critics of security-development nexus 2, 3, 15–19, 20, 23, 30, 53, 153, 181, 185
cross-fertilisation 156
cross-pillar instrument 75, 120, 124, 125, 128, 131, 151, 164
customs 73, 74, 101, 132

DANIDA 49, 165, 180
Dayton Peace Agreement 64
defence 48, 49, 131
demand 44
demand reduction 44, 91, 92, 104, 116, 152, 165, 186, 188
democracy 14, 31, 64, 74, 123, 124, 140, 141, 159, 175, 178, 180
democratic governance 88, 175, 176
democratic institutions 87, 88, 90, 100
Denney, Lisa 36
desecuritisation 2, 3, 17, 186, 189
deterrence 110
development as freedom 38, 92, 161
development: actors 3, 9, 10, 14, 17, 18, 21, 41, 43, 44, 45, 50, 65, 99, 104, 109, 113, 116, 130, 140, 154, 157, 158, 159, 161, 165, 169, 171, 172–81, 188, 189; application of 4, 37–9, 41, 93–5, 126–7, 154–7, 163, 168; conditions for 99; contribution to conflict 9; modalities 16, 41, 158, 159, 160, 161, 171, 173, 179, 181
developmentalisation of security 3, 15, 17, 75, 181
diamonds 67, 107, 112
direct involvement 175, 180, 181, 189
Directorate of External Relations (DG RELEX) 133
disarmament, demobilisation and reintegration (DDR) 10
disjuncture 19, 20, 23, 52, 112–14, 121, 142–3, 161, 162, 168
displacement 12
disruption 115
donors: Canada 7, 165, 166, 180; Denmark 49, 165, 180; EU 7, 23, 41, 42, 44, 49, 64, 74, 75, 121, 125, 128, 129, 131–4, 142, 143, 151, 158, 160, 165, 186; Germany 102, 111; Italy 102; Japan 102; Netherlands 102, 111, 141; state-

based 102, 109; Sweden 102; UK 7, 11, 16, 17, 41, 50, 64, 99, 102, 107, 111, 134, 159, 172, 174, 175, 177; US 7, 41, 42, 111
drug control 61, 62, 101
drug cultivation 61, 113
drug dealers 73
drug policy 42, 59
drug production 61, 78, 100, 102, 113, 115, 144, 161, 163, 170, 177
drug trafficking 22, 48, 51, 60, 61, 66, 67, 68, 69, 70, 72, 73, 74, 78, 79, 87, 88, 89, 90, 91, 96, 97, 100, 102, 103, 104, 109, 110, 111, 112, 113, 115, 120, 121, 122, 144, 151, 159, 162, 165, 175, 176, 180, 186
drug use 45, 70, 71, 91, 99, 100, 104, 106, 108, 152, 166, 172, 173, 179, 186
Duffield, Mark 2, 7, 8, 9, 12, 15, 16, 17, 18, 33, 35, 47, 48, 180

Eade, Deborah 158, 169
early warning 10, 107
Eastern Europe 143
Ebola 67
Economic Community of West African States (ECOWAS) 22, 58, 65, 86, 87–8, 90–1, 92, 93, 97, 98, 100, 110, 151, 155, 163, 164, 188
economic crime 73, 120
economic development 13, 14, 32, 34, 50, 62, 70, 75, 87, 88, 89, 90, 92, 94, 96, 98, 99, 123, 124, 125, 126, 128, 143, 157, 165, 178
economic growth 9, 13, 36, 37, 45, 47, 61, 75, 123, 124
economic security 46, 60
ECOWAS Commission 88, 90, 91, 92, 96, 97, 100, 151, 152
ECOWAS Political Declaration 68, 87, 90, 93–7, 100, 102, 105, 112, 155
education 13, 50, 61, 100, 101, 171
effectiveness 3, 18, 46, 79, 121, 135, 140, 160, 186
efficiency 42, 53, 76, 180
elections 63, 67, 71, 112, 176
elites 7, 67, 79, 112, 142, 143
Ellis, Stephen 66
emancipation 3, 19, 20, 21, 30, 31, 34, 38, 42, 53, 71, 127, 151, 152, 153, 154, 169, 170, 173, 179, 185, 189
emancipatory approach 18, 20, 21, 34, 37, 46, 53, 71, 127, 151, 152, 153, 154, 169, 170, 173, 179, 185, 189

194   *Index*

embedded 46, 169
empire 64
employment 13, 37, 69, 108, 144, 178
empowerment 13, 20, 170, 171, 173
engagement 3, 6, 9, 12, 16, 17, 21, 30, 31,
    38, 39, 43, 44, 46, 48, 49, 52, 60, 64, 65,
    71, 74, 75, 78, 79, 81, 91, 94, 99, 100,
    105, 107, 108, 112, 115, 116, 126, 127,
    128, 129, 135, 139, 141, 143, 150, 153,
    154, 156, 159, 160, 161, 162, 166, 172,
    173, 175, 178, 178, 179, 180, 181, 188,
    189
enlargement 75, 124, 125, 126, 128, 129
enlightened self-interest 17, 47, 49, 161
environment 9, 12, 15
epistemological approaches 1, 19, 21, 150
equipment 70, 102, 103, 106, 114, 177
eradication 44, 128, 129
EU Consensus on Development 130
EU Delegation 124, 125, 128, 139
EU membership 124, 125, 143
EU Police Mission 22, 23, 58, 65, 74–8,
    79, 120–44, 151, 152, 156, 157, 158,
    159, 163, 164, 165, 166, 170, 172, 186,
    187, 189
EU Security Strategy 122, 123, 125, 126,
    129, 130, 141, 153
EUFOR Bosnia 74, 137
European Commission 127, 131, 132, 133,
    134, 158, 164, 165
European Council 122, 131, 132, 133, 134,
    158, 164
European Development Fund 130
European External Action Service (EEAS)
    133
European Security and Defence Policy
    (ESDP) 120, 122, 125, 126, 131, 132
Europol 77, 164
existential threat 11, 31, 44
experts 41, 44, 76, 77, 86, 132, 135, 137,
    139, 141
external security 75, 122
extortion 44, 73, 74
extraordinary measures 12, 16, 33

failed states 8, 47, 166, 185
Federation of Bosnia and Herzegovina 64,
    73, 139, 142
Felbab-Brown, Vanda 53, 60, 79, 180
financial crime 66, 178
financial investigation 69, 106, 144
Flessenkemper, Tobias 133, 135, 160
food security 113, 161, 163, 177
force generation 135

foreign policy 18
forensics 70, 104, 114
fragile states 49, 111, 175
freedom 12, 13, 32, 33, 38, 103, 129, 143,
    161
freelance 66
Freetown 64, 67, 71, 79, 106
Freetown Commitment 87, 88, 90, 94, 96,
    100, 112, 156
Friere, Paolo 171
frontline 46
Fukuyama, Francis 8, 48
funding 7, 32, 43, 47, 99, 102, 103, 105,
    108, 115, 133, 134, 139, 140, 164, 165

gender 8, 14, 31, 77, 78, 122, 128, 189
genocide 9, 36
Ghana 66
Glenny, Misha 52, 66, 72, 143, 144
global security 7, 49
goals 12, 21, 38, 41, 44, 77, 87, 95, 98,
    104, 105, 127, 131, 133, 137, 153, 161,
    170, 179, 187
good governance 11, 44, 121, 123, 124, 125,
    126, 130, 152, 166, 178, 185, 187, 189
Goodhand, Jonathan 167, 175, 176, 177,
    179
governance 10, 11, 44, 59, 60, 64, 68, 70,
    79, 87, 88, 90, 100, 104, 115, 116, 121,
    123, 124, 125, 126, 130, 140, 144, 150,
    152, 161, 166, 167, 175, 176, 180, 185,
    187, 189
grants 44
grassroots development 171
Guinea-Bissau 66, 67, 68, 87, 110
Gulf of Guinea 52

hard security 32, 34, 35, 42, 88, 89, 90,
    121, 122, 123, 152, 165, 168, 187
headquarters 43, 45, 46, 106, 122
health 13, 15, 45, 70, 71, 87, 91, 96, 98,
    99, 100, 167, 171, 177
heroin 66, 73
hierarchy 10, 40, 45, 47, 96, 107, 108, 137,
    138, 155, 158
High Representative 64, 133
HIV/AIDS 8, 91, 116
holistic 11, 21, 75, 169, 170, 174
Honduras 61
horizontal inequality 37
hotline 78, 107, 179
households 17, 100
human development 13, 14, 31, 32, 33, 34,
    36, 42, 46, 65, 86, 90, 97, 151, 165

Index 195

Human Development Index 62, 65, 186
human rights 8, 9, 31, 43, 50, 60, 78, 122, 123, 124, 128, 129, 130, 132, 152, 159, 189
human security 3, 12, 20, 21, 24, 31, 32, 33, 34, 35, 38, 46, 47, 48, 60, 86, 87, 92, 97, 100, 121, 130, 150, 151, 152, 168, 175, 187, 189
human trafficking 121, 137
human-centred approach 14, 33, 35
humanitarian aid 9

ideal types 42–7
identity 35, 42
illegal logging 67, 107, 137
illicit trade 51, 60, 67
illiteracy 96
immanent critique 20, 23, 79, 173, 181
immigration 70, 107
implementation 76, 77, 86, 88, 91, 95, 98, 101, 105, 108, 120, 122, 129, 131, 133, 139, 151, 159, 165, 166, 169, 172, 179, 181, 188
improving lives 153, 161, 162, 165, 166
income 10, 13, 14, 60, 65, 79, 100, 113, 130, 157, 178
independence 13, 43, 44, 103
individual needs 11, 12, 16, 42, 48, 51, 87, 92, 121, 125, 165, 181, 187
inequality 10, 37, 130
inflation 60, 72
infrastructure 9, 13, 50, 66, 100, 176
insecurity 152, 179, 185, 186
interstate wars 8
institution building 52, 89, 127, 128, 129, 135
institutional architecture 41, 43–4, 47, 99, 100–3, 109, 110, 131–4, 157, 158, 159, 160
institutional capacity 22, 45
institutional memory 159
institutional underpinnings 42, 43, 46, 86, 105, 109, 110, 157, 158, 159, 160, 166, 172, 187
institutions 3, 4, 6, 8, 10, 11, 19, 20, 31, 41, 42, 46, 47, 50, 64, 68, 69, 75, 87, 88, 89, 90, 100, 103, 105, 107, 121, 123, 124, 127, 128, 130, 131, 133, 135, 138, 139, 148, 150, 163, 176, 177, 178, 181, 185, 186
Instrument for Pre-accession Assistance (IPA) 133, 160
insurgency 9
integration 2, 3, 4, 10, 11, 17, 19, 20, 21,

22, 23, 24, 30, 31, 35, 36, 39, 40, 41, 46, 48, 51, 52, 53, 58, 62, 63, 65, 68, 69, 74, 75, 78, 79, 80, 86, 93, 95, 96, 97, 98, 99, 115, 120, 123, 124, 126, 129, 130, 140, 150, 186, 187, 189
intelligence 70, 76, 77, 101, 103, 104, 106, 107, 108, 111, 112, 113, 114, 134, 136, 141, 167, 178
interconnected 31, 39, 40, 49, 98, 129
interdependence 129
interdiction 44, 50, 67, 70, 102, 104, 105, 106, 108, 114, 115, 163, 179
interests 7, 12, 16, 17, 19, 33, 34, 35, 48, 49, 50, 52, 59, 79, 87, 88, 91, 102, 103, 110, 111, 125, 131, 132, 134, 136, 142, 143, 158, 164, 167, 179, 181
intergovernmental organisations 11, 32, 132; *see also* specific institutions
internal security 49, 121, 122, 127, 142, 143
internal wars 8, 12, 47
international assistance 136
international engagement 2, 3, 6, 12, 39, 52, 60, 94, 141, 162
International Labour Organisation (ILO) 13
International Monetary Fund (IMF) 14, 32
international organisations 23, 48
international security 12, 15, 33, 47, 48, 49, 50, 51, 52, 89, 90, 92, 93, 110, 111, 112, 113, 114, 115, 116, 125, 144, 152, 153, 156, 160, 161, 162, 163, 164, 165, 166, 170, 173, 179, 180, 185, 186, 188
Interpol 22, 65, 86, 101, 135
intervention 8, 9, 10, 12, 30, 41, 45, 63, 64, 102, 150, 174, 179
intra-state conflict 49
investigation 19, 64, 69, 70, 73, 74, 76, 77, 101, 102, 103, 106, 107, 108, 114, 115, 121, 136, 137, 144, 162, 182
investment 60, 71, 75, 99, 123
Iraq 14, 32, 60

Jamaica 177
Jolly Ambassadors 140
judiciary 107, 132, 177, 178
justice 10, 43, 63, 70, 75, 88, 89, 91, 96, 97, 101, 102, 104, 114, 116, 120, 123, 128, 129, 130, 131, 132, 143, 170, 179
juvenile justice 91, 116

Kaldor, Mary 8, 10, 32, 35, 47, 63
Kelmendi, Nasser 73, 142
kidnapping 44

196 *Index*

Kosovo 73

language 44, 45, 47, 103, 104, 105, 109, 134, 135, 157, 187, 189
latent potential 4, 173, 181, 189
Latin America 66, 67, 111, 160
law enforcement 8, 21, 23, 42, 43, 45, 48, 50, 53, 59, 60, 61, 68, 69, 71, 73, 75, 76, 77, 78–80, 89, 96, 99, 100, 101, 102, 103, 105, 106, 107, 108, 109, 110, 111, 113, 114, 115, 116, 120, 121, 124, 125, 126, 127, 128, 129, 130, 133, 134, 135, 136, 137, 138, 139, 140, 143, 144, 156, 158, 159, 164, 166, 170, 172, 177, 179, 180, 185, 186, 189
Liberia 63, 68, 87, 110, 113
linguistic 44
linkages between security and development 1, 4, 6, 11, 31, 37, 39–41, 62, 86, 95–9, 128–30, 155, 156, 163, 165, 168: hierarchical 40, 96, 107, 108, 137, 138, 155, 158; interdependent 1, 39, 40, 96, 130, 155; interface 41, 160, 187; mutually constitutive 39, 40, 96, 97, 98, 155; sequential 33, 40, 96, 97, 98, 99, 128, 130, 155, 163, 165, 188, 189; synonymous 40, 96, 155
Lisbon Treaty 129, 131
livelihoods 9, 59, 61, 97, 100, 144
local engagement 16, 17, 21, 154, 181
local knowledge 104, 158, 169
local organisations 16, 46, 99
local ownership 52, 64, 65, 77, 144, 173
local partners 43
local perspectives 104, 107, 142
local solutions 78, 106
locus 33, 34, 42, 88, 89, 90, 92, 121, 122, 123, 126
long-term approach 189

Maastricht Treaty 129, 132
Mafia 66, 72, 73
magic wand 180
Mali 66, 175, 176
Mamdani, Mahmood 7
Mano River Women's Peace Network (MARWOPNET) 107
Marshall Plan 7
media 59, 107, 122, 140, 177, 178
Menkhaus, Ken 37
mentoring 89, 108, 109, 137, 138, 141, 189
merging of security and development 1, 49, 52, 109, 131, 137

methodology 2–4, 100
Mexico 66, 68, 178
Middle East 49
middle-income states 65, 130, 157
middle power states 12
migration 27, 31
militaristic approach 20, 45, 165
military 9, 10, 11, 16, 19, 21, 60, 61, 62, 63, 93, 121, 123, 130, 132, 134, 137, 156, 165, 167, 172, 176, 185
military operations 134
military strategies 12, 21, 156
Millennium Development Goals 14, 33, 38, 62, 175
mobile banking 176
money laundering 51, 69, 70, 73, 74, 87, 88, 96, 104, 114, 136, 138, 176
monitoring 12, 89
Montenegro 73
moral imperative 38, 45
motivational drivers 46, 52, 110, 160, 161, 188
motivations 31, 48, 50, 51, 86, 110, 160, 161, 188
motives 18, 46, 50, 60
multi-agency initiatives 65, 68, 86, 100, 120, 151, 172
multi-stakeholder 86
murder 73, 74
mutual interest 49

Naim, Moses 79
narcotics trafficking 74, 111
National Drug Law Enforcement Agency (NDLEA) 89, 105, 106
national security 14, 16, 32, 47, 67, 87, 89, 90, 94, 96, 101, 107, 110, 121, 180
natural resources 52, 107, 177
neoliberalism 14, 32, 33
neutrality 43
Newman, Edward 18, 19, 20, 35, 49, 92, 181
NGOs 1, 12, 17, 23, 32, 33, 70, 71, 91, 104, 107, 116, 124, 139, 160, 171, 174
Nigeria 66, 67, 106
non-state actors 7, 8, 12, 167
normative 20
North Atlantic Treaty Organisation (NATO) 63, 135

Office of National Security (ONS) 67, 69, 89, 107, 112
oil bunkering 66
oligarchs 73

Index 197

Operation Lutka 73
operations 8, 45, 46, 59, 63, 66, 67, 70, 77, 103, 112, 113, 134, 135, 137, 164
opportunity 13, 61, 62, 174
Organisation for Economic Co-operation and Development (OECD) 60, 174
organisational procedures 41
Organised Crime and Corruption Reporting Project (OCCRP) 73, 144
organised crime networks 44, 59, 66, 73, 76, 113, 115, 135, 143, 144
organised crime 8, 37, 48, 49: addressing 2, 11, 21, 22, 23, 33, 34, 37, 38, 39, 40, 43, 51, 58–80, 86–116; approach 42, 43, 45–7, 50, 52, 53, 60, 61, 63, 93, 105–10, 135–41, 151; conduciveness 21, 38, 96, 110, 114, 116, 130, 161, 163, 166, 185; impact 11, 21, 47, 60, 61, 62, 88, 90, 93, 94, 121, 152, 162, 163, 164, 167; in conflict-affected states 59, 65, 113, 181; and development 90, 91, 92, 127, 168, 175–81, 185; and security-development nexus 37, 38, 52, 58–80, 87, 96, 97, 186, 187; presence of 4, 65, 150; prioritisation of 51, 110–12, 141–2; threat 21, 47, 51, 60, 61, 87, 88, 89, 95, 96, 97, 100, 116, 125, 128, 143, 156, 163; understanding of 43, 44–5, 47, 103–5, 134–5, 157, 158, 166, 187, 188
Oslobođenje 72
outreach 78, 128, 189
ownership 52, 64, 65, 77, 120, 143, 173

panic politics 162
Paris, Roland 8, 12, 18, 30, 58
participation 171
partnership 14, 23, 39, 45, 46, 47, 76, 78, 89, 107, 109, 136, 137, 138, 143, 158, 181, 189
patrol 67, 70, 115
patronage 15, 16, 72
peacebuilding 15, 18, 51, 58, 101, 105, 133, 174, 175: critical approaches 2, 18, 166, 167, 185; liberal 34; missions 22, 58, 86, 89, 172; negative peace 12; orthodox approaches 3, 18, 181
peacekeeping 22, 96, 101, 134, 174
people-centred approach 11, 12, 14, 21, 39, 45, 87, 88, 92, 151, 161, 163, 169, 170, 171
persistent conflict 8
Peru 100
pillars 131
police 22, 23, 58, 59, 61, 64, 65, 67, 72,

73, 74, 75, 76, 77, 89, 101, 102, 104, 106, 107, 111, 114, 120, 121, 122, 123, 128, 132, 134, 135, 136, 137, 138, 139, 141, 142, 160, 165, 172, 174, 177, 186
police liaison officers 141, 160
policing 10, 63, 101, 107, 111, 114, 120, 121, 122, 128, 132, 135, 136, 138, 141, 142, 156, 189
policy mantra 1, 35, 37
policymakers 1, 2, 6, 10, 11, 12, 15, 18, 19, 21, 46, 50, 59, 69, 162, 185
Political and Security Council (PSC) 131, 132, 164
politicians 67, 88, 136, 138, 143
politico-criminal nexus 79
ports 69, 108, 109
post-conflict reconstruction 1, 3, 4, 6–15, 20, 21, 22, 23, 30, 31, 34, 41, 42, 43, 46, 52, 53, 58, 59, 60, 63, 64, 65, 66, 74, 101, 114, 150, 164, 167, 175, 185, 186, 188
poverty 8, 9, 13, 14, 15, 16, 36, 45, 48, 60, 62, 64, 68, 69, 96, 97, 99, 103, 104, 114, 116, 124, 128, 129, 130, 150, 157, 171, 175, 186
poverty reduction 15, 16, 45, 114, 130, 186
Poverty Reduction Strategy Process (PRSP) 14
poverty relief 124, 157
practice turn 22, 167
practices 16, 21, 23, 33, 41, 42, 51, 52, 64, 65, 67, 72, 79, 99, 106, 109, 120, 130, 135, 137, 144, 155, 156, 157, 160, 166, 167, 169, 173, 174, 179, 180, 181, 186, 188
practitioners 46, 179, 185
precursor chemicals 73, 110
preventative approach 104, 105, 166
prevention 10, 22, 36, 41, 48, 62, 87, 91
priorities 10, 17, 33, 38, 43, 48, 52, 53, 74, 78, 95, 102, 105, 106, 110, 112–14, 115, 122, 131, 135, 142–3, 156, 161, 162, 164, 167, 168, 169, 170
private sector 14, 32
privatisation 33, 73, 79
problem solving 3, 18, 181, 189
prohibition 42, 61
proliferation 48
prosecution 67, 73, 74, 108, 114, 115, 163, 180
prosperity 7, 49
Protocol to Prevent, Suppress and Punish Trafficking in Persons 62
public health 47, 87, 96, 167, 177

198 *Index*

public information 77, 78, 128, 189
public services 33, 98

quality of life 100

Radončić, Fahrudin 143
reactive bargaining 44, 47, 104
realism 11, 14, 19, 23, 32, 33, 39, 97, 168
reconciliation 10, 58
Red Cross 43
referendum 63
referent object 31, 33, 34, 35, 38, 39, 40,
    42, 45, 48, 50, 51, 87, 88, 89, 90, 91, 92,
    93, 94, 95, 121, 122, 124, 125, 126, 151,
    152, 153, 165, 168, 187, 189
regime security 33, 34, 88, 89, 92, 126
rehabilitation 37, 91, 92, 116, 152, 165
relationships 1, 3, 4, 9, 15, 18, 19, 30, 31,
    35, 36, 37, 38, 39, 40, 41, 46, 50, 53, 68,
    93, 95, 96, 97, 98, 99, 107, 108, 109,
    126, 129, 130, 133, 134, 136, 137, 138,
    139, 140, 141, 154, 155, 156, 158, 163,
    167, 175, 176, 178, 186, 188, 189
reprisals 178
Republika Srpska 64, 73, 138, 142
resilience 33, 35
revenue 60, 107, 111, 112, 113, 164, 177
Richmond, Oliver 18, 20, 35
risk 18, 35, 36, 41, 42, 45, 48, 49, 50, 61,
    69, 70, 79, 87, 99, 102, 137, 157, 163,
    166, 174, 176, 181
rivalry 63, 105, 106
Romania 143
root causes 9, 10, 52, 74, 130, 178
rule of law 11, 44, 60, 62, 87, 88, 89, 90,
    100, 101, 103, 113, 122, 123, 124, 125,
    128, 132, 133, 135, 143, 152, 157, 159,
    163, 164, 167, 174, 178, 185, 189
rural development 61, 100

Šariæ, Darko 73
secondment 141
securitisation: of development 2, 3, 15, 16,
    17, 18, 19, 20, 32, 48, 49, 61, 150, 153,
    154, 160, 166–7, 169, 170, 179, 181,
    185–9; theory 2, 16, 19
security: actors 1, 6, 10, 11, 17, 38, 45,
    110, 131, 154, 157, 160, 162, 164–6,
    167, 168, 169, 170, 171, 173, 178, 179,
    181, 187, 188, 189; application of 4,
    37–9, 41, 93–5, 126–7, 154, 163, 168;
    dominance of 2, 79, 153, 158, 167, 171,
    181; how concieved 8;
    reconceptualisation 12; traditional

perspective of 3, 11, 19, 20, 21, 30, 31,
    34, 37, 39, 41, 42, 46, 52, 53, 65, 70, 71,
    77, 78, 80, 87, 90, 92, 99, 102, 103, 105,
    107, 108, 116, 123, 125, 126, 127, 130,
    133, 134, 135, 136, 137, 138, 140, 141,
    151, 152, 153, 156, 157, 158, 164, 166,
    168, 172, 173, 179, 185, 186, 188, 189
security–development nexus: adoption 2,
    6, 30, 41, 42, 46, 48, 61, 63, 68–9, 74–5,
    109, 114, 150, 154, 157, 160, 167, 173,
    179, 189; barriers 4; critiques 2–4,
    15–19, 30, 48, 53, 153, 185, 186, 189;
    expectations 2, 19; gap between policy
    and practice 6, 71, 150; historical
    linkages 6; implementation 16, 22, 23,
    59; processes 3; and post-conflict
    reconstruction 6–12
security first 99, 130, 156, 173
Security Sector Reform (SSR) 17, 50, 63,
    64, 74, 75, 78, 107, 156, 165, 172, 173,
    174
seizure 67, 112, 178
self-interest 17, 46, 47, 49, 50, 51, 114,
    141, 160, 161, 163, 168, 188
Sen, Amartya 13, 32, 34, 38, 92, 161
sensitisation 70, 104
sequencing 18, 181
Serbia 73
Sierra Leone 2, 4, 9, 17, 22, 23, 37, 38, 40,
    43, 50, 53, 58, 63–71, 75, 78, 79,
    86–116, 125, 126, 127, 135, 143, 150,
    151, 152, 154, 156–73, 179–81, 186–9
Single Convention on Narcotic Drugs 61
small arms 51, 87, 88, 96
smuggling 67, 71, 72, 73, 102, 107, 111,
    121, 137, 144
social capital 8, 167, 178
social cleavages 9, 36
social services 100, 178
social transformation 38, 45, 154
socio-economic development 75, 124, 128,
    143, 178
soft strategies 11
South Africa 7, 66
sovereignty 11, 31, 32, 89, 163
Soviet Union 7, 8
spectrum 21, 30, 31, 34, 35, 37, 40, 41, 42,
    46, 48, 50, 51, 59, 87, 95, 155
speech act 44
spill over 35, 49, 89, 92, 152, 161, 163,
    170
Stabilisation and Association Process 124,
    128
stability 7, 8, 15, 16, 34, 36, 42, 49, 53, 60,

62, 66, 68, 71, 75, 86, 88, 89, 97, 98, 124, 127, 128, 141, 143, 163
stakeholders 86, 104
State Investigation and Protection Agency 64, 121, 135, 137
state security 14, 19, 32, 46, 88, 92, 152, 163, 165, 174
statebuilding 52, 58
Stewart, Francis 36, 37, 50
Structural Adjustment Programmes (SAP) 14
structural deficiencies 103
structural factors 45, 73
structural transformation 45
superpowers 7, 12
surveillance 70, 103, 135
survival 11, 32, 33, 61, 72, 100, 162
sustainability 17, 46, 77, 130, 160, 186
sustainable development 9, 61, 62, 95, 128, 129
Sustainable Development Goals 62

tacit knowledge 167, 168, 169, 170, 171, 172, 173, 179, 181, 188
tactical operations 70, 103
Tadjbakhsh, Shahrbanou 20, 24
Talking Drum Studios 107
tax evasion 73, 74
Taylor, Charles 63
technical assistance 62, 106, 135
technical capabilities 114
technical equipment 70
tensions 2, 4, 18, 21, 22, 23, 24, 30–53, 173, 180, 181, 186, 188: causal 35–41, 93–9, 126–30, 154–7, 163, 165, 168; conceptual 31–5, 86–93, 120–6, 151–3, 163, 165, 168; institutional 41–6, 99–110, 131–41, 157–60, 164, 168; motivational 46–53, 110–16, 141–4, 160–2, 165, 168
terrorism 8, 9, 14, 15, 47, 48, 49, 62, 122
theft 73, 74, 121
threat 2, 7, 8, 9, 11, 12, 15, 19, 21, 22, 31, 32, 33, 38, 44, 45, 47–52, 59, 60, 61, 68, 69, 71, 75, 78, 79, 86–91, 94, 96, 97, 98, 103, 110, 113, 114, 116, 122, 124, 127, 128, 130, 134, 135, 141, 142, 143, 150, 152, 153, 156, 159, 161, 163, 164, 166, 167, 168, 174, 187, 188
threat assessment 59, 115, 134, 142
Togo 66, 68
top-down approach 33, 34, 35, 39, 65, 78, 90, 169, 171
trade 14, 15, 16, 31, 51, 60, 67, 72, 102, 107, 129, 162, 163, 170, 176

trade-offs 34, 35
trafficking 22, 48, 51, 60, 61, 62, 66–71, 73, 74, 78, 79, 87–91, 96, 97, 100, 102, 103, 104, 107, 109–13, 115, 120–2, 137, 141, 144, 151, 159, 162, 164, 165, 175, 176, 180, 186
training 70, 77, 89, 101, 102, 106, 114, 132, 133, 135, 137, 158, 177
transformation 6, 38, 45, 154
transhipment 96
transit 66, 67, 104, 107, 112, 160, 162, 175
Transnational Organised Crime Unit (TOCU) 69, 70, 89, 99, 102, 103, 104, 105, 106, 108, 109, 112, 113, 186
treatment 45, 91, 92, 116, 152, 165, 186, 188
trickle down approaches 90
trust 14, 41, 107, 111, 141
Tschirgi, Necla 1, 3, 9, 11, 16, 18, 38, 50
Turkey 72

UK 7, 16, 17, 41, 49, 64, 102, 111, 134: aid strategy 11, 16; Conflict Prevention Pools 7, 41, 159; Conflict, Security and Stability Fund 7, 42; Department for International Development 7, 11, 16, 17, 41, 50, 64, 99, 107, 159, 172, 173, 174, 175, 177; Foreign and Commonwealth Office 7, 159; Ministry of Defence 7, 159
Ukraine 53
UN 1, 9, 13, 44, 48, 51, 61, 97, 98, 101, 135
UN Charter 142
UN Convention against Transnational Organised Crime 62
UN Department of Peacekeeping Operations (UNDPKO) 22, 101
UN Department of Political Affairs (UNDPA) 22, 65
+UN Development Programme (UNDP) 12, 14, 22, 70, 71, 79, 99, 101, 140, 174, 175, 180
UN General Assembly 61
UN International Police Task Force (IPTF) 23
UN Joint Vision for Sierra Leone 68, 69, 94, 95, 97, 98
UN Office for West Africa (UNOWA) 86, 101
UN Office on Drugs and Crime (UNODC) 22, 43, 58, 59, 61, 62, 63, 65–70, 86, 89–95, 97–106, 108, 114, 115, 151, 152, 155, 158, 163, 164, 172, 185, 186, 188

200 *Index*

UN Peacebuilding Mission in Sierra Leone (UNIPSIL) 22, 58, 65, 70, 71, 86, 89–95, 97, 98, 99, 101, 104, 105, 106, 108, 109, 111, 112, 113, 116, 151, 152, 155, 157, 158, 159, 163, 164, 166, 172, 187, 188
UN Peacekeepers 63, 64
UN Secretary General 1, 9
UN Security Council 8, 51, 68, 120
underdevelopment 9, 10, 15, 32, 35, 36, 37, 47, 48, 49, 51, 61, 62, 63, 69, 70, 96, 97, 99, 116, 129, 155, 171, 185
unemployment 45, 48, 68, 69, 71, 72, 79, 99, 103, 104, 115, 116, 130, 150, 161, 166, 173, 175, 186
unfulfilled potential 23, 173
unintended consequences 52, 53, 59, 177, 180
US 7, 41, 42, 111: Africa Command 102, 111; Bureau for International Narcotics and Law Enforcement Affairs (INL) 42, 159; Department of Defence 16; Department of Homeland Security 7; Department of State 7, 111; Drug Enforcement Agency (DEA) 42; National Security Council 14, 32; National Security Strategy 32; USAID 7, 44, 79, 140, 175, 176, 177, 180, 181

Venezuela 67
vicious cycle 37, 70
victims 91, 116
Viktor Kulivar 'Karabas' 52
violence 3, 8, 9, 10, 12, 44, 53, 59, 67, 68, 96, 135, 159, 167, 176, 177, 178
virtuous cycle 36, 37, 156

Waddell, Nicholas 1, 9, 33, 37, 167
Waever, Ole 19
war crimes 63
War on Terror 16

weak governance 79, 104, 115, 116, 130, 140, 144, 150, 161, 166
weak institutions 68, 69, 150, 186
weak states 8, 15, 32, 49
weapons 10, 48, 67, 72, 79, 96, 122, 137
weapons trafficking 74
wellbeing 9, 13, 14, 15, 16, 17, 31, 32, 37, 39, 92, 113, 153, 186, 188
Welsh School of Critical Security Studies 3, 19, 20, 53, 173, 186
West Africa 22, 62, 66, 67, 68, 79, 86, 87, 89, 91, 94, 97, 100, 103, 104, 105, 110, 111, 113, 115, 178
West Africa Coast Initiative (WACI) 22, 58, 65, 68, 69, 70, 71, 79, 86, 87, 88, 89, 90, 92, 93, 94, 96, 97, 98, 100, 101, 102, 103, 104, 105, 106, 107, 108, 109, 110, 111, 112, 115, 151, 156, 157, 158, 159, 164, 172, 186, 187
West Africa Commission on Drugs (WACD) 67
West Africa Cooperative Security Initiatives (WASCI) 159
Western Balkans 49, 72, 142, 143
Western interests 49
White, Mark 65, 156
Wikileaks 67, 105, 106, 111, 113
winning hearts and minds 16, 167
withdrawal 8, 128
World Bank 9, 14, 32, 36, 60, 65, 130, 175
World Development Report 9, 14, 175
World War II 7, 13

Yemen 16
youth 9, 67, 68, 69, 71, 79, 94, 98, 99, 104, 107, 186
youth unemployment 68, 69, 71, 79, 99, 104, 116, 150, 166, 173, 186
Yugoslavia 63, 65

zero-sum 39